# Marketing in Practice

W. G. LEADER
N. KYRITSIS

Series created by W. G. Leader
Principal of London City College

## Stanley Thornes (Publishers) Ltd

**Dedicated to Katie and James**

First published in 1990 by:
Stanley Thornes (Publishers) Ltd
Old Station Drive
Leckhampton
CHELTENHAM GL53 0DN
England

British Library Cataloguing in Publication Data

Leader, W. G.
    Marketing in practice.
    1. Marketing
    I. Title  II. Kyritsis, N.
    658.8

    ISBN 0-7487-0512-0

This is a net book and should not be sold at a price lower than the publisher's current listed price.

Typeset by Northern Phototypesetting Co. Ltd, Bolton.
Printed and bound in Great Britain at The Bath Press, Avon.

# ACKNOWLEDGEMENTS

The authors acknowledge with thanks the advice provided by Norman Waite, Director of Diploma Studies for The Chartered Institute of Marketing, and The Institute for permission to reproduce past examination papers.

We also thank The Association of Business Executives for allowing the reproduction of their past examination questions.

# Contents

## PART 1 THE INFORMATION INPUT

## PART 2 THE PROMOTIONAL OUTPUT

iv CONTENTS

# PART 3   MARKET PLANNING

# PART 4   INTERNATIONAL MARKETING

# Dear student

With courses becoming more and more intensive there is a greater need for students to have precise study information available so that they can study more efficiently and speedily.

At the same time this enables tutors to devote more effort towards the understanding and analysis of the subject. Rather than give up valuable time dictating and providing notes, they can concentrate more on actively involving students in the learning process.

In this text the authors have covered all aspects of coursework providing:

- a comprehensive text on the subject
- study and exam tips on each topic
- self assessment tests
- past examination questions
- specimen answers to selected questions
- answers to self assessment tests.

The combination of these elements will greatly improve your confidence and performance in the examinations.

W. G. Leader
N. Kyritsis

# General study and exam tips

*In many situations information is so great a part of effectiveness that without information a really clever person cannot get started. With information a much less clever person can get very far.*

*Dr Edward De Bono*

Being successful on a course does not simply result from listening to lectures or reading a textbook. You must become actively involved in the learning process in order to acquire knowledge and skills and perform well in assessments.

There is no reason why you cannot achieve this aim. After all you are on a course of study because an examining authority believes that you have the necessary ability to complete the course successfully. If you are prepared to become actively involved and do the work required, you have every right to feel confident that you can succeed in the final examinations.

These notes are designed to make your study more efficient, to ensure that you use this manual to best advantage and to help you improve both your coursework and your examination techniques. They have been divided into four parts:

1 general study tips
2 improving the quality of your work
3 examination technique
4 studying with this text.

## ■ 1 GENERAL STUDY TIPS

An eminent physicist once said: 'Thinking is 99 per cent perspiration and 1 per cent inspiration'. Take his advice and that of most of us who have had the benefit of a good education. Ignore the advice of those who believe you can prepare yourself for the examination in one or two weeks. Knowledge and skills of any value are not easily learned. For most of us it takes time to understand and permanently remember the content of a subject; instead of forgetting everything immediately the examinations are over. Therefore start working at studying right at the very start of your course and continue at a steady pace until the examinations. Do all the work expected of you by your tutor including homework and mock/mid term examinations. Homework is good practice and the mock exams simulate aspects of the final examination. Doing them as well as you can makes your tutor more willing to help you, as he or she will see that you are playing your part in the learning process.

The knowledge and skills you will gain on your course of study are precisely the kind needed by professional business people. So approach the study of each subject as if you were in real life a business man or woman, or a person following a profession such as accountancy or law. In this way the subject should come alive for you, and your motivation to learn should increase.

To help realise this objective, read a quality daily and Sunday newspaper that has a good business section. By doing this you will discover what is happening on a day-to-day basis and be in a better position to understand the topics you are studying on the course. You will also broaden and deepen your knowledge of the subject. Professional people at work usually read a quality newspaper and monthly or quarterly periodical related directly to their discipline in order to keep abreast of the latest developments. You will probably wish to do the same when you commence work, so why not start now?

Carry a pocket dictionary with you and look up words you hear or read but do not understand. None of us has a complete vocabulary but we can improve it if we really want to be able to read and study more effectively. In the case of students it is even more important because words used in lectures, textbooks or newspapers often become misused in examinations. Some words which cause problems with their meaning or spelling are:

| | | |
|---|---|---|
| aggregate | disseminate | heterogeneous |
| antithesis | distinguish | homogeneous |
| constituent | evaluate | panacea |
| discipline | facsimile | prognosis |

Do you fully understand how these words may be used in the context of your subject? Use a dictionary.

As soon as you start your course, find out if you are going to be given past examination reports for your subject, examiners' reports, specimen answers to previous examination questions and a work scheme. It is probable that they will not all be available at your school, college or university or even from the examining authority. You should, however, obtain as much information about your course of study and the examinations as possible so you know exactly what amount of work lies ahead of you and the academic standard you are expected to reach. This will help in planning your personal workload for the period of your course.

If you do not understand something ask your tutor. Do not assume that you are inadequate because you did not understand something that other students seemed to appreciate. They may be having difficulties too or your lecturer may simply not have explained the point to everyone's satisfaction. If something is overlooked by the tutor, don't be afraid to bring it to his/her attention.

Personal health is something that many students dismiss with comments such as: 'what has health got to do with ability to think?' Studies on the topic have now clearly indicated that general health and mental performance are statistically related. Within four weeks of being given multi-vitamin and mineral tablets students in two separate controlled studies improved upon their written perform-ance in intelligence tests by approximately ten points. Your common sense alone should tell you that you cannot perform at your best if you continually feel tired or have flu or a heavy cold in an examination. Eat a varied diet that includes protein foods, vegetables and fruit, and get some daily exercise even if it is only a good brisk walk home after your day's study.

Contrary to the belief of many students, the best academic work is not done at night-time. Once again research shows that students perform better in the early part of the week, in the daytime – particularly mornings – and in a place where there is natural daylight to read and write by. Therefore plan your study schedule so that it is completed in the day. This will also leave you the evenings and weekends free to relax and enjoy yourself.

# ■  2  IMPROVING THE QUALITY OF YOUR WORK

The earlier in the course you bring your work to a satisfactory standard the more likely you are to exhibit a good standard of work in the examinations. Obviously, academic standards do relate to the thinking abilities of the student but they also depend on motivation, and a logical approach to one's work if effective present-ation at the appropriate academic standard is to be achieved. Here are three tips that will help you develop a logical approach to the presentation of your work.

## Read the question carefully

When undertaking essay or numerical work make sure you read the question very carefully. Underline the key words in the question so that your mind is con-centrated on the essential aspects. For example, distinguish between the two main types of question.

### DESCRIPTIVE QUESTIONS

A descriptive question is one in which you will be expected to describe or explain something and possibly distinguish it from alternative or similar items or ideas. Two examples are:

   a) *Describe* and *distinguish above-the-line advertising* from other forms of *advertising*.

b) *Explain* with the *aid of graphs, how the price* of a product is *determined* in a highly *competitive economy*.

Some of the key words have been emphasised in italics to give you an idea of which words are at the heart of the question. Always underline or highlight the key words yourself before attempting to answer.

## ANALYTICAL QUESTIONS

These include the purely analytical question, or the analytical question that requires you to evaluate a statement (indicate your level of support for an idea/give it value) or only to present your own ideas. Examples of these are:

a) *Solely analytical*: Analyse the contention that there is no such thing as fixed costs.
b) *Analytical and Evaluative*: How far do you support the idea that adult behaviour is predominantly related to one's early childhood experiences?

If you have been presented with a mini case (short story) or case study (extended story) detailing opposing opinions regarding a problem a company is faced with, you may be requested to offer your own solution. In this event your answer should analyse the value of all the opinions offered in the case as well as possibly suggesting your own.

Consider also the way a question is structured. If it is in two or more parts give equal time to each if equal marks are awarded to each part. If more marks are awarded to one part than another, allocate your time in the same proportions as the marks awarded. For example, if a question has marks awarded: part (a) 5 marks, part (b) 15 marks (total 20 marks), you should spend a quarter (5/20) of your time answering (a) and three quarters (15/20) on (b).

Sometimes the time you should allocate to a part of a question is indicated by the implied requirements of the questions, rather than by marks. For example:

**Q1** a) Briefly outline 'actual' and 'ostensible' authority.
b) Brown and Brown Ltd contracted with a married woman for the laying of new carpets. After the work had been done, the woman's husband refuted the contract and refused to pay for the carpets. Advise Brown and Brown Ltd and the woman on their legal position.

By using the words 'briefly outline' the examiner is indicating that much less time should be spent on answering part (a). The question required more marks to be awarded to part (b) as the **analytical** and **applied** nature of this part indicates that it is more difficult to answer.

With numerical type questions, such as in accountancy and statistics, do not assume that all you have to do is arrive at the right answer. Your tutor – or an examiner – will expect you to explain what you are doing as you introduce each set of workings, graphs, illustrations or tables. After all, how is your tutor to know how you arrived at the right answer if you do not explain? Even more importantly, even if you give the wrong answer, at least you will be given some marks for those parts of your calculation which are correct. Such subjects involve a large element of communication and if you do not communicate effectively in your answer what you are doing you will lose marks.

## Construct an essay plan

Always spend a few minutes constructing an essay plan before answering a question. This only requires jotting down a few notes for each paragraph which indicates the approach you will take to your answer and the points you will include. This will make sure that you construct your essay in a logical manner and that you keep to a target when writing your answer.

## Follow up with your tutor

To understand fully what is required when answering questions, ask your tutor about the work you have handed in and had marked if he or she has not commented sufficiently on your script, informing you of where you were right and wrong and why.

## ■  3  EXAMINATION TECHNIQUE

If you are studying at college you can start improving your examination technique in the mock/mid term examination which will help you in the coursework assessment during the second half of the course as well as in the final examination. Here are a few tips on improving your presentation:

- *Always do rough workings*. Use essay plans and/or numerical workings to plan your answer, but on a page other than the one on which you start your answer to the question. Cross through your rough working before starting to answer the question.
- Select the questions you intend to answer and *start with the one you think you will find the easiest* to answer. In this way you may gain your highest marks early in the exam which is very important in case you do not complete the examination.
- *Keep an eye on the clock* so that you allow about the same amount of time for answering each question (unless one is a more difficult, compulsory question). Noting the time in order to complete all the questions you are required to answer gives you a better chance of achieving high marks.
- Allow at least a third to half a page of illustrations or diagrams. In this way they look like illustrations rather than scribblings and you have sufficient space available if you have to return to your illustration to add more detail later in the examination. Always explain what your illustration is supposed to illustrate.
- Unless otherwise instructed, use a complete page of graph paper for presenting graphs and make sure that you provide a title for any entries you have made. Explain what your graph illustrates.

● Do not present workings for numerical subjects such as accounts and statistics without explaining what you are doing and why.

If you would like a deeper understanding of study skills and exam techniques a useful book containing a wealth of tips and examples that will help you to succeed in any examinations is *How To Pass Exams* by W. G. Leader, published by Stanley Thornes.

# ■ 4 STUDYING WITH THIS TEXT

This student text has been specifically designed to act as a study aid for students while on a course, as well as present the contents of a subject in a way that is both interesting and informative.

Use this text as part of your study activities, adding your own or your tutor's notes at appropriate points. Study the text in great detail, making notes on the chief points in each chapter so that the ideas have gone through your own head and down on to the paper in your own words – though perhaps with key quotations from the text.

Don't get bogged down in any one chapter. If you really can't follow the chapter leave it and go on to the next, returning at a later date. What seems difficult at the start of your course in say, September, will be easier by December and child's play by March! You are going to develop as you do the course – so don't give up too early. Perseverance is everything in acquiring professional status.

Do not just read the specimen answers provided at the end of certain sections. Study their content and structure in the light of what you learned in the particular section and what you learned earlier in this section. In this way your skill in answering questions set by your tutor and/or the examination body should improve.

At the end of each section there are examples of past examination questions. Where the answer is to be in essay form jot down beside the question the major points that you think should have been highlighted when answering. Then check back with the appropriate text of the particular section to see if your answer would have been correct. If you are still uncertain, discuss the problem with your tutor.

Talking with the tutor and fellow students is essential for developing the ability to analyse problems.

Always complete the self assessment part of each chapter as this is designed to reinforce what you have learned and improve your recall of the topics. Check your answers with those provided in the manual. As repetition of a process improves one's memory, it is very useful to re-test yourself every few weeks or let someone else read the questions to you and tell you if you got them right.

If the subject covered by the particular manual involves value judgements do not assume that what is mentioned in the manual is the only correct version. Your tutor may have other opinions which are just as valid. What matters is that you have sufficient knowledge of the subject to illustrate a firm understanding of the topic in the examinations.

One of the best ways to study is to buy a lever arch file and make dividing pages from coloured paper for each subject or chapter. File your notes, and your essays and any newspaper cuttings, articles, etc. that are relevant in the appropriate topic position. You will then have an easy-to-revise and lively set of notes. If you find it a bit bulky to carry, use a ring binder instead and then at the end of every week or two weeks transfer the notes you have made to the lever arch file, keeping it at home for safety.

Now that you have read these Study and Exam Tips you should feel confident to continue with your studies and succeed in the examinations. It just remains for ourselves and Stanley Thornes to wish you every success on your course.

# Preparing for Marketing in Practice

It is often the case that people with a fundamental knowledge of the principles and theories of marketing believe that they are equipped for making detailed marketing decisions. The result is that they may make themselves look foolish when confronted by a professional or, worse still, make a decision that adversely affects the life of others. Understanding the principles of marketing is essential but it is also essential that students, or those embarking on a marketing career, learn about the subject as practised and apply their ideas to some case studies before tackling real life situations.

The purpose of *Marketing in Practice* is to provide the reader with a practical understanding of major areas of the subject and to provide necessary foundation for higher studies in the area. To accomplish these aims the book is divided into four parts, each including questions, exam and study tips, past examination questions and/or specimen answers and mini case studies.

The first part, **The information input**, examines the ways marketers obtain essential market information which enables them to make effective marketing decisions. The second part, **The promotional output**, closely examines the major areas of the promotions mix and provides a mini case study for the reader to test his or her newly found knowledge on the topic. Part 3, **Marketing planning**, gives the reader an insight into the thought processes and planning that go into the preparation of a total marketing plan, and Part 4, **International marketing**, introduces the reader to the approaches employed in selling and marketing within an international framework.

The basic principles of marketing will also be touched on to ensure that the reader readily links principles with practice. (See also *Fundamentals of Marketing* in this series, written by the same authors, published by Stanley Thornes in 1989, and which provides an excellent grounding in the subject of marketing.)

PART 1

# The information input

# 1 Introducing research

*A constant supply of relevant, accurate information is the cornerstone of effective marketing.*

Information is possibly the most vital element in the work of a marketing manager. All the decisions which must be made are based on facts and/or opinions highlighting the **needs** of a group of consumers, a product, a company's personnel, a distributor or any other group of interest to an organisation. The word **needs** also represents a very critical aspect of a marketer's working life as marketing is about reconciling the needs of the organisation with those of potential customers. If a meeting point is achieved where customers' needs are met and the company makes a profit then the needs of both parties to the transaction are reconciled. The problem is identifying customer needs; to accomplish this the company itself needs information so that it does not produce something that will not sell, or is difficult to sell.

An organisation remains in business by continually servicing and satisfying customers and the medium to long term task of most marketing managers is to adjust or extend the range of the products and/or services offered in order to meet the customers' needs, wants and expectations.

Adjustments need to be made in line with changes in social trends, fashions, expectations, competitors' activities, economic developments, etc. Accurate information – from internal or external sources – is needed, therefore, to provide concrete ideas as to the **reasons** for and **implications** of the changes taking place, as well as to provide marketing management with information for decisions on advertising, sales promotions, selling approaches to be used, product development and product elimination, etc. Imagine a situation where marketing adjustments would seem necessary and consider some questions which may require an answer:

- What is the exact profile of the customers you are aiming to attract?
- How do customers or potential customers feel about the product/s?
- Have they seen the latest advertisements? Do they understand them? Do they like them?
- Is the price right? Is it set too high or even too low?
- How will price changes (up or down) affect the demand for the products or services?

- What is your company's market share? How can it be improved?
- Can the sales force sell more? If 'yes', who to, when and how?
- Can you introduce new product(s)? What type of products? Who for? What will you name them?
- Are there any opportunities overseas? If yes, which countries? Will the products have to be modified?
- How do consumers perceive competitors' products? Do you have an advantage over them? How do you find out?

It is possible to list hundreds of similar questions but the general theme is likely to remain the same: 'How do you constantly improve in order to maintain profitability through customer satisfaction?'

## ■ MARKETING RESEARCH

Information which can provide the answers to the questions identified can be obtained through a process known as **marketing research** (**MR**), which can be defined as

> the planned and systematic gathering, collation of data and the analysis of facts relating to all aspects of the marketing function

MR offers a solid base upon which marketing planning can be based and it can reduce the area of uncertainty surrounding the way specific markets operate. It would be wrong to assume that marketing research will lead to solutions for all the current or potential problems facing an organisation so it is best if it is treated as a **risk reduction** facility. Accurate relevant information is critical for sound decision-making but the skill in taking the right decision given the information provided still rests with the marketing manager. Many marketing managers will also relate to past experiences, intuition, rumours, personal preferences and biases. Marketing research is not a replacement for valuable assets such as experience or intuition; it is simply a guide to efficient management and a support to effective decision-making. Opinions of managers may be reinforced by research findings. Consider, however, situations where the whole future of an organisation may depend on your decision. Would *you* follow an opinion, suspicion or belief or would you rely on solid findings from the market within which your company operates? Running an organisation – large or small – without adequate marketing information reduces business decisions to guesswork. It is common practice to divide marketing research into two general areas: **market research** and **other marketing research**. This division is shown in Table 1.1.

Market research may be further divided into **consumer market research** and **user/industrial market research**. It has also become common practice to name research in accord with the element of marketing that is being researched such as **advertising research**, **product research** and **sales research**.

**Table 1.1** Division of marketing research

| | |
|---|---|
| **Market research** may be defined as research involving current and potential customers who constitute a market. Major areas of interest include the study of: | **Other marketing research** may be undertaken by companies to improve marketing decision-making. Major areas of interest include the study of: |
| 1 The size and location of current and potential markets<br>2 Buying habits of potential and/or current customers<br>3 The segments that may be part of the market<br>4 Personal characteristics of the consumers<br>5 Structure of the market<br>6 Current and future demand and purchasing trends<br>7 Attitudes of consumers towards the product or promotions<br>8 Analysis of market shares<br>9 Influencers and deciders in the buying decision. | 1 Analysis of the strengths and weaknesses of competitors<br>2 Product design and development<br>3 Study of distribution (channels and physical)<br>4 Economic, social, legal and technological changes and trends<br>5 Pattern and effectiveness of the marketing effort, such as: sales force, routing, PR expenditure, etc.<br>6 Cost effectiveness of advertising<br>7 Trade attitude towards the company, its product and its competitors. |

# ■ DATA AND INFORMATION

Many people confuse two simple research terms which carry their own distinct meaning, namely **data** and **information**.

## 1 Data

Data represents a series of facts, figures and opinions which have not been statistically processed. Thousands of people have opinions that may be important to us but those opinions remain raw data until we have discovered what they are and arranged them in a way that we can understand. Data may also take the form of statistics, questionnaires that must be analysed, or statements made by people, the implications of which are not yet established. Data collected will need to be collated (or rearranged) in a meaningful way before it becomes an understandable set of findings, i.e. 'information' that is understandable to the marketing manager.

## 2 Information

Information represents the meaning and implications of the data collected. It could take the form of tables, graphs, correlations, summaries, etc., or virtually any form provided that it is understandable. Hopefully, if the right research was undertaken, in the correct manner, the marketing manager will be able to take a decision to forward or protect the trading position of the company on the strength of the information obtained.

# ■ PRIMARY AND SECONDARY DATA SOURCES

Marketing managers can rely on a number of information and data sources which can be classified as either **primary sources** or **secondary sources**.

1 **Primary (first hand) sources** of information or data represent findings the company obtains direct from **respondents** (people answering our questions or questionnaires). They generally tend to involve direct contact with groups of consumers, distributors, suppliers, etc., with the intention of collecting information which has not previously been recorded or collected. When a company – or research agency – collects data direct from the respondents this is referred to as **field research** or **survey**.

The methods of research may include personal interviewing, group discussions, observation, in-depth interviews, etc., which are examined in detail in Chapters 2 and 3 of this book.

Primary research may be:

a) **Ad-hoc**. One-off research designed to obtain specific information of relevance at a particular point in time. A company, for instance, may wish to find out how consumers respond to its latest price reduction, new package or recent advertisement. Interviews may be organised to collect the necessary information which can aid a particular marketing decision.

b) **Continuous**. As the name implies, a company seeks continuous information on market developments usually by subscribing to research programmes operated by specialist research organisations. This area of research is extremely attractive in the case of markets which are constantly changing. Consider, for instance, the ever changing taste in regular foods. It involves participation in continuous retail audit and consumer panel surveys which are discussed in detail in Chapter 3.

2 **Secondary sources** of information, on the other hand, represent information which has already been collected and collated by other organisations or individuals. These reports and/or statistics are often readily available, for instance statistics regarding particular industries, published by the Government.

Secondary sources can provide a company with a wealth of information which may answer many of their questions and possibly solve some of their problems without incurring the higher costs associated with primary research. It is advisable, therefore, to locate and evaluate secondary information **before** considering primary research. Extensive savings, in time and money terms, may be enjoyed; the embarrassment of collecting information already available will be avoided, and primary research, if needed, can be left to concentrate on the additional information required in order to update, refine or supplement the secondary information obtained.

Secondary information from other organisations or internal to the company can often be obtained by phone or post with out the researcher leaving his or her desk and such research, therefore, is often referred to as **desk research**.

Secondary information can be divided into three types:

- Abstracts
- Lists
- Statistics.

All three types can be found or generated **internally** as well as **externally**.

## Internal sources

Internal sources of information are those generated internally by a company as it trades, and may include:

- Accounting records, e.g. creditor/debtor gap, speed of customer payments
- Costings on products and/or services, delivery costs, etc.
- Marketing and administrative expenses
- Cost of after sales services
- Total sales by product, area, time, period, etc.
- Number, nature and frequency of customer complaints
- Materials used by the production department
- Production capacity
- Levels of stock currently held by the company
- Advertising expenditure
- Consumer response to sales promotions previously used
- Sales achieved by sales staff, product, area, etc.
- Personnel records
- Labour turnover
- Productivity levels

The above represents just a small sample of the information which can be generated internally and the key to success is the continuous and harmonious interaction and co-operation of all the departments within the company.

## External sources

External sources of secondary information are those generated by organisations other than the company itself, such as the Government, media owners, trade associations, banks, embassies, academic institutions, specialist research organisations, advertising agencies, etc., and can be used by individuals or companies as part of their research programme. Sources include: statistics compiled by the Government, international organisations, specialist and business publications, etc. For greater detail on these sources refer to the Appendix to Chapter 1 on page 11.

Non-government statistics, such as lists or abstracts produced by a particular industry, may prove of greater value to specific marketers because **trade** sources concentrate on particular industries and thus tend to provide more relevant information.

A major limitation of secondary information is its **reliability**. Information may be out-of-date, incomplete, inaccurate or biased due to the methods of information collection used by others. Mistakes may not be detected easily and necessary information and relevant additions may not be evident. It is essential to evaluate secondary information very carefully by checking information from different sources and the methods employed in collecting the raw data. Any discrepancies witnessed may highlight areas of weakness in the information obtained and may provide the incentive to seek new, up-to-date, relevant and accurate supplementary information through primary sources.

Data obtained through marketing research may be:

1 **Quantitative:** i.e. objective data, such as the number of cars that pass a particular site for a proposed petrol station in any one week
2 **Qualitative:** i.e. subjective data, such as the attempt to assess people's attitudes or motivations.

## ■ RESEARCH PROCEDURE

Having identified the types of information used by marketing management and having listed the variety of sources of information, there is a need to concentrate on the actual approach used to collect the necessary facts and figures. The sheer variety and complexity of information demands a serious, careful and well-planned procedure. Like every aspect of business, marketing research needs to have a clear **directive**, a well-defined purpose and a proper objective. The directives are likely to vary from company to company but they can serve as vital guides for the complete research programme to be undertaken. When undertaking research it is necessary to know:

- What information is needed to be able to take a decision concerning a particular topic/problem?
- When the information is needed?
- Why it is needed?
- What are the likely sources of such information?
- How much is already known? There may already be sufficient information to take a reasoned decision without the expense of planned research.
- How much more information is needed?
- What is the level of accuracy sought?
- What is the research budget?
- Will external advice be sought?

These general questions can be supplemented by more specific questions to cover a company's special problems or expectations, but they nevertheless highlight the major questions being faced by marketing research managers and reinforce the need for clearly laid down objectives.

Once the major directives have been established, decisions need to be reached on the *methods* of collecting information to be used. For example, whether to simply observe consumers' behaviour or to seek to establish the reasons behind their behaviour? Should an ad-hoc research programme be used or should a continuous information flow from the market be looked for? Whatever decision is arrived at, the research – or survey – will involve one or more methods for collecting information; these are considered in Chapters 2 and 3.

Collecting information may prove costly, time-consuming and strenuous for the people involved but it can also be a rewarding experience if the information collected proves to be of value to a company. To achieve this, the information must be handled correctly. It needs to be classified accurately, processed patiently and evaluated properly. Findings need to be presented professionally and the implications of the findings communicated to all concerned.

This is a stage of research which is often underestimated or even avoided by marketing researchers, with the result that many valuable facts are lost or misunderstood. The steps in the ideal research programme can be summarised as follows.

1 **Definition of the purpose of the research**
   a) Identification of information needs
   b) Setting of research objectives
   c) Definition/selection of target market to be researched and sources of information to be used

2 **Information collection**
   a) Decision between census and sampling
   b) Selection of the type of respondents to be sought
   c) Evaluation and selection of survey methods to be used
   d) Questionnaire design

3 **Collating, analysis and reporting**
   a) Classification of findings
   b) Evaluation of information collected
   c) Implications of the information
   d) Reporting on findings

Note: Marketing research invariably affects most aspects of the marketing mix because **information** represents the most important part of a marketing manager's working life. The following chapters cover advertising, sales promotions, personal selling, marketing planning, international marketing and sales forecasting – all major decision-making areas within the sphere of marketing, all with a common need: accurate information to be supplied by the marketing research function of the company.

# ■ STUDY AND EXAM TIPS

**1** Be prepared to discuss the **value** of information to marketing decision-making, not simply the types of research or information available.

**2** Distinguish data from information and be prepared to discuss the relationship between the two terms.

**3** Avoid treating research as the solution to all marketing problems. Treat it as a risk reduction approach and do not hesitate to identify and discuss the likely limitations of the information which could be collected. You will become more able to analyse opportunities and limitations of research as you read the next two chapters.

# ■ SELF ASSESSMENT QUESTIONS

Answer the following questions and then refer to the answers given at the end of the book in order to determine your score. Award yourself one mark for each complete question that you answer correctly. If you scored seven or less re-read the relevant parts of the chapter. Answers are on page 237.

**1** Complete the sentence: 'Marketing research may be defined as the planned and systematic ....................................................................................................................................
....................................................................................................................................
.............................................. and the final consumption of goods or services.'

**2** One source of internal information is the accounts department. Name four more.

  a) ....................................................................................................................................
  b) ....................................................................................................................................
  c) ....................................................................................................................................
  d) ....................................................................................................................................

**3** Name three external sources of information other than specialist publications.

  a) ....................................................................................................................................
  b) ....................................................................................................................................
  c) ....................................................................................................................................

**4** Identify three types of secondary data.
   a) ................................................................................................................
   b) ................................................................................................................
   c) ................................................................................................................

**5** There are two types of marketing research information, namely, primary and ..................

**6** Primary research may be ................. or continuous.

**7** Identify the three main stages of a research programme:
   a) ................................................................................................................
   b) ................................................................................................................
   c) ................................................................................................................

**8** Marketing research is solely concerned with the analysis of the market itself. YES ☐ NO ☐ (tick appropriate box)

**9** Complete the sentence:
Marketing research helps more with risk ................. than with providing absolute answers to marketing problems.

**10** Complete the sentence.
   a) Marketing research may involve both quantitative as well as ................. findings.
   b) There may be field research and ................. research.

# ■  APPENDIX TO CHAPTER 1

External sources of information (using the UK as an example):

## 1   Governmental

For example:

a) Censuses – production, distribution, population
b) Annual Family Expenditure Survey
c) Statistics on income, prices, employment and production
d) National income and expenditure – *The Blue Book*
e) Overseas Trade Accounts
f) Accounts relating to the Trade and Navigation of the UK
g) *Monthly Digest of Statistics*
h) *Annual Abstract of Statistics*
i) *Economic Progress Report* (monthly – Treasury)
j) *Trade and Industry* (DTI magazine)

## 2 International organisations' publications

For example:

a) *United Nations Yearbook*
b) *UN Monthly Bulletin of Statistics*

## 3 Specialist publications (by subscription only)

For example:

a)   Economist Intelligence Unit publications
b)   *Nielsen Indices* (food, drugs, etc.)
c)   *Statistical Reviews of Advertising Expenditure*
d)   Detailed Media Listing – *British Rate and Data (BRAD)*
e)   Dunn and Bradstreet (Market Directories, Status Reports, Guide to Key British Enterprises, Register)
f)   Moodies Services Ltd (Company Accounts Interpretative Service)
g)   *Kompass Register*
h)   *Kelly's Directory*
i)   *Stock Exchange Yearbook*

## 4 Business publications

For example:

a)   *London and Cambridge Economic Bulletin*
b)   *Times Review of Industry and Technology*
c)   *Economist, Financial Times*
d)   *Harvard Business Review*
e)   *British Marketing Journal*
f)   *Marketing*

Visit your college library or a good public library with a commercial section and analyse some of the publications mentioned so that some basics of desk research become familiar to you.

## 5 Other sources

For example:

British Institute of Management (BIM), Confederation of British Industry (CBI), British Standards Institution (BSI), DTI Export Intelligence, British Overseas Trade Board (BOTB), Central Office of Information (COI), National Economic Development Council (NEDC), Economic Development Committees (EDCs), Trade Associations (e.g. ABPI), Chambers of Commerce, banks (e.g. Barclays, Klainwort Benson), Consumers Association (publishers of *Which?*), embassies and consulates.

# 2 | Research methodology

*The accuracy of research findings can be directly related to the effectiveness of the research methods employed.*

In the first chapter we distinguished between data and information, identified and discussed the importance of research to marketing decision-making and outlined the research procedure. This chapter examines in detail every stage of the recommended procedure and identifies the problems which may be encountered during implementation. All research programmes should allow for a series of activities which may be divided into three distinct sections:

1 Defining the purpose and objectives of the research
2 Determining how the data or information will be collected
3 Collating, analysing and reporting on the findings.

## ■ DEFINING THE OBJECTIVES OF THE RESEARCH

The purpose for which MR will be employed will depend upon the information the marketing manager needs in order to take a decision. For the newcomer to marketing some of the purposes for which MR may be employed are outlined below.

## Product research
- New product screening
- Product acceptance by selected target markets
- Packaging, e.g. colour, shape, size, texture, etc.
- Pricing, e.g. what price to launch with and what pricing structure should be followed?
- After-sales service, e.g. will repair services be needed if sales are to be made?
- Examination of the 'product concept' (the benefits offered and the overall product 'personality').

## User market research

- Size of current market
- Market potential
- Trends within a market
- Analysis of market shares amongst suppliers
- Users' opinions and beliefs.

## Sales research

- Sales force effectiveness and incentives used
- Sales achieved on product, area or customer basis
- Attitudes of distributors towards the company and its products
- Sales and profitability trends
- Contributions of product lines to overall profit
- Sales to overseas markets; determining the best country or countries to market in
- Sales forecasting.

## Communications research

- Effectiveness of advertising campaigns
- Company image
- Product image as perceived by segments of the total market
- Publicity generated
- Popularity of sales promotions.

## Economic and business research and its effect on an industry

- Economic trends and forecasts
- Political trends and forecasts
- Social trends and developments
- Inter-industry and inter-firm comparisons, etc.

By now you may have realised that some of the above information may be obtained via desk research. It is always policy – for the sake of speed and costs – to check if secondary sources are available before becoming involved in field research.

## Setting research objectives

Determining the purpose of the research leads to a clear understanding of the ultimate objectives of the investigation. A clearly defined objective marks a goal to be aimed at, while a poorly defined or incomplete objective will mean that it is difficult to direct the investigation in a satisfactory way. Companies may wish to know **who** buys their products, **how often** they buy, **where** they buy, **why** they buy, **who else** may buy, etc. On a more negative note, they may wish to find out why they don't buy, or whether there is anything wrong with the marketing approach used by the company. Thus, the *purpose* may be to examine the pricing structure used by the company but what *objective* should there be?

Take for instance an advertising campaign: extensive, costly and well-planned research may reveal that only 1 in 50 people have seen the advertisement in question or have heard of the company's products or services. A problem has obviously been discovered but the **cause** of the problem remains unknown. Did the company use the wrong advertising media? Were the right advertising media used at the wrong time? Was the advert shown often enough? Was the message clearly understood? Did consumers confuse the adverts with those of competitors?

Many similar questions may have to be asked before the **relationship** between the advertising campaign used and low consumer awareness levels is clearly understood. It is vital, therefore, to be as precise and as detailed as possible when setting objectives for a research programme.

## ■ DEFINING THE 'TARGET MARKET'

A target market is a group of consumers or organisations of special interest to a marketing organisation. It could be the current product users, the distributors, the company suppliers, potential users or a combination of some or all of the above. Usually, however, when a company is speaking of its target market it is referring to the people to whom it wishes to sell or does sell whether it be a consumer, user market or both. From the point of view of researchers they need to know how to identify a target market to know who to interview. Audiences can prove very difficult to define and quantify due to their size, geographical dispersion, variety and complexity. For example, a life insurance company wishes to introduce a new policy for people over 50 years old. A number of important questions will have to be answered before they can proceed:

- What is the size of the target market?
- What is the geographic dispersion or concentration of the target market?
- What are the occupations and income levels associated with this age group?
- What are the names, addresses, telephone numbers, etc. of the people in this target group?
- Who will influence and/or decide on the purchase of the insurance policy – the person who will have the policy, their spouse or the company for whom the potential policy holder works?

It is clearly important to define the target market as precisely as possible so that the characteristics identified can be used to guide the research activities, e.g. choosing the right people to interview, in the right number, at the right time and place, for accurate results and lower research costs. Students asked to consider where they would interview pregnant women have said 'on the streets' instead of pre-natal clinics, health centres, etc., where they naturally conjugate and may answer in the security of known surroundings. Thinking carefully about who to interview and where best to interview respondents is fundamental to efficient, cost-effective research.

To identify the right target audience to research, **market segmentation** techniques are used, whereby marketing researchers seek to identify clearly defined groups on which the research programme will be implemented. A full discussion of market segmentation is beyond the scope of this book but for our purposes the following is a reminder of the most popular methods of segmentation.

Target markets need to be defined according to:

- *Demographic variables*; i.e. consumers are classified according to age, sex, occupation, etc.
- *Psychographic variables*; i.e. beliefs, attitudes, perceptions, etc.
- *Geographic variables*; i.e. geographic location, city, district, country, etc.
- *Buyer behaviour*; i.e. where purchasers buy; how they buy – cash, credit, etc; how much they buy, e.g. heavy, light, occasional or non-user; social behaviour, i.e. what they like to do and where they tend to go – they may like football but some watch it on TV while another segment goes to local matches.

One method of segmenting a market may not lead to a truly homogenous target market so some or all of the methods are often combined for a detailed identification of the target market. If, for instance, only demographic variables are used you may – as an exaggeration to prove the point – have a target market consisting of men, 30–40 year olds, who work for banks. This definition may be sufficient in certain cases but no reference is made to any other characteristics. Behaviour patterns may differ from area to area. It is possible to have 30–40 year old, male, bank employees in London who may prefer wine while their counterparts in Glasgow may be beer drinkers. These additional characteristics could be vital to the research so a combination of as many relevant characteristics as possible is encouraged when a target market is defined for research purposes.

Organisations on the other hand are classified according to the industry they operate in, the end-user/consumer markets they serve, their size, their geographic location and the variety of products or services they offer.

## Disadvantages

The methods of segmentation identified and the criteria they utilise fail to allow for certain practical problems which could be faced when attempting to define a target market. For example:

1  Geographic areas cannot always be defined precisely; perhaps because of the lack of clearly defined boundaries. For instance, assume that you wish to interview marketing students living in the Greater London area. Where does this area start and end? Different people will have different ideas and opinions on this matter as it is difficult to define a large city precisely.

2  Demographic segmentation utilises criteria such as income, occupation, sex,

age, religion, as a means of dividing large, dissimilar audiences into smaller audiences having similar profiles. There may be no problem in identifying sex, age group or religion but researchers will face problems in defining income groups or occupations. Income is very personal and respondents often lie about their earnings, assets and expenditures. Worse still, titles given to jobs are vague and often misleading. Business people may have impressive titles, e.g. Marketing Executive, Chief Executive, Director of Operations, which do not depict the true nature of their positions. The words 'advisor', 'consultant', 'co-ordinator' and 'programmer' have become very popular, assuming many different meanings within different industries or individual companies.

3 Retail and other sales outlets fall into many different business categories because they offer a wide range of unrelated products. Some Tesco supermarket outlets sell groceries, records, pharmaceutical products, clothes, DIY goods, toys, cosmetics, etc. and consequently a description of the outlet or the company as simply a 'retailer' becomes totally inadequate.

When problems of this nature are faced marketing researchers need to **set their own definitions** of the criteria being used for segmentation purposes, and these should be communicated to all parties involved in the research programme so that accurate samples may be drawn.

# ■  SAMPLING

The success of a research programme will be largely determined by the quality of the sample of respondents used to seek answers or opinions from. If you consider the large size and wide geographic dispersion of most consumer markets you can appreciate the need to obtain relevant information from a relatively small group of respondents who represent the values, opinions, beliefs and expectations of a much larger group of consumers.

A marketing research sample, therefore, can be defined as:

> *a representatative proportion (number) of a given target market used in the collection of information consistent with a pre-determined research objective.*

Think of a popular brand of biscuits and try to visualise the millions of consumers who may be buying or eating the biscuits every week. It is impossible to get opinions from *all* the users so we have to rely on the information we can collect from a small but representative cross-section of that market. If, for instance, 10 per cent of the users are children, 5–10 year olds, then you should seek to have a sample of total users, 10 per cent of which is children of this age group. *Note*: Marketing researchers often refer to the target market as 'the **universe**', i.e. the total market from which the sample of the people to interview will be taken.

## Sample size

The size of the sample to be used during the research will be affected by a number of variables. A sample of 100 respondents drawn from a population of one million people who drink a particular brand of coffee is unlikely to lead to unbiased and solid findings, as the sample is too small and does not effectively represent the values, beliefs and expectations of everyone. It is possible to select a representative number of people (the sample) from consumer markets because they tend to be large in number and homogeneous. Most importantly they abide by two laws of statistics that must apply when selecting a representative sample from a larger group. These are:

1 **The law of inertia of large numbers** which asserts that large groups of people are less likely to rapidly change their patterns of behaviour than small groups. A survey may take several weeks to complete and if the market from which the sample is being taken is constantly changing in its behaviour the findings will not be representative of the current behaviour of the market.
2 **The law of statistical regularity** which maintains that a large enough sample of a very large group of people (or items) will be representative of the characteristics of the large group.

While these laws underpin the theory of sample selection the actual real life decision regarding the sample size and mix necessary to be representative of the market will depend on the following:

- Statistical determination of the right number of respondents (interviewees) to approach
- Nature and size of universe being investigated; for example, only a few major companies in an industrial or retailer market may need interviewing, plus a small sample of other companies in the industry, in order to determine, for example, the reaction to a proposed price change
- Budget available
- Time available – where fashions change rapidly, research should be short (in time) before it becomes unrepresentative
- Type of research – desk or field?
- Skilled research personnel available
- Fieldwork problems expected – particularly when large numbers of respondents need to be interviewed over a short period of time
- Tabulation requirements; masses of information collected from large samples of respondents may take a long time to be classified, analysed and understood, during which time the information becomes less attractive because consumers may have changed their minds, competitors have altered their marketing approaches, etc.
- Accuracy sought – the more precise the information required, the larger the sample needs to be
- Number of people to be interviewed (respondents).

# Sampling methods

### RANDOM (PROBABILITY) SAMPLES

A random sample implies that the items or persons who constitute the universe each stand the same chance of being selected to be part of the sample. Therefore, a purely random sample requires that all items or persons who represent the universe are available or known. As a simple example, if you have a large bag of thousands of marbles of various colours it is reasonable to assume that if you extracted several handfuls of marbles they would have similar characteristics to those remaining in the bag. In marketing, random samples are usually selected by computer.

A problem when using random samples for MR surveys is that they may consist of too many people with a particular characteristic. An extreme example of this would be to select a sample of men and women in the USA of various races to interview, which may have 70 per cent of white women with no black people included in the sample at all.

### NON-RANDOM SAMPLING

Unless all the items that constitute the universe are known then a purely random sample cannot be used; instead a non-random sample is needed. This does not mean that a non-random sample is less representative than a random sample, as it may take account of differences in the importance of people, organisations or items that can be selected. A non-random sample will invariably be more cost-effective than random samples when used for MR purposes. Non-random samples would include:

1 **Stratified sampling.** The universe is divided into strata/segments that collectively represent the whole universe. For example, house-owners may be stratified into owners of detached, semi-detached, terraced houses, etc., and their numbers estimated. A randomly selected proportion from each stratum may then be obtained for research, thus ensuring that in the total sample you are obtaining proportions in relation to the total universe.
2 **Systematic sampling.** The first item is selected randomly, and then additional items are selected by equal intervals, i.e. house number 11 may have been selected randomly, and then each tenth in the district thereafter will be used for research.
3 **Multi-stage sampling.** Multi-stage sampling is based on defined regions/areas. Regions of a country may be selected randomly and thereafter areas within these regions. For example, counties or states may be selected at random; then local authorities within the counties or states selected; then streets within the local authorities' areas; then families in the streets; and finally individuals within families.
4 **Cluster sampling.** This is similar to multi-stage. Representative clusters of people are selected randomly instead of by a staging process based on society's defined areas. For example, apartment blocks or streets may be used. Every person in the apartment block or street that has been randomly selected will

then be interviewed.

5 **Quota sampling.** This is possibly the most popular method used by marketing researchers. The universe/population is stratified and interviewers are then given specific numbers (a quota) of types of people to interview, such as, ten house-owning teachers, 13 house-owning managers, etc. The attributes essential to typicality of respondents is more important than location or random selection. Therefore, if you wanted to interview red-headed women about a proposed new hair dye you may send interviewers to a city in Wales (a country where there are many red-headed people) to cut down costs of the research and provide each interviewer with a **quota** of women of different ages to interview.

Because of costs and the need to ensure a representative sample, non-random sampling is the more popular method of sampling in MR. Bear in mind, however, that most non-random samples have an element of random selection in them, but they are not purely random samples as all items, or people, did not have the same opportunity of being selected. You may, in fact, find some books referring to certain non-random sampling methods as **modified random sampling**.

**Table 2.1** Advantages and disadvantages of the two sampling methods

| Random sampling | Non-random sampling |
|---|---|
| *Advantages* | *Advantages* |
| • Knowledge of the universe's characteristics is unnecessary | • Relevant sections of the universe can be selected in the proportions they appear in the universe |
| • Bias which may be caused by the selector is eliminated. | • Geographical concentration can be achieved thus reducing costs |
| | • It is usually a more practical method for MR sampling. |
| *Disadvantages* | *Disadvantages* |
| • Certain groups of people may be selected more than they should be, i.e. bias in the final sample | • Detailed initial information of the universe is needed |
| • Errors can be difficult to detect | • Errors in sample selection can easily occur by the research organiser or/and where the interviewers are expected to identify appropriate respondents. |
| • May be costly, particularly where people in remote districts are selected. | |

## User market sampling

The above sampling methods are rarely used in researching user markets because companies constituting a market (e.g. the industrial market) are often so few in number that it may be possible to interview all the companies involved, or a small proportion of companies that account for the majority of supply by the particular industry, plus a small proportion of the remaining companies. Where, however, a method of sampling is possible the method used will invariably be non-random.

## Sampling frames

If field research is to be used, there may be a list or table of the details of the universe, known as a **sampling frame**, e.g. a mail order list, or a new car register. Sampling frames may provide the major characteristics of the universe and are helpful for any MR, but particularly for selection in random sampling. If a frame does not already exist the company may have to develop its own sampling frame, or they may be purchased from companies specialising in compiling and selling sampling frames, although these can be very expensive and may be drastically out-of-date, incomplete or inaccurate in other ways. It is worth remembering that sampling frames may be viewed as secondary data and they subsequently may suffer from the limitations of secondary data already discussed on page 6.

# ■ CENSUS

The term census implies counting or collecting information from **every** member of the universe. The census of population, for instance, involves the actual checking of the number of people living in a particular country while a census in the marketing research context implies interviewing every member of a **given** universe. You may feel that carrying out a census is an impossible task so it is worth considering the following:

1 Some consumer markets are relatively small or easily definable, so a census could be the most attractive option. How many people own a private jet or a Rolls Royce in this country? The number is small and therefore the extraction of a sample becomes meaningless.
2 Consider the limited number of students attending courses at your college, university or school. Is sampling justified? Would it be possible to ask every student to answer some simple questions regarding the college services? If yes, then a census becomes a much more reasonable and effective alternative.
3 Industrial and retail markets have certain characteristics which make a census a necessity rather than a luxury. It is worth reviewing the main features of industrial markets:
a) Many industries are small in size. Consider the number of car, television or computer manufacturers within one country. The number may even run into hundreds but it is still possible to carry out a census.
b) User markets often consist of individuals or organisations of unequal purchasing power. Think of multiples (companies with a large number of outlets) which dominate various retailing markets. It is possible to have five multiples which account for, say, 70 per cent of the annual turnover in a particular market while the remaining 30 per cent is shared among thousands of small retailers. It will be pointless to carry out any research designed to evaluate the whole market if the multiples refuse to provide the information required. They may dominate the market for a low price good, affecting the trends within the market and attracting the main customers of a particular manufacturer's

product. If a census is used involving all the multiples, supported by a sample of the remaining small retailers, then adequate information for a marketing decision will probably result.

c) Some industrial markets are geographically concentrated. Consider the car industry: if car manufacturers are located in a particular area you may find that many manufacturers of component parts used by the car manufacturers could be located nearby (tyre, battery, windscreen wiper manufacturers, etc.). This reduces distribution cost, minimises delays and improves the daily communications between the companies. Thus, the geographic concentration existing may make a survey bordering on a census cost-effective assuming that the companies are willing to respond to any request for information.

# ■ PILOT SURVEYS

In some cases a **pilot survey** of one or two hundred people in a universe may be used to gain a fair idea of characteristics of a universe and how often such characteristics may occur. For example, a few hundred of the targeted universe may be interviewed to determine what proportion are fresh juice drinkers, thereby determining the proportion of fresh juices that probably exist in the total universe and, therefore, what size sample must be used (perhaps thousands) to ensure the final findings are accurate within defined limits.

# ■ OBTAINING DATA FROM RESPONDENTS

Having selected a sample to obtain information from, there are four main methods which can be used to collect the information/data:

1 **Postal questionnaires**
2 **Personal interviewing**
3 **Telephone interviews**
4 **Observation.**

## Postal questionnaires

Questionnaires are posted to the selected respondents, along with clear directives on the purpose of the research, the importance of the research to the respondent, the address to be used in returning questionnaires (stamped and addressed envelopes should be used) and the time limit within which questionnaires should be completed and returned. The effectiveness of this method will be determined by the accuracy of the mailing lists used, the interest levels achieved and the quality of the questionnaire used (see page 28).

## ADVANTAGES

- Wide distribution is possible. Respondents in all parts of the country may be reached.
- Respondents have time to consider their answers, consult colleagues, friends and members of their family – unless they are instructed not to consult with others before and when answering the questions on the questionnaire.
- Respondent anonymity may encourage individuals to answer the questions truthfully.
- Respondents will usually be asked to enter their name and address, telephone number, occupation, etc. Research programmes may relate to personal or confidential matters, in which case a coding system used by research companies classifies the questionnaires they receive, which will not identify the respondent but will provide a guide as to the age group, location, sex, etc. Having names and addresses helps the company to develop mailing lists for future research or promotional purposes such as sending promotional material by mail (direct mail).
- It is a relatively inexpensive method of distributing questionnaires but the actual cost should be determined in terms of the number of completed questionnaires returned. Each questionnaire mailing may cost the company 30p, which is very attractive. However, if 10 000 questionnaires are sent out and only 100 are returned then the cost per 'completed interview' increases dramatically, e.g.

$$10\ 000 \times £0.30 = £3000 \text{ (Total cost of mailing)}$$

Cost per completed questionnaire however, is:

$$\frac{£3000}{100 \text{ questionnaires returned}} = £30 \text{ each.}$$

This cost would compare unfavourably with alternative methods of contact, like personal interviewing. Therefore, pre-planning, effective design and writing of the questionnaire, stimulating letters of encouragement, reminder cards to respondents to prompt replies and pre-paid methods for respondents to answer through the post are all important.

- Letters can be addressed to the 'occupant', 'manager', etc. Personalised letters are obviously more effective but when complete and up-to-date mailing lists are not available a more general approach can be used.
- Bias that may result from an interviewer being present is eliminated.
- A team of researchers is not required. A skilled researcher may on his/her own arrange and implement the survey.

## DISADVANTAGES

- Questions used must be kept simple. Respondents will not spend a lot of time answering complex questions demanding in-depth answers. As a result the information collected may lack depth.
- Many people are often worried about their handwriting, spelling and general

vocabulary. Wherever possible questions should therefore be accompanied by pre-set answers which only require the respondent making a tick, e.g. Have you ever drunk alcohol? YES/NO (please tick the appropriate answer).

- The questionnaire itself must be kept as short as possible which again detracts from the depth of research. It will be unreasonable to expect respondents to spend more than 15 minutes filling in a questionnaire. The longer respondents have to spend completing the questionnaire, the fewer questionnaires will be returned.
- Reasons for non-response cannot always be determined. Reminder letters and covering letters may be used to maximise interest levels in the research, but respondents cannot be forced to reply nor can they be encouraged to reply by an interviewer.
- Low response is a major problem with this method of research and researchers need to decide in advance whether they would be happy with 10–15 per cent response levels (this does not imply that reasonable response rates may not be higher or lower).
- Lack of face-to-face contact makes the evaluation of whether the respondent is precisely the type wanted impossible. For example, if people with a particular type of curly hair are required to respond, or people with more than $x$ amount of tooth fillings, there is no guarantee that the right respondents are answering.

## Personal interviewing

Research is often associated with personal interviews because it is a form of collection everybody encounters some time on the streets. Personal interviewing – indoor or outdoors – involves interviewing one or more respondents. The interviewer's questions are often guided by a questionnaire and directives will be given by the MR manager as to who to interview.

**ADVANTAGES**
- Many methods of formal or informal approach are possible. Potential respondents can be stopped in the streets, interviewed in shops, visited in the office or at home, etc.
- Body language' (facial expressions, body movements, general reactions, etc.) can prove extremely informative. Respondents may claim that they agree with a particular way of behaving, but their overall reactions may imply that they are uncomfortable with the answer given.
- Typicality of the respondent can be more readily ascertained, e.g. potential respondents who have a certain hair colour, way of dressing.
- Interviewers may be given the freedom to pursue lines of questioning outside the questionnaire used. A particular answer may be unexpected, surprising, controversial or unique so well-trained interviewers seek to determine the reasons and implications of such answers.
- The product, special offer, advertisement or service under investigation can be explained and product samples, copies of the advert, business literature, cards, etc., can be used in order to inform or remind the respondents.

- Difficult questions can be explained by the interviewer.
- The face-to-face situation may facilitate the introduction of lengthier interviews because interest can be maintained more easily. References to the weather, the news, children when they are present, etc., may break the monotony, relax the respondents and 'buy' more time for answering more questions.

## DISADVANTAGES

- Personal interviews can prove difficult to arrange; managers may have a busy schedule, housewives carrying heavy shopping may avoid interviewers, poor weather will restrict street interviews and many members of the public simply do not like being interviewed.
- It is a very costly method of collecting information; interviewers and travel must be paid for.
- It is difficult and extremely costly to cover large geographical areas.
- Interviewers need to be trained well. Untrained interviewers have been known to stand in doorways when rain starts interviewing only those visiting the premises, resulting in biased findings.
- The face-to-face situation may lead to bias. Respondents may not be willing to give the full facts, may dislike the interviewer, may be shy, may react angrily to certain questions or may be ashamed to tell the truth.
- Sometimes – particularly in surveying user markets – an interviewer may only have sufficient time to interview two or three respondents a day, so the survey may be quite extensive.
- Interviewers may interpret respondents' reactions wrongly, may select the wrong respondents or may fail to observe vital clues given during the interview. An interview has to be treated as a 'social event', involving two or more people, with the aim of exchanging information. Careful preparation and professional handling of the conversation will maximise the collection of information and will leave the respondent feeling happy and possibly important. Some useful **tips** to follow during a personal interview include:

  - try to create a friendly and relaxed atmosphere by being polite, by speaking slowly and clearly and by relating to the profile of the respondent
  - explain clearly the purpose and likely duration of the interview
  - listen to the answers given and record all information provided
  - leave enough time at the end of each answer to ensure that the respondent has finished
  - do not show any emotions about the answers given by the respondents
  - avoid thinking of the next question while the respondent is still answering the last one
  - plan the ending of the interview as carefully as you planned the initial approach; try to finish in a courteous and friendly manner
  - write up your observations immediately on completion of the interview.

To ensure that respondents have actually been interviewed most MR managers will phone a random selection of respondents to check or, if phone numbers and addresses are not being collected, visit interviewers while they are interviewing.

## Telephone interviews

Telephone interviews can be carried out from a 'central location' (the office of a research organisation for instance) or from the home of an interviewer. Computer Administered Telephone Interviewing (CATI) is also widely used. Interviewers can use TV monitors which display the questions to be asked and a series of pre-coded answers; the researcher then keys the responses received directly into a computer at his/her office. This saves time and mistakes associated with pen and paper telephone interviews can be eliminated.

### ADVANTAGES
- A large geographical area can be covered in a relatively short period of time.
- Respondents who cannot be reached during the normal business hours can be reached at home during the evening.
- The response rate is much higher than for postal questionnaires, sometimes as high as 90 per cent.
- Responses can be collected and analysed fairly quickly.
- Travelling expenses associated with face-to-face interviewing are eliminated.
- It is particularly useful for industrial and retailer market research as most respondents will have a telephone.

### DISADVANTAGES
- There is no face-to-face contact so it is difficult to assess the typicality of the respondent.
- Not everyone has a telephone so the sample may not be totally representative.
- It is difficult to establish rapport with the respondents and interviews tend to be kept rather formal.
- Expenses can rise rapidly where respondents are widely dispersed and daytime phoning is necessary.
- Lengthy interviews cannot be carried out and complex research programmes cannot be accommodated by this method of contact. Respondents may not be willing to spend too much time speaking on the phone to somebody they don't know or cannot see.
- Sampling frames used are often biased. Telephone and business directories are *not* complete or up-to-date, thus the quality of the sample used may be adversely affected.
- Some people are suspicious of telephone interviews because they cannot establish the true identity of the caller. Questions about ownership and use of household items, product preferences, hobbies, occupation and absence from the house may worry respondents.

## Observation

Observation represents one of the most neglected and least understood methods of collecting information. The lack of an interview obviously limits the scope of this method but it is ideal when dealing with very young children, animals or adults who cannot be interviewed, e.g. motorists driving past a given site.

## ADVANTAGES

- It is a relatively inexpensive method of collecting information because it does not involve the arrangement of expensive, time-consuming interviews.
- It can cover a large geographic area, because many observation points can be set up in different areas. However, the research may relate to one spot, for example checking the number of people who pass by the proposed location for a large supermarket at various times of each day.
- As little time is usually necessary to observe, information from a large sample can be collected. For example: the percentage of motorists using children's car seats can be observed by the researcher standing at traffic lights.
- Bias resulting from face-to-face, and possibly telephone interviewing is eliminated.
- Visual communications from subjects not able to communicate orally are established. For example, a dog's reaction to a given brand of dog food, or an infant's handling of a toy.
- Physical typicality of what is being observed can be determined.
- Bias emanating from respondents' replies is eliminated.

## DISADVANTAGES

- Researchers can only observe current behaviour; no information as to past behaviour is known. This could lead to dangerous generalisations or wrong assumptions because current, observed behaviour is often taken as being representative of past or likely future behaviour.
- Reasons behind a pattern of behaviour observed cannot be determined.
- Satisfactions or dissatisfactions delivered by products or services are not known – only whether a person purchased or didn't purchase.
- Respondents may realise they are being observed and change their normal pattern of behaviour.
- Verification of findings is often difficult as the MR manager cannot contact respondents to check if they were observed.

# ■ TYPES OF MARKETING RESEARCH QUESTIONS

Respondents may be asked only four types of questions, whether orally or written. These are:

1 **Dichotomous questions**. These are close-ended, two-sided questions, in that the respondent can only answer 'Yes' or 'No', 'True' or 'False', etc. The respondent can choose from only two options.

   *Example*
   Q. Do you smoke? YES/NO    Please circle your answer.

2 **Multiple choice questions.** Again close-ended but the respondent is given more than two possible choices.

*Example*

| Q  If you smoke, on average, how many cigarettes do you smoke each day? Please circle your answer. | 1  1 to 9 <br> 2  10 to 20 <br> 3  21 to 30 <br> 4  31 to 40 <br> 5  41 or over |
|---|---|

Thus multiple choice questions are a compromise between the inflexibility of dichotomous questions and the possible vagueness of open-ended questions.

3 **Semantic differential scales**. Semantic differential scales go further than multiple choice questions as, while they limit the reply the respondent may give, they do allow freedom of response within the governing extremes on the scale.

*Example*

Q  Mark with a cross 'X' the point on 'Scale A' which reflects your liking of the ice-cream that you have just tasted.

SCALE A

I ............................................... I

Hate it                                    Adore it

4 **Open-ended questions.** It may be justifiably reasoned that open-ended are the best types of question for obtaining opinions. However, the main problem is the effective interpretation and collation of answers, which may be vague and extensive. For this reason respondents are often asked to limit their replies to a set number of words. Open-ended questions are very useful where a company is attempting to determine if there are aspects of respondents' attitudes and/or behaviour they may not currently appreciate, but skilled researchers are required to analyse the replies.

*Example*

Q  What, do you believe, is your main reason for smoking? Please write your answer below.

.........................................................................................................

.........................................................................................................

.........................................................................................................

# ■ QUESTIONNAIRE DESIGN

Questionnaire design has a direct effect on the overall quality of the research programme. Questionnaires are not just a list of questions; they represent a carefully compiled, logical sequence of questions for achieving a well-defined research objective. Selecting the right sample, deciding on the most appropriate survey method, employing experienced interviewers or planning the method of approach to be used may be totally wasted if the wrong questions are asked, if the wrong sequence of questions is used or, worse still, if the 'right' questions are not asked at all.

A well-planned approach is vital to questionnaire design and the following five steps are recommended:

1 Decide carefully upon the information to be collected
2 Carry out informal interviews
3 Draft the questionnaire
4 Pilot test the questionnaire
5 Determine the final design.

Each step involves a series of activities, as follows.

# 1  Decide upon the information to be collected

The information required can only be determined after a careful study of the objectives of the survey and the variety of information that may result. If, for example, the purpose of the research is to determine the popularity of a particular brand of tea bags, questions which may be created at this stage could include:

- Do you drink tea?
- Do you use Brand X tea bags?
- Have you tried other brands of tea?
- What do you consider when you select a particular type of tea?
- What do you think of Brand X?
- Etc.

Many questions of this nature will be listed for general reference purposes. Each will need questions to be tested, placed in a logical sequence and evaluated in terms of its usefulness to the survey. Additionally, the team of researchers will have to consider the:

- Logic of presentation of the questions selected
- Understanding of the vocabulary used
- Quality of possible answers generated
- Possible respondent reactions to individual questions
- Additional questions which may have to be introduced
- Length and time needed to complete the proposed interview(s) or complete the questionnaire if it is to be posted to respondents
- Adequacy of instructions to the respondent and, where applicable, to the interviewer.

# 2  Carry out informal interviews

The objective during this stage is to evaluate the draft questionnaire developed along the lines identified in the previous stage. A small sample of representative respondents (say 10 to 20) should be selected for the purpose of informal interviewing designed to determine **how** the respondents react to the points raised, **what** they think of the questions asked, whether they **understand** the words used and whether the questionnaire maintains an acceptable level of **interest** in the respondent. Feedback (answers, comments, facial expressions, body movements, etc.) will help the researchers to adapt questions and offer the researcher the opportunity to get a more intimate feel for the subject. By meeting and talking to a small sample of the target market he/she can establish the type of vocabulary and method of approach which can best serve the research programme.

## 3  Drafting the questionnaire

Information collected through the informal interviews will affect the actual content and design of the questionnaire but irrespective of the topics covered, certain principles must always be applied.

a) Each question used should only cover one point. In order to explain the principle let us look at a couple of poor questions:

*When and where did you buy this brand of baked beans?*
There are obviously two questions in one sentence which ought to be separated in order to avoid confusion and misunderstanding.

*Why do you prefer this particular make of car?*
This type of question could involve a series of answers, ranging from price to reliability, to speed, to cost of parts, etc. Each area should be considered separately because it is likely to have a direct effect on the marketing mix to be used by the company in the future. The component parts of a question should therefore be identified and should be used in the framing of separate questions, each covering a specific point of interest. Advice on this point is to keep questions as short and as simple as possible without insulting the intelligence of the respondent.

b) Avoid leading questions. The question, 'You do use this marketing book, don't you?' put to a group of marketing students is likely to lead to a biased answer since it is implying that 'Yes' is the right or acceptable answer. A questionnaire should not be designed to collect information which the sponsoring company would like to see; it should concentrate on collecting information representing facts.

c) Avoid third party questions. Asking a respondent about products used, satisfactions obtained and selection criteria used by somebody else, even a member of his/her own family, will lead to an **opinion** rather than facts. If the third party is vital to the research then he/she should be asked instead of the selected respondent.

d) Select intensive phrases carefully. Everyday words used by the members of the public assume different meanings from person to person. Think of the words 'expensive', 'cheap', 'good', 'bad', 'rich', 'poor', etc. We all know what they mean but we all use them differently because of differences in personal circumstances, perceptions, decision-making criteria, moods, etc. A £400 car could be seen as very expensive by somebody who is unemployed or facing financial problems while the same car could be treated as a real bargain – or not worth purchasing – by somebody in full employment earning £25 000 per year.

If a response along these lines is needed then a range of answers should be provided so that the respondents can tick off or select the appropriate answer.

e) Avoid ambiguous questions. Every question asked must lead to one inter-pretation. Think of the question 'Do you study your lecturer's handouts?' This is a very ambiguous question because it could imply 'every day', 'every week', 'Do you understand them?', etc. A more precise set of questions should be used covering specific subjects, time periods, frequency of use, student selectivity, etc., each one having only **one** possible meaning.

f) Avoid questions which place too much strain on memory for an answer. Any questions relating to events, activities or purchases which took place a long time ago are likely to generate answers which do not represent the truth. Respondents cannot always remember accurately and may unintentionally give the wrong answer or best opinion of what they think happened. Questions relating to the distant past must be limited as much as possible or they should relate to major events or purchases which the respondents are likely to remem-ber fairly well.

g) Utilise the working vocabulary of the target market. All questionnaires should involve clear and precise words or statements which can be understood easily by the respondents. The language used on an everyday basis by the members of the target population is the best guide, and may include technical terms or even abbreviations as long as they are fully understood by the respondents. PLC to a marketing student should automatically imply 'product life cycle' while to a layman it may not mean anything at all.

h) Seek a logical sequence of questioning. The questions used should follow a pattern which allows the respondent to summarise his/her thoughts. Some simple and general questions about the respondent and the general topic of investigation should be used at the beginning followed by more specific or complex questions which tackle the major issues of the research. Therefore, keep like questions in the same section and keep personal questions to the end. Make the questionnaire pleasing to look at and easy to complete.

## 4  Pilot test the questionnaire

Considerable errors can still occur after the questionnaire has been designed if a researcher does not check the first draft with other researchers and with respondents in the target market. To test the questionnaire the researcher must:

a) Make allowance for his/her own bias by ensuring that researchers with different opinions analyse an outline questionnaire and then assist with the final construction of the questions and questionnaire design.

b) Conduct some free-ranging interviews with representative individuals or groups of respondents to ensure there are no unforeseen problems, such as difficulties in obtaining typical respondents.

c) Conduct a pilot survey and include the method of double interviewing (interviews in which the interviewer asks the question on the questionnaire and after the response asks the respondent what he or she thought the question was trying to determine: respondents often infer different things about the same question).

## 5  Final design

After pilot interviews are completed all interviewers involved should discuss their views and impressions, in order to finalise:

- The instructions (to the interviewer or the respondents)
- The numbering of the questions
- Covering letters which are needed if postal questionnaires are to be used
- The actual length of the questionnaire
- Pre-coded answers used to identify age group, sex group, income group, etc.
- Actual vocabulary to be used
- Overall presentation of the questionnaire.

Once the questionnaire is finalised, it can be introduced into the research programme and the actual process of obtaining the desired information can begin. It is possible for further adjustments to be carried out on the strength of new findings during the actual fieldwork, but it is worth remembering that the conditions to effective questionnaire design should still be obeyed.

## ■  COLLATING, ANALYSIS AND REPORTING

The last stage in the research procedure is the actual collating and evaluation of information. Collating involves statistical methods and techniques which will enable researchers to understand the implications of the findings.

Classification of data, establishment of correlations, determination of averages and reporting on actual findings using tables, graphs, charts, etc., are beyond the scope of this chapter and reference should be made to statistics textbooks on this subject.

Marketing decisions to take action or not, may be made on the strength of the survey's findings by senior management. As indicated earlier in the chapter, information remains the key to success in marketing and the research methodology discussed offers the reader an insight into a systematic, professional, logical and effective way to keep contact with and assess the needs of the people that matter most: actual and potential customers.

## ■ STUDY AND EXAM TIPS

**1** Examiners tend to ask specific questions on certain aspects of marketing research. Read the questions carefully, identify the aspect/s to be discussed and concentrate your recommendations on these aspects.

**2** Always allow for the fact that research will not offer perfect solutions to any problem so present your thoughts along the lines of risk reduction.

**3** Be willing to identify and discuss both advantages and limitations of techniques used in research programmes.

**4** Allow for the marketing orientation to filter through your discussion by never forgetting the role of MR in helping to determine the right marketing mix to use in satisfying customer needs.

---

## ■ PAST EXAMINATION QUESTIONS

### The Institute of Marketing

**1** What market information should be collected by a marketing manager planning to launch a new product? How will he collect and use it?

**2** Why is quota sampling extensively used in survey research, in preference to the theoretically superior random sampling?

**3** Researchers may collect primary data in face-to-face interviews, over the telephone or through the post. Discuss the advantages and disadvantages of these methods.

**4** What factors should be taken into account when designing questionnaires to be used as part of market surveys?

---

## ■ SUGGESTED ANSWER TO QUESTION 2

It is rare to find situations where market researchers are able to carry out a complete investigation covering the full target market of their choice. Information is usually collected from a small but representative proportion of the target market and the degree of representation will determine the quality of the findings. This process is called sampling. Two laws that must be obeyed when selecting a sample are;

1 The sample should contain the properties of the total population under investigation (a spoonful of coffee should be the same as the rest of the coffee in the jar).
2 The sample should be big enough in relative terms so that the properties of the total population exist in the sample.

Both needs can be allowed for in all sampling methods available to researchers but a decision needs to be reached as to the sampling technique to be used.

Two general techniques which dominate the theory and practice of research are random and non-random sampling.

## Random probability sampling

Using this method *all* members of the population are given an equal chance of being selected, thus, it is believed, bias is removed or at least minimised. This belief is not necessarily correct in practice, however, because of the following:

1 For all members to have an equal chance of being selected, a complete, up-to-date list (sampling frame) needs to be compiled. Although in the last few years there has been a rapid growth in the availability of lists, it is impossible to obtain a complete list of members in consumer markets. It could be possible in the case of some industrial or retail markets but you will then face the problem of members having **unequal** purchasing power.
2 Even if you assume a complete list is compiled, there are no guarantees that the sample extracted at random will not be biased. Some minority groups may be completely missed or over-represented, so there will be different degrees of representation between total population and sample population.
3 Non-response from sample respondents selected could lead to further bias unless researchers can, or are willing to, replace them with potential respondents with similar characteristics.
4 Selected respondents may be geographically scattered and as a result data collection may become cost-prohibitive.

From the above you can see the practical limitations of a theoretically sound technique, which forces researchers to seek a more practical, cost-effective approach such as non-random sampling, of which quota sampling is one method.

## Quota sampling

This approach allows for pre-determined percentages to appear in the sample. In other words assuming a total universe of one million people is to be researched, the profile of the segments must be identified, as follows:

Figure 2.1

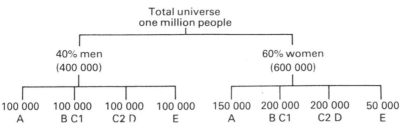

The percentage of the population is used as the percentage breakdown of the sample. Assuming the sample size is determined at 2000 people, the samples may be broken down as follows, in the same proportions as the universe.

Figure 2.2

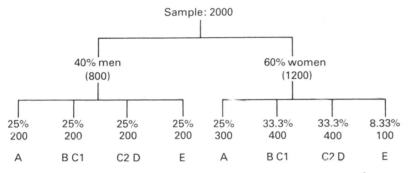

Interviewers are then given **quotas** of respondents in relation to the sample breakdown without any specifications as to name. For example, they may be instructed to interview 200 males in the socio-economic groups B and C1. In the same way, of course, the proportion of women in the sample would be divided by their characteristics, i.e. socio-economic groups, as shown in Fig. 2.2.

This technique controls over- or under-representation of groups and it does not need a complete sampling frame of the total population, although it cannot be seen as the perfect alternative to random sampling since it suffers from certain limitations:

1 The percentage breakdown of the target population is not always available or up-to-date.
2 The technique relies heavily on interviewers' professionalism. It assumes that the 'right' respondents will be selected but subjective assessment or deliberate mistakes by interviewers are always a major threat.

As may be noted by interviewers it is not possible to obtain a perfect solution to a business/marketing problem but one needs to seek risk reduction. In marketing research random sampling is often subject to bias while quota sampling offers the opportunity to control some bias occurring. Practising researchers often prefer a theoretically inferior technique which gives them greater control and consequently research quality – hence the popularity of quota sampling.

# 3 Continuous and motivation research

The research methodology discussed in the previous section revealed the major steps to be followed in the implementation of a research programme and identified the likely benefits and problems which may be associated with each stage of research.

It was assumed that a company, or a market research agency on behalf of the company, was carrying out just one piece of research (*ad hoc*) at one point in time, to discover specific information about the market which was needed at a particular time by that company in order to make a marketing decision. It would be more useful to a company, however, to have such information on a continuous basis so that it would be immediately aware of any changes or trends within the market. **Continuous research** is considered in the first part of this section on research.

We will then consider the deeper or subconscious reasons why people purchase – or don't purchase – by looking at some techniques of **motivation research**.

## ■ CONTINUOUS RESEARCH

*Continuous research is about constantly keeping our finger on the pulse of the market*

Some information regarding aspects of the market are difficult or costly to obtain, such as the continuing market share of a particular brand. In other words the number of products sold by a company in relation to all other competing brands. If, for instance, consumers in the USA buy 20 million packs of coffee per month and a particular brand accounts for 2 million units per month, then the market share for this brand is obviously 10 per cent. But over several months the brand's share of the total market may adversely change and if the company cannot analyse the changes monthly it may not discover why changes are taking place in time to take corrective action. The problem facing marketing management is how to obtain such continuous information for monthly analysis, in all regions in the country, using a representative sample that includes people who purchase competitors' brands. It may also require research in retail outlets throughout the country, to check the amounts of each brand sold. A very costly operation, particularly for any one company.

A company may also wish to receive continuous information to provide the answers to these questions:

- What is the market share of the company's brand in each region?
- Which outlets account for most of the company's sales?
- How often do consumers buy the company's product?
- What is the level of unsold stock currently in the hands of the distributors (wholesalers and retailers)?
- How fast do consumers use the company's product?
- Is there a group of consumers who are switching to products offered by the company's competitors?
- How well are the products of the company's competitors selling?

As the cost of obtaining such information is high many medium to large sized companies pay specialist market research organisations/agencies to receive the information needed. Such agencies continuously research markets to collect specific information which is collated and sold to those companies (subscribers) willing to pay for it.

Each market research agency provides different types of market information but most are concerned with the areas of research discussed below.

## Retail audits

This method of information collection concentrates on the sales achieved by a **representative sample** of retail outlets. Probably the best known audit operation in the UK is A.C. Nielsen, which employs over 250 auditors and uses a sample of 1400 shops from the UK retail industry. Audits are carried out every two months and involve checking the store's purchases, using invoices from suppliers, and despatch notes for goods received and stocks that remain unsold. With this information the auditors can determine the amount of each product that has been sold by using the following formula.

| Closing stocks of each product determined at previous audit | + Purchases during the intervening period between the two audits | − Unsold stocks currently held in the store/s | = **Sales** for the period for each product |

From the information collected the auditors can determine:

- Total sales for individual product groups by adding up the total sales of all brands
- Market shares of individual brands (national or regional basis)
- Levels of unsold stock with individual distributors – useful for production planning purposes: marketing managers can identify areas and types of outlets over- or under-stocked

- The effectiveness of certain types of outlets in selling specific types of products, e.g. specialist outlets may be more effective in selling certain products than non-specialist outlets
- Sales and market share trends to compare company performance against competitors
- Seasonal variations within specific markets or for specific product groups, e.g. it is known that sales of ice-cream drop during the winter months, but a company may need to know the precise periods of maximum and minimum sales.

A.C. Nielsen is in the process of introducing various reforms to its retail audit operation. Subscribing companies will be offered monthly audits as well as telephone links to their audit data base at Nielsens. More frequent reporting and simplification of data evaluation will improve the system and should encourage more companies to subscribe.

## LIMITATIONS OF RETAIL AUDITS

The major limitation of retail audits is that they do not identify who buys a particular product or why they buy. For example. A brand may have achieved sales of 200 000 units in a period of two months in a specific type of retail outlet. Theoretically, this figure could represent 200 000 customers buying one unit each or 100 000 customers buying one unit each, twice or, as an extreme case, one customer buying 200 000 units. The characteristics of customers are unknown, repeat purchases and the rate of repeat purchases are not highlighted and the level of consumer satisfaction is also unkown.

These limitations should not detract from the value of the research. The evaluation of a retail audit to a company should be based on what information the audit *can* deliver as against what it *cannot*. What they can offer – as detailed above – may prove extremely valuable to a company's marketing efforts, particularly in the areas of advertising, distribution and personal selling. Information collected can be analysed more closely by collecting other kinds of information through other MR methods so that a full understanding of the market situation and on-going developments is achieved.


# Consumer panels

This method of research provides continuous information about the purchases of different groups of respondents who are regular consumers. Each group of respondents is referred to as a panel, hence the term, 'consumer panels'.

Representative samples of consumers throughout the UK fill in diaries provided by the research agency and complete questionnaires concerning major aspects of all their purchases. Information collected may include:

- Products purchased (brand names, sizes, flavours, weights, prices paid, etc.)
- Frequency of product purchases
- Types of outlets used for specific purchases
- Composition of household (number of adults, children, pets, etc.)

- Location of household
- Television programmes viewed
- Other media used (newspapers and magazines, radio, cinema, etc.)
- Hobbies and spare time activities of the members of the household
- Opinions on products and satisfaction obtained through product application or use.

The information collected through the diaries and/or questionnaires may be supplemented by meters attached to television sets which record the actual use of television on a daily basis. Viewing of certain programmes and likely exposure to television commercials may be correlated with the purchasing of specific brands. This may in turn encourage further research into likely relationships, such as a recently introduced commercial TV advertising campaign for a new brand of instant coffee. Consumer panel findings may show that many members of the panels used have watched programmes at the times the adverts were shown. At the same time, the diaries indicate purchases of the new product by panel members. One cannot assume that the adverts actually generated the sales achieved because many other marketing functions such as PR or/and personal selling efforts could have contributed to the acceptance and purchase of the new product. There is enough evidence, however, to suggest that advertising may have had a positive effect on the purchasing behaviour of consumers and the company may now seek to determine the actual impact of the adverts shown by introducing a series of interviews involving the panels' members.

Reports on the findings are sent to the subscribing organisations and the information generated can be used in determining:

- The type of consumers purchasing specific brands
- Degrees of loyalty towards products by particular types of consumers
- Sales trends
- Seasonal variations
- Sources of supply preferred by consumers
- Marketing shares (brand or geographic basis)
- 'Switchers' (consumers switching from one brand to another as a result of promotions, competitors' activities, price changes, etc.).

## THE SUPPLIERS OF THE SERVICES

There are two major consumer panel operators in the UK, namely: AGB (Audits of Great Britain) and BMRB (British Market Research Bureau) – Target Panel. BMRB use a sample of 25 000 adults who only supply information about their usage of **major advertised brands**. The information received is used in the compilation of the **Target Group Index** (TGI) which identifies changes in product usage by socio-economic, geographic, age and sex groups. TGI can improve the efficiency of advertising campaigns by identifying particular groups of potential consumers who can be treated as 'key prospects'.

AGB gathers information about ownership and purchases of more than 30 categories of consumer durable products. A sample of 35 000 households is used and the audit falls into six different categories:

1  Major durable goods – cars, motorcycles, caravans, etc.
2  Small kitchen appliances – toasters, mixers, percolators, etc.
3  Leisure appliances – TVs, radios, hi-fis, etc.
4  Heating appliances – electric fires, gas fires, central heating systems, etc.
5  Personal appliances – personal listeners, watches, lighters, etc.
6  Other equipment.

AGB also use the **people meter** system; panel members are provided with special wrist watches or brooches, containing an electronic key which records the wearer's presence in a room where a television is on. The wearer presses a button on the remote handset used on leaving or entering the room. The information is recorded electronically and is transmitted by telephone wire to AGB. It is useful in the measurement of television audiences but is not totally reliable as people may forget to carry or start the handset.

Panels are a very effective method of information collection and help marketing managers in identifying the trends within the market in which their company operates, although there are some drawbacks:

a) Panel members are aware that they are under review so may behave differently, becoming untypical of the population from which they were randomly selected. For instance, members may behave in a manner that they believe the panel organisers expect.
b) Exploratory research of panel members is difficult due to the structured design of the questionnaire.
c) As members are willing participants they may be different from the population from which they were selected.
d) It is difficult to replace members who leave the panel, and few people remain members of a panel for more than two years as they are unpaid or receive only a minimal payment.

## Omnibus surveys

Omnibus surveys are carried out by research agencies on a weekly, monthly or quarterly basis. Companies are offered the opportunity to 'buy' individual questions or a section of a questionnaire for a pre-agreed fee. A survey, with questions from many different clients who each bear a relatively small part of the cost, can then be carried out. Omnibus surveys are one of the cheapest and easiest ways of collecting specific information and are particularly suited for companies with limited research needs or for companies wanting to assess the power and value of market research for the first time. Research findings are passed on to the subscribing organisations and some research agencies also provide their own assessment of the information collected for subscribers. Omnibus surveys may also involve personal interviews, telephone interviews or postal questionnaires.

# ■ MOTIVATION RESEARCH

*When we know why people buy or don't buy we have some idea of how our product should be changed or/and what message we should use when promoting.*

So far we have been mainly concerned with quantitative research to obtain such information as what people buy, when they buy it, how and who they buy it from, etc. Sometimes, however, we need to discover **why** people are motivated to buy or not buy certain goods or services. This research is referred to as **motivation research** and it attempts to determine the subconscious causes for people's behaviour. During conventional interviews respondents may claim that the major reason for not purchasing is the price of the product. This may be true but it is also possible that a promotion may have caused potential customers to perceive the product in a different way to that intended by the supplier of the product, thus causing potential purchasers to consider the product unfit for its intended purpose, too cheap or too expensive, etc. Some products have even been known to sell more as a result of a deliberate increase in the price.

In motivation research researchers can use techniques designed to reveal consumers' decision-making criteria, perceptual biases and expectations, leading to a better understanding of the actual drives behind consumers' purchasing behaviour.

The most widely used methods in motivation research are:

1 Word association tests
2 Sentence completion tests
3 Blind tests
4 In-depth interviews
5 Group discussions.

## Word association tests

Selected respondents are given stimulus words which depict the product name or general concept. If a brand of perfume is under examination, words like beauty, hope and youth may be used to reveal consumers' reactions and perceptions. Words are introduced in rapid succession and the respondent is asked to provide an alternative word which in his or her mind has the same meaning as the word forwarded by the interviewer, or summarises a relationship. Words that are constantly revealed by respondents may be used as part of advertising messages, but more immediately can provide a framework for the evaluation of the strong or weak aspects of the product or concept under consideration. If, for instance, respondents associate the word 'speed' with words like 'lightning', 'rocket', 'turbo', 'flash', etc. and the car under examination, which is supposed to be speedy, is called 'Princess' – representing a stately, reliable name – then a possible reason for marketing failure in a segment of the market may have been identified, or anticipated if it is a proposed new model.

## Sentence completion tests

Respondents are asked to complete sentences designed to determine a respondent's true attitude or opinion. A similar method formed part of a 'picture association' test developed in America in order to discover why young men did not volunteer for military service. One young man was seen asking another why he thought their friend didn't volunteer. Respondents, who were also young men, were then asked to write the reply, which indicated the respondent's own thinking on the subject.

Care should be taken in the design of the sentences for the sentence completion tests so that they do not 'lead' the respondents to specific answers. For instance, if you need to determine respondents' perceptions of the speed of a car, it is pointless to ask them, 'A turbo-charged car is . . .?' The phrase 'Turbo-charged' may lead the respondent to the word 'speed', even though the car under examination is not generally considered to be particularly fast.

# Blind tests

The objective of this technique is to evaluate the physical elements of a product as perceived by respondents free of interference from the name, the package, the price and the other elements of the marketing mix that may influence potential purchasers.

We can take a brand of ladies' scent as an example. A group of respondents may be asked to evaluate four or five alternative brands, including the one under examination, which are presented to them in plain, unmarked containers so the respondents do not know which brand they are trying (hence the use of the word 'blind'). The scents are then rated by the respondents according to the factors they are asked to evaluate, such as pleasantness of odour, strength of odour, duration of odour, etc. The process is then repeated by presenting the same products in their normal, labelled bottles, to the respondents. It is possible for a brand to be ranked top during the blind test and bottom after the presentation of its true identity.

The differences in rankings submitted can highlight the impact that name, colour, shape, size, texture, etc. have on consumer preferences, and information collected can be used in the improvement of a product's and/or pack's personality.

Blind tests can be followed by personal interviews or group discussions designed to identify the reasons behind the selections made by the respondents.

Respondents often find their own blind test choices and ranking surprising and on occasions they even accuse the interviewers of switching products or changing the rankings, etc. In fact, consumers are affected by a variety of promotional stimuli, from the design of the label to a full marketing campaign.

# In-depth interviews

An 'in-depth' interview allows each respondent to discuss with an interviewer a particular subject freely and in confidence, instead of answering specific questions. It involves the analysis of one person with the objective of revealing as much as possible about that person's perceptions, expectations, preferences and other decision-making criteria. The technique is widely used by research agencies because it can probe deeply the motivations of potential consumers. It can, however, prove extremely expensive and time consuming because expert direction is required by a professional interviewer and a normal interview may last between 30 minutes and two hours. It is popular however – as is group discussion – for the initial preparation of a questionnaire to be used in a full field survey.

## Group discussions

The group discussion is a modification on the in-depth interview in that it involves groups of respondents rather than individuals. The product, service or idea under examination is discussed by the members of the group with the interviewer discreetly guiding the discussion and acting as a stimulant to the discussion while, most importantly, studying the way the individuals react to one another and the way in which personal attitudes towards a product or service are influenced by other people present.

Group discussions can prove particularly useful in identifying the areas which questionnaires for formal surveys should cover or in revealing topics which merit closer examination. However, consumers, their values and their expectations, change all the time so any findings may need to be re-assessed at a later stage in the marketing programme.

A major objective of all motivation research is to identify the stimuli which can help with the successful promotion of products or services through identifying a product's strong and weak points as perceived by consumers. The future of such research depends on the ability of its exponents to develop and produce reliable techniques which can deliver information that will help in measuring the hidden motives of consumers.

It cannot be treated as a precise research tool and certain areas of uncertainty should be left to the intelligence, intuition and experience of individual marketing managers. Nevertheless, when findings of such qualitative research are matched with findings of quantitative research, the combined findings can provide marketing management with very detailed information, thus reducing the risk of taking a wrong marketing decision.

## ■ STUDY AND EXAM TIPS

**1** Concentrate on the type of information which retail audits, consumer panels and motivation research can provide. Examiners often identify a problem or a purpose for a research programme and then expect examinees to recommend the most appropriate methods of obtaining the information.

**2** Be prepared to identify one or two organisations involved in continuous research.

**3** Familiarise yourselves with the actual operations of retail audits, consumer panels and omnibus surveys so that you have a clear understanding of their operation and do not confuse one with the other

**4** Do not confuse in-depth interviews and group discussions with formal personal interviews (discussed in the previous chapter). Personal interviews in surveys are strongly directed by a pre-designed questionnaire and may involve a large team of interviewers.

---

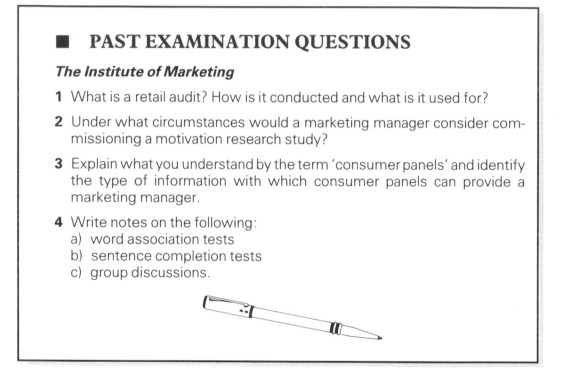

■ **PAST EXAMINATION QUESTIONS**

*The Institute of Marketing*

**1** What is a retail audit? How is it conducted and what is it used for?

**2** Under what circumstances would a marketing manager consider commissioning a motivation research study?

**3** Explain what you understand by the term 'consumer panels' and identify the type of information with which consumer panels can provide a marketing manager.

**4** Write notes on the following:
   a) word association tests
   b) sentence completion tests
   c) group discussions.

---

■ **SUGGESTED ANSWER TO QUESTION 4**

The three research methods mentioned all represent qualitative research methods designed to determine the motivating factors behind people's behaviour, though each adopts a different approach.

## Word association tests

A representative sample of respondents are given a number of stimulus words and are asked to mention other words which they associate with each of the stimulus words. The words are usually verbally presented to the respondents in rapid succession so that they are not given an opportunity to think carefully about their answers. The objective is to discover those words which spring to mind without detailed consideration because they may reveal the respondents' attitudes or opinions regarding the words mentioned by the researcher.

The list of stimulus words actually used will have a direct effect on the quality of information collected and it is vital therefore to prepare a list which relates directly to the problem, product or service under investigation. If, for instance, the research relates to the operations of a bank, it may be considered that the following stimulus words could prove helpful:

| Money | Overdraft | Loan |
| Account | Capital | Deposit |
| Interest | Bills | Withdrawal |
| Credit | Cashier | Interview |

The words mentioned by the respondents in relation to the above words could facilitate the development of promotional campaigns, identify areas of strength and weakness and likely areas of improvement in service and merchandising of the bank's services and corporate image.

Respondents may unknowingly indicate via their replies that they find interest rates too high, overdraft facilities difficult to obtain, credit cards extremely tempting, etc. A promotional campaign may then be designed to defend the way the bank operates or to emphasise friendly staff and speedy, professional service.

## Sentence completion tests

This method is also designed to reveal the underlying cause/s of consumer behaviour. The sample of respondents used in the research are given a number of partly completed sentences and asked to complete them in whatever way they feel is appropriate. The sentences actually used will relate to the product, service or problem under examination and should be designed in a way which examines the concept or concepts under investigation.

For example, respondents may be asked to complete a sentence similar to the following: 'I like men's clothes that project . . .'. When respondents complete the sentence or sentences they knowingly or unknowingly indicate their deepest opinions or emotions on the subject which can help marketers in designing or altering a product, or in constructing advertising slogans.

## Group discussions

Group discussions involve a small group of respondents who are asked to discuss products, services, problems, concepts, ideas, organisations, or any other areas relevant to the investigation. The comments made by participants are recorded, the reactions of individuals are observed, the counter-arguments used are closely evaluated and the general decisions reached by the group are summarised by an expert researcher.

Group discussions have proved very beneficial to marketing research managers in revealing the reactions of individuals to questions, opinions or ideas presented to them by others. It is often the case that we have realised we were wrong or amended our assessment of a situation, a product or a person when provided with the opinions of other people. This is of vital concern to marketers because consumers will come across competitors' advertisements, advice from distributors, offers from salespeople, opinions of friends or relatives and new information from other relevant sources before they decide on purchasing. All of these may reinforce opinions and beliefs, but on occasions may change them and, in turn, the attitudes, expectations and general buying behaviour of current and/or potential customers.

This method may bring to the surface decision-making criteria used by individual consumers which may not be revealed in a face-to-face, one-to-one situation. It can serve as a means of evaluating information collected through personal interviews or it can initiate a series of interviews designed to further evaluate the information collected.

The motivation research techniques discussed cannot be relied upon as perfect guides to consumer motivation but they are, nevertheless, important, as they can remove some of the uncertainties surrounding the reasons behind consumers' actions and obviate too much guesswork by marketing managers. Findings may also be compared with quantitative research of the company so that a more complete picture of the situation under review is obtained against which marketing decisions may be taken.

# ■ SELF ASSESSMENT QUESTIONS

Answer the following questions without reference to the section and award yourself one mark for each complete question you answer correctly. If you score 12 or less re-read the relevant parts of the section. Answers are given on page 237.

**1** Complete the sentence: The target market from which researchers select a sample is referred to as the ...........................................................................................

**2** Complete the sentence: Target markets need to be defined in terms of demographic, psychographic and geographic variables as well as by ...............................

**3** Complete the sentence: A marketing research sample may be defined as 'a representative proportion of a given target market used in the collection of information ...........................................................................................................................

**4** Complete the sentence: The selection of a proportionate random sample depends on two laws of statistics referred to as 'the law of inertia of large numbers', and 'the law of ...........................................................................................................

**5** Complete the sentence: Two forms of samples exist, namely random (probability) samples and ...............................................................................................................

**6** One form of non-random (or modified random) sampling is quota sampling. Name three more:
  a) ...........................................................................................................................
  b) ...........................................................................................................................
  c) ...........................................................................................................................

**7** Complete the sentence: Possibly the most popular form of non-random sampling is ................ sampling.

**8** Complete the sentence: Carrying out research that involves every member of the universe is referred to as a .............................................................................................

**9** There are four methods by which we can obtain information/data from the sample, one of which is via personal interviews. Name three more.
  a) ...........................................................................................................................
  b) ...........................................................................................................................
  c) ...........................................................................................................................

**10** Complete the sentence: Most pilot surveys involve using a ................ interviewing technique.

**11** Which heading would motivational research come under; quantitative or qualitative research? ...........................................................................................................

**12** Complete the formula:

| closing stocks of each product determined at the previous audit | + | Purchases from the previous audit to the current audit | − | Unsold stocks currently held in the store(s)/shops |
|---|---|---|---|---|

**13** The formula outlined in Question 12 refers to an audit. What is it called?
.............................................................................................................................

**14** Complete the sentence: When consumers keep diaries concerning all their purchases and complete questionnaires, they are usually members of a ................

**15** One form of motivation research explained in Chapter 3 was 'group discussions'. Name four more.
  a) ...........................................................................................................................
  b) ...........................................................................................................................
  c) ...........................................................................................................................
  d) ...........................................................................................................................

## ■ MINI CASE STUDY

This exercise offers you the opportunity to try answering your first mini case study in marketing research. Read the case study and then try answering the question at the end in note form.

## John Brown's Bookshop

John Brown, a well-paid electrical engineer, earning £30 000 a year, is a bit of a bookworm. In an effort to fulfil his most treasured ambition he is contemplating the purchase of a fifteen year lease to a clothes shop in order to turn it into an educational bookshop. The shop, which covers two floors of approximately 2000 square feet, is near to the centre of the city.

The asking price for the lease is a one-off payment of £20 000 followed by £10 000 per annum paid via monthly payments of £833. In addition John has had estimates around £20 000 for the refurbishment and stocking of the shop to make it suitable for the sale of books.

To pay out the initial £40 000 (£20 000 + £20 000) John realises that he will have to put up the family house as guarantee. John's wife is supportive of the venture but is concerned that the house could be lost if the venture fails and she has no current means of support – of her own. They have three young children which she prefers, at the moment, to look after herself, thus she is unable to take a full-time job.

John talked over a potential loan with his bank manager who is prepared to make the loan and has put John in contact with a local solicitor and an accountant conversant with the problems of new companies. However, the bank manager has also suggested to John that he carries out as much marketing research as possible to determine if the venture will succeed, as once he signs the lease he will be responsible for paying the £10 000 per annum for 15 years.

John, accepting the sound advice of his bank manager, has now telephoned you, his life-long friend and marketing manager of a medium-sized company to seek your advice as to what to research and how the research can be done.

**Note:** Use the knowledge that you have gained from having read the first three chapters of this book, relating it to John's circumstances and bringing your own common sense to bear. When you have jotted down your proposed advice to John compare it with that suggested on the next page. You are not expected to research legal aspects or costs of setting up the business for the purposes of this case study. You will have an opportunity, in later chapters, to check your ability to handle other mini cases.

## ■   SUGGESTED ANSWER TO MINI CASE STUDY

Advise John of the following:

## The market

1   Check the number of pedestrians who pass the site where the bookshop is to be and compare it with the pedestrian traffic passing a busy bookshop in another part of the city.
2   Check the number of bookshops – especially educational ones – in the city and in particular the local area, and evaluate the services they supply, i.e. postal service, delivery service, type of books sold, magazines, newspapers, image of

shop, hours of opening and closing, etc. If any are limited companies check with the registrar of companies to determine the profits they make and the sales levels they experience. This will help in assessing the number of customers needed, the difficulties in becoming established and the profits possible.

3  Through local job agencies, magazines for the book trade, an association or society of booksellers, etc. obtain some idea of what salary staff of various levels in bookshops obtain and how to recruit quality staff and motivate them.

4  Through statistics of publishers', authors' or booksellers' associations/ societies, check who are the main purchasers of books, i.e. men, women, children, age and socio-economic groupings, etc. Check sales trends in the market indicating which types of books sell the most, which have the highest mark-up etc. to determine if specialising in educational books is a good idea, or if other, related, items are growing fast in sales and are profitable, such as magazines, computer software, audio and video tapes.

5  Check the records at county hall and/or with a small friendly local advertising agent – who may want your business – to discover where the main book reading population (as determined above) in the area tend to live and the numbers that make up each group. Also check where local schools and colleges buy their books and if they have their own bookshops or order direct from publishers; or students buy from book retailers.

6  Talk with a senior person in any booksellers' association to discover if they can envisage pitfalls or provide additional useful information. Identify any needs in the bookselling service and/or market that are not presently serviced.

## Products and prices

7  Check with the booksellers' association and with some publishers the credit time publishers allow booksellers and any sale-or-return services they provide. Discounts allowed to bookshops at various levels of purchases and the time needed to allow for delivery should also be established.

8  Check the position with regard to books arriving damaged.

9  Check sources of all books by obtaining a directory of publishers and consulting with the publishers' society/association.

10  Check where out-of-print or withdrawn books may be purchased and approximate prices.

11  Check if books have to be sold at a price set by the publishers.

12  Can discounts be used with effect when selling to the public?

13  Do particular customers require credit?

14  What is the procedure for accepting credit cards? What is the percentage loss to the bookseller accepting credit card payments?

## Promotions

15  Discuss with the booksellers'/publishers' associations the best media in which to advertise the bookshop and its services.

16 Check with a small local advertising agency the best way to promote in the locality – and beyond if direct mail is to be used.
17 Check if there are local clubs, societies, etc. through whom special services may be promoted, such as books for golfers or anglers.

## Collation and analysis

18 Then collate the information and analyse what it all means in relation to obtaining the necessary sales levels and profit margin.
19 Relate the information to the original idea to determine if specialisation in educational books is still best and what the profile of books offered should be and the image and personal service of the shop.
20 Prepare a feasibility report (business plan) on the venture for yourself and the bank manager, relating research findings and sales forecasts to finances, type of books to be sold, equipment and human resources needed.

Only then should you determine:

a) If the idea is feasible
b) If you should continue in line with the information provided from the research
c) If you should continue but in a modified form, e.g. continue with the engineering job and employ an experienced manager to initially build up the business of the shop.

PART 2

# The promotional output

# 4 Advertising

*Even the best product cannot reach its full sales potential without promotion.*

## ■ ADVERTISING IN THE PROMOTIONAL MIX

The first part of this book concentrated on marketing research and how marketing oriented companies identify potential markets and customer needs, and monitor changes in the markets they serve by collecting, analysing and evaluating relevant information. The remaining parts will focus on the likely applications of the information collected, and developing a marketing plan. Part 2 examines the ways in which organisations communicate their commercial message to their markets by studying the **promotional mix**:

> *Promotions encompass all the tools in the marketing mix whose major role is persuasive communications.*

The term **promotional mix** is used to summarise the four main means of communication which companies rely upon to communicate messages to potential audiences, and the way they are mixed and applied to obtain the best promotional effect. These are:

1 **Advertising**
2 **Sales promotions and merchandising**
3 **Public relations (PR)**
4 **Personal selling.**

The relationship between these four methods of communication is illustrated below.

Figure 4.1

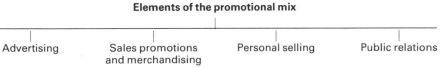

Elements of the promotional mix

Advertising    Sales promotions and merchandising    Personal selling    Public relations

Every organisation must consider the effect of communications passing between itself, its customers, its competitors, its suppliers, the general public, its shareholders, the media owners and, possibly, the government. It is important that the Marketing Manager knows how to effectively combine these elements in order to achieve his or her marketing objectives. The first, advertising, is discussed in this chapter.

> *Advertising. The art of determining the right message and making it known to the right target audience.*

Everyone is exposed to advertisements every day, encouraging people to purchase new products, switch from products already used, visit specific outlets, take advantage of special offers or even warning people about the dangers associated with the use of certain products. Companies may also be advertising the company itself to enhance its image (corporate advertising), to recruit staff or to buy particular items. You may advertise your second-hand car for sale or an agent may advertise your house for you.

In short, advertising has become part of our daily lives and has assumed the role of a major information service within society. Just consider the number of products and services you get to know every day through advertisements and you can appreciate a small fraction of the contribution of advertising.

Many people question the effect that advertisements have on their purchasing behaviour and often criticise the way products or services are presented. Even though some criticism aimed at advertising may be valid the fact remains that it is a marketing strategic tool which can offer rewards to its users. This chapter examines the major issues relating to advertising, the advertising industry, the most popular media currently available and advertising planning.

## ■ THE ROLE OF ADVERTISING WITHIN THE MARKETING MIX

Advertising can be defined as a:

> *paid form of non-personal presentation of ideas, goods or services by an identified sponsor.*

A number of key words are included in this definition, which attempts to distinguish advertising from other forms of communication used by a company. The words **paid form** distinguishes advertising from any free publicity which a company or a product may be subject to. A publishing company, for instance, may advertise a newly launched book by paying for advertisements to appear in certain newspapers or magazines while an institute or association may recommend the book to its members as essential reading. The first situation relates to straightforward advertising while the latter is free publicity.

The words **identified sponsor** used in the definition are also vital because they imply that all advertisements should identify the person or company with a vested interest in the product or service being advertised. It again facilitates the separation of advertising from free publicity and explains to the interested parties *who* is responsible for the benefits which can be derived from the purchase, hire or use of a product or service.

The distinct advantages of advertising over other forms of promotion are:

- The exact same message may be regularly or irregularly communicated to the target market.
- Images, drama and atmosphere useful in promoting the product/service, not possible with other promotional methods, may be used.
- Customers may be persuaded without pressure.

Advertising in the independent media (e.g. the press and TV) is referred to as **above-the-line media advertising**, as adverts are there for anyone to see, hear or read. Advertising directed at people in certain places or jobs is referred to as **below-the-line advertising** and includes such methods as direct mail and mail drops, point-of-sale displays, sales literature, sky advertising and trade fairs and exhibitions.

Advertising contributions to effective marketing operations include:

1 The introduction of new products into the market by announcing the features, benefits, applications and general attractions of the new product.
2 The introduction of changes in a company's marketing mix by informing target markets of package changes, special offers, new sizes, introduction of new ingredients or components or even identification of new product applications.
3 Increasing consumer understanding of products, services or company operations. Many advertisements are designed to inform the general public of the successes enjoyed by a company, the wide variety of products they offer, overseas expansion plans or even their excellent employee relations.
4 Aiding sales staff during new product launches, 'off-peak' periods or when expansion into new geographic markets is undertaken. Many people fail to appreciate the impact that advertising might have on the activities of the sales force by ignoring the fact that unknown products, with unknown benefits, offered by companies unfamiliar to the public, are not likely to succeed. An advertisement can establish awareness, interest, understanding or even curiosity which can generate sales leads, lead to salesperson acceptance by the potential customer and afford sales staff the necessary time to contact interested parties.
5 Many advertisements introduce popular 'catchphrases' which facilitate understanding, memorisation and often product or service acceptance through their entertainment value. Just consider the number of advertising catch-phrases *you* have found amusing, the number of times you used them in everyday conversation and more importantly the number of times you remembered a product through the catch-phrase rather than through its benefits, name or actual advert.
6 Advertising can also play a defensive role within a company's marketing mix by helping to maintain the interest and confidence of existing customers. In

highly competitive markets many new products may be introduced by competitors and companies must seek to keep their existing customers by reminding them of past satisfactions or by reassuring them about the quality, reliability and value of what they are currently buying.

7  Advertising can be relied upon as a means of dramatising products or services; they can be presented as modern, up-market, tailor-made to specific needs, advanced, improved, traditional, youthful, etc.

8  Advertising campaigns may contribute to increased market penetration by attracting new buyers or users of products and services. Creation of favourable word-of-mouth testimonials from satisfied customers, well-known personalities' recommendations, or presentation of special incentives, can all contribute to increased sales.

9  Distributor acceptance can also be facilitated because advertising has the ability to 'pre-sell' products to the general public by performing the tasks already identified. Consider the situation where customers begin to demand a product (possibly for trial purposes) as the result of their exposure to an advertisement. Consumer interest is likely to encourage distributors to stock the product, providing the company with additional sales channels and so increasing sales of a product.

10  There are numerous products and services which cannot be sold on the strength of an advertisement. Cars, television sets, banking services, education, etc. are extremely complex purchases and interested parties must collect enough information before they finalise their selections. Advertisements in such circumstances, however, can be used in order to generate enquiries for additional information, bring to the surface likely buyers who could not otherwise be identified, encourage personal visits and introduce 'no commitment', 'free' trials designed to allow potential buyers to understand and witness the benefits to be derived from the purchase.

11  The last few years have witnessed the rapid growth of advertisements designed to sell products **directly** to consumers without the use of any distributors. This can be attributed to the increased ownership of credit cards, the acceptance of direct-response advertisements by the media owners, the growing ownership of bank accounts and cheque books and the greater confidence of consumers in shopping through the post. Popular newspapers and magazines carry a large number of direct response advertisements and it is possible to buy clothing, books, kitchen utensils, watches, furniture, etc. by simply making a telephone call or posting off a coupon to a specified company.

12  A major role of advertising literature is to create the backcloth against which sales and PR personnel should work. Advertising can be used to explain to staff the major benefits of the product or service. Staff will then be guided by such claims although they may add additional ones as directed by senior management.

Where advertising is solely intended to make sales the advertiser will generally – but not always – follow a **push** or **pull** policy. Push policy advertising is aimed at the channels of distribution to encourage them to stock and sell and usually implies a profit opportunity. Pull policy advertising is aimed at the final customers (e.g. the consumers) designed to bring them to the point of sale (e.g. the super-market).

# ■ ADVERTISING MEDIA

Advertising should be approached with caution as it is one of the most costly, complicated and unpredictable elements of marketing. The difficulties associated with advertising can be appreciated by examining the advertising media available to marketing managers.

The five principal mass media, independent advertising channels (above the line advertising media, see p. 55) available to the prospective advertiser are:

1 **The press** (newspapers and magazines)
2 **Television**
3 **Posters**
4 **Cinema**
5 **Radio**

Each medium provides prospective advertisers with different advertising advantages, so it is essential to analyse the main considerations associated with each medium category.

## The press

The press includes national and regional newspapers, magazines and periodicals, trade and technical (T & T advertising) journals. The types of advertisement published include:

    a) **display** – advertisements with a border mainly designed and placed by manufacturers and retail distributors (or their advertising agents);

    b) **classified** – advertisements in the same type and format (line advertisements) as the editorial such as, miscellaneous wants and sales, property, motor cars and, increasingly, jobs vacant and wanted advertised by companies and the general public respectively, representing the main classified advertisements;

    c) **financial** – company reports, prospectuses and so on.

Display advertising is the most important and accounts for about two-thirds of the total expenditure on press advertising. The national newspapers get the largest share, followed closely by regional newspapers and magazines and trade journals. Classified advertising accounts for the remaining expenditure with regional newspapers carrying by far the greatest load. You only have to open your local paper to see how much space is given to classified advertising and it will become clear why many regional newspapers are much more financially secure than the nationals. Advertising is a major source of revenue in the newspaper and magazine publishing business: without it your newspaper could cost at least three times as much.

## 1  NEWSPAPERS AND GENERAL INTEREST MAGAZINES (PERIODICALS)

Selling advertising space used to be a fairly passive activity in as much as publishers were able to sit back and wait for the advertisements to flow in. Nowadays there is much more competition not only from other newspaper publishers but also from other media, such as commercial radio and television.

There are usually two departments in newspaper or magazine publishers concerned with advertising. The Advertising Sales Department handles the advertising space selling activities and is often divided into display and classified sections. The Marketing (or Publicity) Department is responsible for newspaper sales and circulation and also for promoting the newspaper as an effective advertising medium.

Not all advertisements in newspapers and magazines are an actual part of the publication; loose leaflets (flyers or inserts) may be inserted to attract the readers' attention. In some cases the product itself, e.g. face cream in a sample sachet, may be attached to a page.

## 2  TRADE AND TECHNICAL (T & T) PUBLICATIONS

A vast number of magazines are issued weekly, monthly or quarterly for particular trades, industries or professions. Some journals are for the 'users' of those trades such as engineers, tailors, electricians, while others are for the 'dealers' such as retail chemists, grocers and hardware dealers. Firms whose products are used only by certain trades advertise exclusively in these media. Generally T & T publications are relatively inexpensive to advertise in and the target audience can be pre-defined quite accurately. Individual copies may be read by more than the one purchaser as they are often circulated round a firm's staff, doctor's clinic, or a shop and are often available in public libraries.

## 3  SPECIAL INTEREST MAGAZINES

There are many publications in this category, covering fashions, gardening, photography, music, etc. A wide range of products are advertised in these journals, depending on the particular market in which they circulate.

## 4  LOCAL PUBLICATIONS

There is a vast choice of local publications, such as local newspapers (daily or weekly), church magazines, local chamber of commerce publications, town or regional magazines, local guide books and telephone directories or commercial directories, programmes of theatres, cinemas, fêtes, and sporting events. These are particularly suitable for firms in the retail trade who want to advertise their local shop/s and for hotels, restaurants, banks, insurance companies, etc. operating in the area. This medium is relatively cheap and effective for purely local trade.

# Television

This medium is the most sophisticated and costly – in terms of initial production costs. In most countries it is used on a nation-wide basis although it is possible in some countries for advertising on TV to be purely regional.

The independent television companies are financially dependent on advertising revenue and they have their own sales departments concentrating on selling advertising time to interested companies.

TV advertising represents a creative medium offering a wide variety of opportunities to present products and services in an exciting, informative and entertaining manner. Planning for effective TV adverts should involve the following:

a) Ensure that the name of the product, service, company being advertised is clearly and regularly presented to the viewers so that memorisation is maximised.

b) Seek to create adverts which are different and unique. Audiences should be exposed to different ideas so that interest and curiosity in an individual advert is developed.

c) Use sound, movement, colour and personalities in order to dramatise the presentation.

d) Keep adverts as realistic as possible so that audiences can relate to them.

e) Make adverts topical in order to relate to current needs, trends and expectations.

f) Try to initiate favourable emotions by explaining the functions, benefits, applications, qualities and satisfactions which can be derived as a result of the purchase.

g) Repeat advertisements as often as possible – within the promotional budget – in order to ensure retention of the message by the viewers and maximise overall impact. Research has indicated that 95 per cent of viewers forget an advertisement's exact message within six weeks; hence the general preference for short adverts constantly repeated.

The main audience for commercial television programmes is from the C2, D and E socio-economic groups. State TV, e.g. the BBC in the UK, attracts more A, B, and C1 viewers. To overcome this companies may attempt to reach the higher socio-economic groups by advertising in weekly TV magazines, e.g. *Radio Times*. Companies may also use the magazines as 'support media', supporting the main advertising being shown on television.

Television is currently undergoing some dramatic changes which are likely to change the viewing habits of consumers world-wide, see pages 65–8.

# Posters

Posters are not as widely used as they were a few years ago as fewer sites exist. They are generally used for nation-wide advertising of products with wide consumer appeal, e.g. soft drinks, food, cars, newspapers as well as local advertising of musical, sporting or political events. They may be static, i.e. on stationary **billboards** or on, or inside a vehicle, e.g. **transport posters** on buses.

**Advantages**
- Large posters have considerable visual impact on the environment within which they appear.
- Proximity to the point of sale is possible and often essential for consumers to respond to the information.
- Cost per viewer is relatively low.
- Opportunities for creativity.

**Disadvantages**
- Larger sites are over-demanded and are not always available when needed.
- Difficult to select the audience.
- Damage is inevitable so frequent poster changes are necessary.
- Limited to simple messages because audiences will not spend a long time reading posters.
- Limited to daylight hours, although some sites also provide the user with floodlights or other means of illumination.

Posters are a good support medium reminding the general public of a longer advertising message they may be seeing on TV or in newspapers. They are not usually used as the sole means of advertising goods and services, unless the company advertising is located close to the poster site.

**NEON SIGNS**

Relatively little use is made of this medium in the UK outside of the centre of major cities such as London, but it is widely found in such places as Brussels, New York and many South American cities, where almost every building top lights up at night with adverts. Cost varies according to the complexity of the design, e.g. whether it is still or animated, the range of colours, the size, and the location of the site. Again this form of advertising is aimed at the public at large and is unsuitable for specialised or technical products, except where it is located on the shop which is selling them.

As with posters, messages are generally short. In particular, neon signs are useful at night-time when ordinary posters cannot be seen, making them popular with services close to the sign and which operate at night-time, e.g. theatres and cinemas.

# Cinema

This medium is used less in the UK nowadays than was once the case but it is still important in other countries. The cost varies according to the type of film, its length and sophistication and the class of cinema where it is shown. The medium can be used for products with a wide appeal but the current trend is for local trade adverts, e.g. restaurants and car dealers, rather than national suppliers. The multi-screen complexes of modern cinemas have maximised seating capacity and given advertisers a wider option of film packages. A drawback, however, is that audiences tend to be between approximately 16 and 34 years of age.

# Radio

Over the last few years radio as an advertising medium has become less popular as a result of the growth of television and home video, etc. It is often considered the least creative medium because it only provides sound, but it is perhaps underestimated; creative advertisers can use the radio effectively if they are willing to consider the following:

a) Can voices used in the advertisement raise people's curiosity regarding the product or service being advertised? A voice may be ideal for the advertising of cosmetics for women: it may communicate 'mystique', 'personal satisfaction', 'beauty', 'class', etc.

b) Some products or services can be 'sold' on the strength of a description. Consider car tyres, for instance, and you may appreciate that safety, reliability and proven track record can be identified without the need for visual presentations.

c) Some radio audiences, such as motorists, can be easily reached during rush hours or throughout the day as they are isolated from most other forms of advertising while driving. Similarly, many people listen to the radio while working but may not be able to be reached by other advertising media during these times.

d) Radio adverts are relatively inexpensive to make so a variety of messages can be introduced.

e) There are many local and ethnic radio stations excellent for reaching these audiences.

Unfortunately, listening to radio does not always require the full attention of the listener so advertisers do not always achieve the impact they expect.

# ■ DIRECT MAIL AND CONSUMER LOCATION SYSTEMS

Direct mail describes the practice of posting advertisements to people in their homes. Leaflets, prospectuses or letters are sent to people to encourage them to respond to a specific promotional offer. How companies obtain names and addresses for a direct mailing, determine potential consumers, and the value of direct mail companies will be examined in this section.

Direct mail represents one of the fastest expanding sectors of advertising. Most of its growth can be attributed to the following factors:

a) The growing appreciation by companies of direct mail's creative potential and its value as a method of reaching closely defined target audiences.

b) The ability to mix direct mail with campaigns appearing in other advertising media in order to achieve an effective interaction.

c) The increasing availability of 'mailing lists' which provide lists of addresses of target audiences for various products and services.

d) The availability of new mailing preparation techniques which are making the medium easier and more effective to use.

e) The fact that the media owners, and in particular the Post Office, have gained a far better understanding of the contribution they can make. For instance, the **Consumer Location System**, introduced by the Post Office, is a means of effectively targeting advertising material sent through the post. This has been achieved by bringing together the BMRB's Target Group Index (TGI) and ACORN. The TGI is published annually, and analyses the responses of some 24 000 adults to a comprehensive questionnaire concerning purchasing habits, covering 4500 brands/services from over 500 product fields. ACORN is an acronym for 'A Classification of Residential Neighbourhoods'. The central idea of ACORN is that a set of areas shown by the census to have similar demographic and social characteristics will, as a result, share common lifestyle features and present similar potential for the sales of any product. ACORN defines these different types of areas and where they can be found.

## ACORN TYPES OF AREAS

A 1 Local authority and new town housing, high wage areas
A 2 Mixed housing, young families
A 3 Recent council housing
A 4 Modern low cost private housing
B 5 Modern private housing, medium status
B 6 Modern private housing, young families
B 7 Military bases
C 8 Mixed housing, older areas
C 9 Older terraces with low unemployment
C 10 Mixed development, often in country towns
D 11 Inner areas, low quality terraced housing
D 12 Low quality housing, declining areas
E 13 Villages with some non-farm equipment
E 14 Rural areas with large farms
E 15 Rural areas with own account farmers
F 16 Peripheral low income local authority estates
F 17 Small local authority family houses
(Scotland and North-east)
F 18 Urban local authority estates, low unemployment
F 19 Terraced local authority houses (often mining areas)
F 20 Local authority estates with older couples
F 21 Low income local authority estates (often high-rise)
F 22 Local authority estates with aged (often high-rise)
G 23 Local authority estates with most stress (Glasgow)
G 24 Tenements and non-permanent dwellings
H 25 Victorian low status (Inner London)
H 26 Multi-let housing with immigrants
H 27 Terraced housing with immigrants

I 28   Student areas/affluent Inner London
I 29   High income areas with few children
J 30   Modern private housing, high income
J 31   Medium status private housing
J 32   Established suburbs of high status
J 33   Established rural commuter villages
J 34   Very high status areas
K 35   Areas of elderly people, private housing
K 36   Areas of elderly people, flats and homes

BMRB fitted their TGI results into ACORN neighbourhood types and discovered that consumers belonging to different ACORN groups responded differently to similar products or services. The levels of discrimination which can be achieved by the ACORN system are usually far more sensitive than those provided by conventional social classifications.

If, therefore, the brand or product category with which the marketer is concerned is one of those measured by the TGI it is possible to establish the extent to which its market is likely to be concentrated in any ACORN neighbourhood type. This concentration is expressed as an **index figure** from which it can be seen whether or not the product in question is above or below the average national consumption of the product (which is the index figure, called **direct target index**) and can be used to make comparisons with other advertising media for effectiveness in terms of reaching the target consumer groups. See Table 4.1.

**Table 4.1** Table wine drinkers

| ACORN type | Target market | | Total adults | | Penetration | Direct target |
| | 000 | % | 000 | % | % | index |
| --- | --- | --- | --- | --- | --- | --- |
| I 28 | 76 | 2.5 | 454 | 1.1 | 16.7 | 235 |
| I 29 | 173 | 5.7 | 1090 | 2.5 | 15.9 | 224 |
| etc. | | | | | | |
| Total | 3054 | 100 | 43198 | 100 | 7.1 | 100 |

The left-hand column refers to the ACORN type; reading across you can see the total number of table wine drinkers within this type (I 28) is 76 000, which accounts for 2.5 per cent of the target market (3 054 000). In the next column the total adults figure for ACORN type I 28 is 454 000 representing 1.1 per cent of the adult population, out of a national total of 43 198 000 adults. The next figure (penetration) represents the number of table wine drinkers within I 28 in relation to the total population of the group. The penetration figure can be obtained by dividing 76 000 by 454 000 to give the penetration percentage of 16.7 per cent which appears in the example. The same process is repeated for all ACORN types and a national average penetration figure of 7.1 per cent is obtained. If the national figure of 7.1 per cent is used to divide the ACORN type I 28 penetration figure of 16.7 per cent the index figure is obtained:

$$\frac{16.7}{7.1} \times 100 = 235 \text{ (Direct Target Index)}$$

This is the **Direct Target Index** which is used to classify the ACORN types according to the degree of product use. The highest users will carry the highest Direct Target Index and will be listed first, while the lowest users will be listed last. Marketing managers in possession of such information will be in a position to decide upon the ACORN groups they would like to contact with a direct mail campaign.

It is worth bearing in mind that the ACORN types with the highest Direct Target Index are not always the most attractive target markets because marketing managers may feel there is no room for increased use of a particular product. Other ACORN types showing much lower usage rates may represent better targets or may be seen as having greater potential for increased product use.

Direct mail, as a means of passing the advertising message, has several advantages over other media:

a) It enables the advertiser to approach the prospective consumer directly without the confusion of many competing adverts appearing together, as in a newspaper.

b) It can be a very selective medium. Marketers can decide who to write to, how often and when to write.

c) A high degree of topicality is possible.

d) The detail of the advertising message is not restricted by the limited space available within other advertising media.

e) The quality of the direct mail shot is almost unlimited.

f) Colour can be used effectively.

g) A direct mail campaign is to a large extent confidential.

h) Direct measurement of effectiveness is possible, because responses, orders or requests for further information are a guide to effectiveness.

i) Results are generally known quickly.

j) A direct mail campaign can be speedily executed.

The flexibility of direct mail can be highlighted by examining the areas to which it can be applied.

## INTERNAL TO THE ORGANISATION

- Building morale of employees by keeping them regularly informed about what is happening within the company both socially and economically
- Stimulating sales staff to greater efforts by offering incentives, advice or information.

## BUILDING NEW BUSINESS BY DIRECT MAIL PROMOTIONS TO POTENTIAL CUSTOMERS

- Securing new dealers
- Obtaining direct orders

- Developing sales in territories not covered by the sales force
- Bringing the buyer to the showroom
- Paving the way for sales staff
- Securing interviews for sales staff
- Keeping contact with customers
- Following up presentations
- Welcoming new customers.

## ASSISTING PRESENT DEALERS
- Helping present dealers to sell more by mailing potential customers in their area
- Educating dealers on superiority of products
- Referring enquiries to local dealers.

## APPROACHES TO THE CONSUMER MARKET
- Creating a need or demand for a product
- Increasing usage of a product
- Attracting customers to the point of sale.

## GENERAL
- Building goodwill, e.g. keeping shareholders informed of company developments
- Stimulating interest in forthcoming events such as a trade fair or exhibition.
- Distribution of samples
- Announcing a new product
- Correcting present mailing list by seeking latest address of persons on the mailing list
- Raising funds, often undertaken by charities.

**Mail drops** may also be used, where advertising literature is posted through letter boxes, without using the mail services. Alternatively advertising literature may be handed personally to people in the street or pushed under windscreen-wipers of cars. This system is costly, involving a number of staff, but has the benefit of identifying a target audience, e.g. people with certain types of cars or young women only.

## ■  ADVERTISING MEDIA DEVELOPMENTS

Some major changes have taken place over the last few years that have already affected the advertising media which companies will need to use for their products and services. These include:

## Freesheets

Freesheets are newspapers and magazines carrying mainly advertising which are distributed to the public – free of charge – through letterboxes or handed to people personally in public areas. They may provide:

- An additional, free information service to the public.
- Regional information (e.g. local suppliers and services).
- Cheap advertising space for producers and readers.
- A complementary publication to the national media, with local news or information on local businesses.
- A local information service that can personalise advertisements, and concentrate on what is available or what is needed within a community.

There are presently over 1500 freesheets/magazines in England alone, and they normally consist of 10 per cent editorials and 90 per cent adverts (including classified adverts). Many are specialist publications (property, DIY, etc.). Advertising charges relate to the potential circulation of each freesheet. Established local publications sell some of their production capacity to freesheets, and publishers of regional newspapers use their own facilities to print freesheets to generate additional revenue.

### ADVANTAGES
- Entire communities can be reached.
- 'Local themes' can be used.
- Attractive in the case of local promotions because offers can be made directly to well-defined audiences or communities.

### DISADVANTAGES
- High degree of duplication is possible because more than one freesheet can be published within one geographic area.
- Adverts are lost in the mass of adverts appearing.
- The amount of actual readership is questionable.

## Teletext

Teletext is a television information service available to viewers with TV sets adapted to receive it. Information provided includes new summaries, weather forecasts, stocks and shares movements, holiday and shopping information, etc.

### ADVANTAGES
- Quick reference to topical issues.
- Permanence of information.
- Armchair shopping is facilitated.
- Up-to-date information is offered to consumers.
- Pictorial information is possible.
- Pages on the screen can be divided into several sections to maximise the impact of the presentation.

### DISADVANTAGES
- Only a small percentage of viewers have teletext facilities.
- Very few viewers look at all the information teletext offers.

# Cable television

Cable television is popular in Benelux countries (Belgium, Holland, Luxemburg) and the USA but a number of franchises have also been taken up in the UK. Consumers who want cable TV are given a viewing 'package', e.g. a film channel, music channel, sports channel. At present it appeals to viewers who tend to be interested in specific types of programmes. As an advertising medium it is able to reach specific target groups, so psychographic factors can be used. The number of subscribers to cable TV in the UK is at present relatively small but as it increases franchisees are expected to reduce fees and be more reliant on advertising funds. Although cable means further fragmentation of the total TV viewing audience, research can be more accurate, as subscribers are known by name, address, occupation, etc. and targeting advertising is therefore easier.

# Satellite television

A satellite orbiting the world receives programmes from the ground and transmits them over large areas to viewers with satellite dishes. A wide variety of entertainment is offered and the advertisements are shown to an international audience. Satellite TV provides advertisers with the opportunity to advertise international brands to many different countries.

The initial success of satellite TV in the UK is questionable because:

a) The national television network is strong, with quality programmes, so the incentive for more programmes is limited.
b) There are many entertainment alternatives in the UK (this is not so in other European countries where satellite is more popular).
c) UK consumers are not, as yet, accustomed to national media overlap, i.e. programmes aimed at several countries with viewers having to select from 20 or 30 channels.
d) FMCGs (fast moving consumer goods) for home consumption are nationally based, therefore satellite will be of little use in this area.
e) It will lead to further fragmentation of the media.

# Current and future implications

Developments in advertising media having been identified, the marketing implications must be considered. Marketing management must respond to the behavioural changes of the media and its public(s) and should take account of the following when planning advertising campaigns:

- Public opinion is gaining in strength and as a result marketing managers must be more careful with media selection and advert presentations.
- Media proliferation within countries is unavoidable and will grow.
- Media overlap between countries is increasing.
- Growth of international publications.

- Audience fragmentation as a result of a wide variety of media options.
- More media must be used in order to reach selected audiences.
- Harder to control overall advertising themes.
- Stricter media selection criteria need to be used.
- Specific audiences can be reached more easily through specialist media.
- National audiences must be reached through conventional media (newspapers in particular).
- Freesheet and local publication offer easier targeting.
- Emphasis on 'local needs' will gain in importance.
- Sponsorship of sporting events or other major events offers easy access to large dispersed audiences.
- Codes of practice are becoming stricter. New codes to be introduced for new media.

# ■ MEDIA SELECTION CRITERIA

Choosing the most appropriate media for a particular product or service is difficult, but a number of criteria can be applied in order to help you through the media maze. The most widely used criteria include:

a) The size of the advertising budget available compared with the cost of each medium, e.g. companies with limited budget cannot usually afford television for national promotional campaigns.

b) Suitability of individual media in terms of the target audience.

c) Availability of particular amount of space at the time required.

d) Suitability of media in terms of editorial and entertainment content – every medium has its own 'personality' and the advert must be consistent with the overall environment/atmosphere of the media selected.

e) Nature of information to be communicated – some products or services may benefit from the creative dimensions of television while others may be presented effectively in a magazine.

f) Familiarity with specific media through previous use – successes, or even mistakes, in the past can form a useful guide to future media selection.

g) Time constraints associated with the advertising campaign – if audiences need to be informed immediately TV advertisements, where time slots may have to be booked in advance, may not be suitable in comparison with, say, newspapers.

h) Nature and scale of competitors' media activities.

# ■ ADVERTISING PLANNING

Before starting work on any form of advertising, the following questions must be asked:

1 At whom is the advertising to be directed (the target audience)? – the general public, a particular trade, car drivers, teenagers or newly married couples, etc.

2  What is the objective of the campaign? To introduce a new product? To increase sales of a particular line? To attract a new type of customer? To introduce a new form of packaging?
3  What timing would be appropriate? e.g. summer holidays mainly advertised in the December–February period, camping equipment in the spring and the summer, garden tools at the beginning of the year.
4  What medium or media is available?
5  How much repetition of the message is necessary?

Whatever objectives are set for advertising strategies, it must be remembered that the primary objective of advertising is to increase sales. As the advertising budget represents a marketing expense, companies have to determine the cost-effectiveness of the cash investment in the advertising process, so planning the advertising effort becomes of crucial importance in ensuring the highest return on investment as possible.

The main decision areas in planning advertising are as follows:

1  Which part of the promotions task is advertising suitable for and what level of expenditure is appropriate?
2  What combination of media should be used?
3  How should the plan be phased during the year, taking into account seasonality and communication needs.
4  What message should be used and what degree of repetition?
5  What are the best means of determining what is being accomplished with the advertising?

Marketing managers must be aware of the mysteries surrounding advertising that may prevent a perfect understanding of this element of the communication mix. These mysteries can be identified by examining some of the major **problems** associated with advertising planning.

## Non-linear effects

High expenditure on promotion does not necessarily mean proportionally higher sales. Advertising 'overkill' is one of marketing's most expensive mistakes. Advertising is **one** of the many influences on consumer decision-making and a sale, or lack of sales for that matter, cannot always be attributed to advertising. As a consumer you are exposed to many advertisements, you follow friends' recommendations, seek advice from a retailer and finally decide by using your own assessment of a situation, product, company, or service. Advertisements represent one, and only one, element of this assessment.

## Threshold effects

Advertising may have little or no effect unless a minimum level – the 'threshold effect' – is reached. Low levels of expenditure may mean that the audience will not receive the message frequently enough for it to have any effect, while too much reminding may lead to boredom or even hostility among consumers. A fine balance must be sought between effective market coverage and adequate reminding; this is an area where research can prove invaluable to marketing communicators.

## Carry over effects

The effects of advertising are spread over time and the memory/associations of the campaign often carry through to the next. Consumers may become aware of a product this year but decide to buy it twelve months later. The information in the advertisement may be recalled and a sale is achieved by an 'old' advertisement. This cannot be measured, or pre-determined, so advertising planners must allow for a certain level of 'information carry-over'.

## Decay effects

Advertisements, like everything else in life, will suffer from decay after they have been used for a certain period of time. Consumers get bored, information becomes repetitive, interest declines and the element of surprise disappears. Advertisers should develop different adverts to replace presentations which have lost their popularity and impact.

## Marketing mix interaction effects

Advertising results are affected by the rest of the marketing mix, e.g. the price, distribution and product and other parts of the communications programme, like sales promotions, public relations and personal selling. It is impossible to separate the influences of each factor in the mind of each consumer, so one must seek consistency in all elements of the marketing mix.

## Competitive effects

The impact of advertising messages/programmes will be affected by the pro-motional campaigns of competitors. Consumers may perceive a competitor's presentation as more exciting, informative or realistic, and respond accordingly. Advertisements should be designed to give a company a unique image, and yet may still have to be altered to respond effectively to competitors' advertising tactics.

## Quality effects

The quality of advertising, its timing, presentation and the media used will clearly affect the sales response.

To measure sales after a commercial has run for a few weeks and attributing sales to one particular commercial are not realistic. Equally, to dismiss all advertising measurement as ineffective is also unacceptable. To arrive at a sales objective you must know where you are going and how to get there, which requires knowledge which in turn requires research. The research methods used by marketers in order to improve or measure the effectiveness of their campaigns are examined below.

# ■ ADVERTISING RESEARCH

The type of research which must be carried out in order to contribute effectively to advertising planning is determined by what the advertiser is trying to accomplish. Objectives may include:

1 To affect the act of purchase (this is the ultimate objective of most advertisements)
2 To determine any correlation between advertising and sales, e.g. specific occasions during the year, weather, change of legislation, inflation rates, etc.
3 To determine whether the advertising is communicating the intended message
4 To discover or unearth new prospects
5 To achieve intended levels of awareness, coverage, interest, etc.
6 To change attitudes towards a brand.

Measuring effectiveness can be related to two distinct areas of activity, **pre-testing** and **post-testing**, which must be examined separately.

## Pre-testing

The emphasis here is placed on evaluating creative ideas and subsequently selecting the most effective adverts and/or messages to be used.

Two measures of effectiveness are:

1 **Interest** – stimulation (informative, imaginative, startling, etc.)
2 **Liking** – enjoyment (amusing, entertaining, etc.)

Though we may seek those aspects highlighted here, it may soon be the case that some of these factors are not important. For example, we may sell perfume or after-shave on an emotive basis without any real information regarding the integral quality of the product.

a) A representative sample of consumers targeted are asked to examine adverts in terms of content, presentation, consistency, etc. and then **rate** adverts presented to them. Rating can involve numerical figures given to each advert or a simple ranking of adverts in order of preference
b) Group discussions to concentrate on general evaluation of advertisements developed
c) Portfolio test – a dummy magazine is used containing dummy adverts as well as the advert being tested. Recall and impact of the pilot advert is then determined through exhaustive questioning.

## Post-testing

The emphasis here is placed on determining the actual impact of adverts already used. The main measures used include:

1 **Recognition/identification** Recognition greatly improves the possibilities of persuasion but it cannot be used as a definite means of measuring advert effectiveness. The best known technique is the **starch recognition method.** Over 100 000 people are interviewed (calls are made at home) per year and adverts under consideration are classified under:
   a) Noted (respondents remember vaguely)
   b) Seen-associated (advert read/seen in part)
   c) Read-most (respondent remembers most of the advert).

2 **Recall** (how well respondents remember the main message of the advertisement) Recall as a measure of assessing the effectiveness of advertising has been a bone of contention for many years. We can only measure whether people remember a particular advert rather than whether it has a good or bad effect on attitudes or sales. Respondents are asked to recall adverts they say they have seen. Tests for recall can be aided or unaided (spontaneous) with researchers seeking to determine how many people actually remember the product that was advertised rather than just the advert.

   A popular and reliable technique currently in use is **triple association tests.** Respondents are given the generic product, e.g. the cigarette and the advertising theme/message, and requested to identify the brand name.

3 **Comprehension** (understanding of the main message) This measure of effectiveness of the advert is always given a high rating in the list of priorities because it represents a vital condition to effective communication. Techniques used include:

   - Personal interviews
   - Word association tests
   - Sentence completion tests

   For information on these research techniques refer to Chapters 2 and 3 on marketing research.

4 **Believability** Although some researchers still use this measure as an indicator of effectiveness, it has to be treated as a minor method. Claims made by advertisers are often exaggerated or adverts are presented beyond 'believability', so consumers rarely take advertising claims literally but accept them as a guide. When examining believability the researchers should try to determine whether consumers believe what they were specifically intended to believe rather than fully accepting all advertising claims. For functional products, where advertisers need to make rational appeals to the consumers in relation to the product's features, benefits and general 'unique selling propositions', this method assumes even more importance. It can also be used to determine the credibility

individual advertisers carry within a particular market and it may contribute to the adjustment of future claims. Techniques used to determine believability are similar to the techniques used to measure comprehension (see **3** above).

## TIR and AIDA

Whether you are a student of marketing undertaking a case study involving advertising or a practitioner in marketing never provide answers to advertising/ promotional problems without first considering TIR and AIDA.

### TIR (Target audience, Impact and Repetition)
What is the target audience you intend reaching? If you know the audience characteristics and how many people you need to reach you will have an idea which elements of the promotional mix are best for reaching that audience. The next thing to consider is how to achieve maximum impact. What should the main message be? Is there a need for colour, sound, movement, size and detailed copy? Once these aspects have been considered, evaluate the degree of repetition (repeat showings) needed to maintain effectiveness. This may not mean repeating regularly but may demand repetition only at particular times of the year such as during the summer, or just before a national event. Applying these sorts of question will help you decide which media to use and the form of the advert.

### AIDA (Attention, Interest, Desire, Action)
The advert should be able to obtain people's Attention, create Interest in the product, arouse Desire to know more or purchase and motivate them into Action, i.e. to purchase. Finally look at cost-effectiveness of the various methods selected in relation to the amount that can be spent, so that some methods can be eliminated and the best approach can be decided upon.

## ■ STUDY AND EXAM TIPS

**1** Be prepared to select or recommend advertising media by applying the media selection criteria discussed, especially when attempting mini case studies.

**2** The term 'advertising effectiveness' is meaningless unless it is linked to the specific communication objectives of an advertising campaign. Always keep this in mind when answering questions concerning the planning of an advertising campaign.

**3** Avoid historical information on the media in the UK (or the country of your choice or origin); concentrate on the value of the different media to an advertising campaign.

**4** Remember ACORN groups are not an alternative to or the same as 'geographic segmentation'. They represent 'clusters' of like consumers living in similar neigh-bourhoods throughout the country.

**5** New media are being introduced in many countries, e.g. satellite TV. Be prepared to mention them where you feel they are appropriate to show that you keep up to date with changes in advertising media.

**6** Check whether the examining body whose exams you are sitting uses the term 'communications mix' or 'promotions mix'. Communications mix refers to a broader concept encompassing non-expressed communication such as setting high price to imply that the product is of high quality. Questions set on the 'communications mix' invariably relate to the 'promotions mix' where the communication method employed is expressed and the communication function is controllable.

## ■ SELF ASSESSMENT QUESTIONS

Answer the following questions without reference to the text and then refer to the answers given at the end of the manual to determine your score. Award yourself one mark for each complete question that you answer correctly. If you scored eight or more you are reading efficiently. Where you have answered wrongly check back in the chapter to see what the answer should have been.

**1** One of the elements (promotional tools) of the promotions mix is advertising. Name three more.
a) ....................................................................................................................
b) ....................................................................................................................
c) ....................................................................................................................

**2** One independent advertising medium is cinema. Name four more.
a) ....................................................................................................................
b) ....................................................................................................................
c) ....................................................................................................................
d) ....................................................................................................................

**3** The only advertising undertaken in newspapers is by companies advertising their products or services for sale. True or false. ................?

**4** Complete the following sentence. T&T stand for ................ and ................

**5** Newspapers may be international, national, regional, local or ................

**6** Direct mail refers to promotional material sent through the post whereas a ................ ................ is where promotional material/literature is given to the respondent, pushed through letterboxes, under car windscreen wipers, etc.

**7** Complete the sentence.
ACORN is an acronym standing for: A classification ............................................
................................................................................................................................

**8** TGI stand for ................................................................................................................

**9** BMRB stands for British ................   ................ Bureau.

**10** Advertising research can take the form of pre-testing or ................

**11** Complete the following:
a) Word ................ tests
b) Sentence ................ tests.

---

# ■  PAST EXAMINATION QUESTIONS

### *Chartered Institute of Marketing*

**1** Compare and contrast methods used to measure advertising effectiveness.

**2** 'The high cost of advertising works against consumer interests by creating a barrier to entry into many large markets.' Discuss. (Refer to the suggested answer to this question which appears after these past examination questions.)

### *Association of Business Executives – Advanced Diploma in Marketing (Advertising and Sales)*

**3** What objectives do media planners have to consider when selecting media aimed at consumers?

**4** What research might a company use before and after an advertising campaign? Give examples.

---

# ■  SUGGESTED ANSWER TO QUESTION 2

The question implies that advertising media are costly, which is a dangerous generalisation. Admittedly, television, national newspapers and large centrally situated posters are extremely costly but one must not forget the availability of relatively inexpensive media options open to smaller companies, such as escalator poster panels in underground stations, local newspapers, freesheets or certain magazines with highly specialised audiences.

Most small to medium sized companies prefer to service one or two segments of a large market where they can optimise their return on advertising expenditure. Even large companies with a wide product/service range often prefer to service a variety of segments rather than advertise nationally so that they 'cream off' profitable segments of the market and leave less profitable segments for others to service.

Small businesses implement plans of action which are affordable and relate to their capacity to produce. Take, for instance, the owner of a small restaurant. The capacity of his business is extremely limited, the finances available are likely to be restricted and the target market is likely to evolve around a given community within a specific radius. There is no need or intention to reach large, dispersed audiences, so the high cost of certain advertising media is irrelevant.

The barrier to entry is not necessarily the advertising cost but the company's own limitations and aspirations, which determine the course of action the business can undertake. It must be remembered that advertising is a marketing tactic employed to achieve specific marketing goals; it does not set the goals. There may be other methods, e.g. PR or personal selling, that may be more useful in reaching certain markets. If small companies use the right business mix they should grow and, as they do, require advertising campaigns that may be national. Therefore, growth and the type of advertising needed generally go hand-in-hand, and a successful company breaks down any barriers – including national advertising – as it meets them.

The second implication of the question is that certain companies, especially small businesses, cannot afford to advertise and consequently consumers do not get to know about the products and/or services they have to offer. As a result of this, consumer needs are not satisfied and the cost of advertising, acting as a barrier, should carry the blame. However, it would rarely benefit consumers if small companies did advertise nationally, as production and distribution capacity would probably be insufficient and over-trading may result. Having said this small companies selling products with a high mark-up may benefit from direct mail, and may also advertise nationally to stimulate enquiries. Thus, product line, size of company and the profitability in advertising nationally are often more important than costs.

There is an element of truth in the implications of the question as everyone would like to know what is available from every company. However, there is a saying: 'There is no such thing as a large company; only a successful small one'. The reason many companies can advertise nationally is because they have been able to supply consumers with a good product at the right price – an important factor when considering if the cost of advertising is detrimental to consumer interests. The high cost of advertising nationally, when looked at as a proportion of the cost of the product, is invariably low and therefore many companies elect to use it: mass production ensures the price of the product is kept low as adequate levels of profitable sales are achieved.

# 5 | Advertising agencies

*There is a tendency for advertising people to fall in love with their
own advertising.*

*Jack Wynne-Williams*

In Chapter 4 you were introduced to the complex subject of advertising media and
advertising planning and specific guidelines were offered as to the correct selection
and use of specific advertising media. Students often ask, however, 'Who are the
people who actually plan, prepare and test advertising campaigns?' If you consider
any advertisement you have come across in newspapers, magazines, television or
any other advertising media you will find that parts of the advertisement involve
skills which one does not normally associate with marketing management, e.g.
photographs used, filmlets forming the actual advert, actors appearing on adverts,
musical themes or poems used as part of an advert, etc. Are they created by
marketing men and women?

   In order to answer this question one has to examine the operations of **specialist**
organisations which concentrate on the preparation and implemention of advertising campaigns on behalf of clients. These organisations, the **advertising
agencies**, are examined in detail in this chapter.

## ■ REASONS FOR USING SPECIALIST ORGANISATIONS

Many large organisations have the necessary marketing skills and resources to
enable them to operate efficiently on a day-to-day basis, but it is becoming
increasing common for companies to seek assistance from a number of different
types of professional services. In earlier chapters you saw that the marketing
research needs of organisations are often satisfied by marketing research
specialists or agencies; a similar situation is seen in the case of the advertising and
promotional needs of companies. A well-qualified, experienced Marketing
Manager will be able to identify problems and opportunities being faced by the
company and should be capable of devising plans of action designed to help the
company *respond* to problems or opportunities; however, the specialist skills
needed for the creation and implementation of an advertising campaign may not

be available within the company. Car manufacturers, major retailers or baked bean manufacturers are unlikely to employ the following skilled personnel:

- Cameramen
- Photographers
- Printers
- Copywriters
- Actors and actresses
- Cartoonists
- Filmlet directors
- Musical directors, etc.

These are just some of the skills needed to create an advertising campaign. Maintenance of such skills on a full-time basis is *not* cost-effective for most organisations because they will be under-utilised most of the time. Advertising agencies provide many of these skills to potential advertisers, either from within their agency or from outside, e.g. specialists such as printers. They offer a professional, structured approach to the creation of advertising campaigns, supplementing the skills from within marketing organisations, providing a cost-effective option to advertising and providing creative ideas on delivering the right message to the market. Advertising companies are therefore an extension of a company's own operations and competence.

## ■ THE ORIGINS OF THE ADVERTISING AGENCY

The function of the modern advertising agency, to help a company to market and advertise its goods or services efficiently, is fundamentally different from the function of the original advertising agents who were agents for the newspapers and magazines rather than the advertisers. The original agents acted as media brokers selling advertising space to anyone they could persuade to advertise and receiving commissions from the publications for the space they sold. It was realised that it was easier to sell space to an advertiser if they could provide the suggestions as to what should be said in the advertisement. Agencies began to employ **copywriters**, to think up and write effective advertising copy. Then, as it became more important to make advertisements stand out from the editorial and from an increasing number of other advertisements, **graphic artists** were employed to design distinctive layouts, select typefaces, and provide illustrations. Finally, **production staff** were employed to order the printing services, ensure the best possible reproduction of advertising literature, arrange for TV and radio adverts to be produced and to keep costs within budgets allocated for the provision of the service.

For some years these staff made up the advertising agent, but gradually the emphasis of the agent's work began to change. As companies began to undertake advertising with agents on a regular basis the agents developed a loyalty towards the companies, which was often in conflict with their loyalty to the publishers for whom they were selling space. Thus, they were forced to make a choice; to sell space for publishers, or to advise the companies wishing to advertise – impartially – as to which publication they should use to advertise products or services. They chose the latter.

In order to advise a company (the client) it was necessary for the agency to employ staff with knowledge of the types of people reading different publications and who could negotiate with the publications regarding position, price and date of appearance; these staff are the **media planners.**

The owners of the publications continued, however, to grant commission to those agencies which they recognised as being efficient and financially sound and which gave certain guarantees, such as a promise not to rebate any part of the commission to an advertiser. The media acknowledged that, although the agencies were no longer selling their space, they were still providing them with considerable benefits. Successful agencies centralised the orders from many hundreds of advertisers, and so reduced the publishers' own administrative costs and financial risk. The expertise of the agencies also enabled them to create effective and economical advertising, stimulating an increased volume of advertising, to the advantage of the publishers.

# ■ ORGANISATION OF A TYPICAL ADVERTISING AGENCY

The structure of advertising agencies provides a basic understanding of the classification of the different skills available and highlights the variety of services offered.

It is impossible to present one structure which represents all advertising agencies so a summarised version of the structure of a typical advertising agency is given here. Agencies may consist of just one person, or hundreds of people. Complex structures are difficult to understand and memorise for examination purposes and, generally speaking, marketing examiners will only look for evidence of understanding of the topic. Figure 5.1 (page 86) illustrates the basic elements of the structure of an advertising agency, followed by a description of the major activities associated with each department.

## Account management

As indicated in Figure 5.1 the term 'Account' refers to an agency's client and summarises all operations which must be carried out to satisfy the client's expectations.

**Account Directors** have overall control of accounts, and **Account Executives** are responsible for the daily activities associated with the preparation of specific advertising or promotional campaigns. Typical activities include:

● Detailed interpretation of the client's needs and promotional expectations

Figure 5.1 *Advertising agency structure*

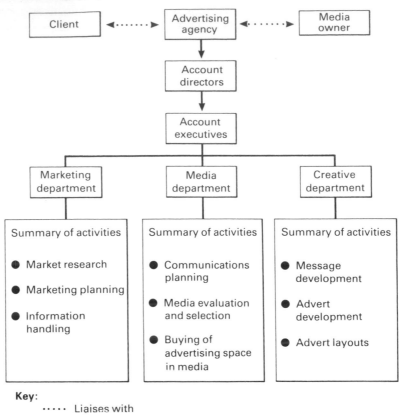

- Briefing individual members of staff on the work they must carry out
- Ensuring that all departments are co-ordinating their efforts towards the development of a specific campaign
- Maintaining contact with clients in order to up-date them on progress or to obtain additional information which may be required
- Ensuring that budgets are adhered to
- Offering marketing or promotional advice to clients
- Ultimately assessing the effectiveness of the campaign developed.

Account Executives or Account Directors need to have wide business knowledge and sound judgement on marketing, promotional and selling issues. They should also be effective managers, able to plan, organise, delegate, motivate, co-ordinate and control all members of the staff.

## The media department

The media department has possibly the most critical function within an advertising agency as it is involved in the **planning** of advertising or promotional campaigns and the **booking** of space in the media selected. Media Planners receive detailed information from the Account Executive covering the product or service to be advertised, the likely buyers or target markets, the budget available, the current competition being faced by the client as well as information on past advertising campaigns used by the client.

This information forms a useful background for the development of a **media plan**, which defines the media to be used, the frequency of use, the timing of the adverts and the total cost of the campaign. The media planner must therefore have access to a vast amount of up-to-date information about every major advertising medium available and the viewing, listening, circulation or readership figures of each. Media planning involves extensive statistical work so planners should be skilled in the use of analytical and statistical techniques. They are also required to have a sound business sense: space and time buying is a purely commercial function involving negotiations and often hard bargaining with the advertising departments of newspapers, magazines and television companies is required.

## The creative department

The creative department will normally consist of **copywriters** who plan and write advertisements; **visualisers** who think up original advertising messages and images; **typographers** and **graphic artists** who design the advertisement and provide finished drawings; and **producers** who ensure the printing and screening is done correctly and within the constraints of the budget. Copywriters must be imaginative and able to present their ideas clearly, in written form. They must understand the people they are trying to influence and the motives for buying. They should also have some degree of artistic ability; effective adverts are often the result of the correct combination of pictorial and implied presentation. Modern advertising campaigns rarely depend on sudden flashes of insight or inspiration; more often they are the result of lengthy discussions between client and agency personnel, involving the use of detailed market information, hours of writing and sketching, and the frustration that results from failed ideas. This is particularly the case with TV adverts, where every word counts and is chosen carefully to match the action and background music.

## The marketing department

Many agencies offer clients the services of a separate marketing department, which is concerned with the following areas of research:

1 **Product research** involves detailed evaluation of the product or service to be advertised and utilises a number of research techniques to reveal consumer perceptions, unique selling points and limitations. These factors are carefully considered before an advert is developed.
2 **Sales research** relates to the evaluation of the activities of the client's sales force or sales potential and concentrates on sales statistics, sales force effectiveness and sales forecasting.

3 **Market research** takes a wider view of the client's operations, concentrating on market size, market trends, market share, user characteristics and the overall sales potential of different consumer segments within the market.
4 **Communications research** concentrates on the evaluation of adverts, the quality of 'point of sale' material, packaging and name tests and provides useful information to be used in justifying or amending promotional activities undertaken.
5 **Economic and business research** focuses on the total 'business environment' of a client's operations, covering social, political, economic and technological developments within a market and their impact on the client's business.

Much of this information can be obtained from official statistics, some can be supplied by the clients, while the remainder may have to be obtained by field research among consumers and/or retailers.

Larger agencies may also have a marketing or advertising **planning** function, which looks beyond the immediate campaign to see how the advertising fits into the wider, long term market problems and needs of the advertiser and defines the overall business strategy to which the campaign should contribute.

# ■ EVALUATION, SELECTION AND BRIEFING OF AGENCIES

A major problem for a Marketing Manager is the identifying, evaluating and selecting of a suitable agency to fulfil the company's marketing and communication needs. A well-planned approach is required in evaluating and eventually appointing the right agency. A professional approach will involve the following:

1 Define the company's needs (e.g. market research, advertising, packaging, PR, new product development consultancy).
2 Identify potential agencies through:
   a) desk research, or
   b) the Advertising Agency Register which provides an impartial service offering video presentation of the services of over 100 agencies.
3 Seek and evaluate business/promotional literature of the potential agencies selected (the agency itself will usually provide this literature). It may help to check their service with client companies who have used the agency before. When evaluating alternative advertising agencies, the following factors should be examined:
   a) Services offered
   b) Track record of top personnel
   c) Creative ability
   d) International services offered
   e) Reputation
   f) Handling of competitors' accounts. Agencies involved in the communication campaigns of competitors should be rejected to avoid conflicting interests

g) Business and financial status
h) Media specialisation (if any)
i) Experience/s with client's market/industry
j) Total billings, client names, industry groups, etc.
k) Basis of remuneration, internal method of costing, allocation of overheads and charges made.

4 These evaluation points should lead to the elimination of unsuitable agencies; the most attractive agencies should be shortlisted. Ideally, the shortlist should consist of four to six agencies, for further evaluation.

5 Arrange for personal visits to the shortlisted agencies and seek to meet the people who could be working on the company's campaign, if the appointment is made. An informal approach is encouraged at this stage so that an understanding of an agency's capabilities, personnel credentials and overall professionalism is established. This is one of the most important factors in selecting an agency as the client must feel confident of the agency's key staff and their ability to have sound but creative and original ideas.

A young graduate applied for a job as a copywriter with an advertising agency. The Accounts Director who was to interview him forgot about the interview, until he was passing the waiting candidate on his way to the toilet. On his return the Director placed a roll of toilet paper in front of the amazed candidate and asked him to write an advertising copy for it. The candidate wrote, 'Our toilet paper is tops with bottoms'. He got the job. Being constantly creative is not easy but being creative in a way that fits in with the marketing strategy of the client company is even more difficult. 'The real thing', the catchphrase for Coca Cola, reminds people that Coca Cola is the original and, therefore, implying it is the best. But it is also intended to imply that consumers should not purchase substitutes, and is therefore a counter-strategy against close competitors.

Advertising agencies will also evaluate potential clients and it is possible to be rejected by an agency even though, as a client, you feel that they represent the most suitable option. In order to understand the likely grounds of client rejection by an agency, the criteria which agencies use in evaluating potential or current clients are listed here:

a) Size of client's budget
b) Reputation and track record (within the industry or with previous advertising agencies used)
c) Financial stability
d) Nature of client's business
e) Compatibility of personnel
f) Expectations and time allowed.

Once a client is accepted a continuous evaluation will take place. The criteria listed above will still apply but the following may be added:

g) Sales growth

h) Changes in client's personnel
i) Satisfaction or dissatisfaction with advertising effort or agency services in general
j) Lateness in payment of bills
k) Creative freedom actually allowed.

If the agency is to provide a good service to a client, integrity demands that it makes certain the client is right for the agency and the agency has the resources to provide the client with a good service.

6 Invite agencies shortlisted to 'pitch' for the account.

Campaign 'pitches' refer to the submission of ideas, reports or proposals by agencies to prospective clients in an effort to convince them that they are creative enough to provide the client with an attractive and effective advertising campaign.

It is important to seek campaign pitches because clients must examine the agency's ability to understand and handle the product or service to be advertised.

A word of caution is necessary at this stage because although some agencies may be willing to offer campaign pitches free of charge, in order to gain the account, most agencies expect to be paid an agreed fee which aims to cover the expenses incurred in relation to the campaign pitch.

7 Evaluate creative efforts relating to campaign pitches or past agency advertising efforts.
8 Rank agencies, prepare report and present findings to company board.
9 Gain agreement from board and offer account to agency selected. Get agreement, finalise working relationships, agree upon payments, appoint formally, announce appointment and finalise brief.

Many advertising agencies belong to international groups which offer an additional advantage to their clients. Products may be launched in several different countries and experience with a client's operations and products make the development of suitable advertising campaigns far easier. Information is passed from one agency to another and international programmes can be effectively implemented. Caution is necessary, however, as certain products may need distinct advertising campaigns for each country they are marketed in, which allow for a direct relationship with the expectations of the consumers. International agencies may be helpful but additional 'local' expertise is also required.

## Agency briefs

A **brief** is a written document which represents a client's expectations in relation to research, media selection, creative work, etc. A brief should be agreed upon by both parties and the following information should be included:

1 Short history of client's operation/s
2 Information on the products or services to be marketed, e.g.
   • Sales performance

- Samples
- Market segments operating in
- Client's product mix in total, etc.

3 Identification of client's direct and indirect competitors and general outline of the industry (information on this can be added to, through additional research)
4 Size of budget
5 Time constraints (negotiable)
6 Marketing objectives
7 Communication objectives or expectations
8 Determination of the work to be carried out by the agency
9 Other contingencies of relevance to a particular situation.

Never accept advertising or promotional mix suggestions of an agency at face value. Make the agency justify how effectively the goals of the promotions will be pursued so that each one can be considered in cost-effective terms. Advertising people tend to fall in love with their own creations and a few will attempt to sell as much to the client as possible.

# ■ ADVERTISING AGENCY REMUNERATION

Advertising agency remuneration revolves around two basic sources of revenue:

1 **Fee payments** relate to non-media work carried out by the agency. The agency may be expected to carry out research, design a new package, advise the company on general promotional activities, organise consumer promotions, offer consultancy services on public relations activities undertaken by the company or simply design a new logo. All these activities incur expenses which the agency has to recover from the client. A profit margin will also need to be considered and a final invoice submitted to the client.
2 **Commission payments** Media owners offer advertising agencies a commission for adverts booked with them, representing the major source of revenue for nearly all agencies. Commissions paid by media owners vary considerably and an agency with a large advertising budget at its disposal will enjoy a major advantage. As a rule of thumb, however, 10 per cent commission on the money spent with the media would be a reasonable guide. If the advertiser only requires the agency to book a few thousand pounds worth of space or time the agency may charge them slightly more.

  The advertiser could book direct with the media to save cost but they usually prefer to use the booking services and advertising skills and knowledge of an agency. Most agencies can provide the client with a detailed schedule of international bookings and keep a check that adverts have appeared – saving even most small companies considerable time and expense. Therefore, agencies may often receive a **commission and fee**, for providing a client with both media and non-media work. Fee payments often represent a major source of conflict between agencies and clients because creative work or general consultancy services are difficult to quantify. For example, an agency may charge what a client thinks is an inordinate amount for the design of a new package which looks extremely plain and simple. The client may fail to appreciate that hours, days or even weeks of hard work could have gone into its development and that numerous alternatives may have been developed or considered beforehand. Clients should be reasonable in their expectations in terms of creative work and monetary charges. Some simple rules can help in controlling or, on occasion, even removing the conflict situation. Seek to develop mutual trust and respect. Both parties should be aware of each other's expectations. Frequent reporting on progress made can prove extremely helpful and willingness to evaluate proposals or creative work completed in an unbiased and professional manner contribute towards a successful client–agency relationship.

# ■ ADVERTISING CODE OF PRACTICE

Any advertisements created by an advertising agency on behalf of a client need to comply with certain rules, designed to protect the interests of the general public. As a viewer or a reader of adverts, you have probably questioned the truthfulness of some of the presentations made to you. You may even have felt that you have been intentionally misled. There are, however, certain moral, ethical and professional duties expected of advertisers in most countries which should, to some extent, protect the consumer from dishonesty or misrepresentation in advertising. For example, British advertisers must comply with the **British Code of Advertising Practice**, which was launched at the Advertising Association Conference in 1961, and seeks to define practices considered to be undesirable. It also stated that 'All advertising should be legal, decent, honest and truthful'. A committee was set up to operate and update the Code, known as The Code of Advertising Practice Committee (CAP). In 1962 the independent Advertising Standards Authority (ASA) was established; its objective was 'the promotion and enforcement in the United Kingdom of the highest standards of advertising in all media'.

## The advantages of the code

1 It has become well-known and respected as a guide for the governing authority of the advertising industry.
2 It is flexibile and adaptable to changing circumstances, e.g. appendices deal with the advertising of alcoholic drinks and cigarettes.
3 It has increasingly unified the advertising industry.
4 It is tantamount to reversing the burden of proof of innocence and goodwill (substantiation of products or services) on to the advertiser: claims, descriptions and comparisons in advertisements must be proved to the ASA and CAP – this would be unacceptable in the present legal system of control.

In theory advertisements that could reduce the public's confidence in advertising are not permitted but in practice there will always be people who believe some adverts are misleading or should not exist. Values and knowledge within society are constantly changing; for instance, many people believed for years that cigarettes should not be extensively advertised and this is now being accepted. The guidelines set apply to the present and are not absolutes for all time and every situation.

In order to appreciate the role of the Code of Advertising Practice, we can examine some of its key points. For example, advertisements should not:

- Contain statements or visual presentations offensive to public decency
- Exploit superstitious beliefs
- Play on fear, without justifiable reason
- Contain any descriptions, claims or illustrations which directly or by implication are misleading about the product or service advertised
- Contain anything which might physically, mentally or morally harm children
- Denigrate other products or companies. In Britain an advertiser is free to compare his products with that of a competitor as long as comments made for comparison purposes are truthful.

There is still some way to go before advertising controls are working towards the majority of environmental and social aspirations of our time, e.g. protecting the environment or reducing alcoholism. The ASA's own advertisements encourage people to write to the ASA with their concerns regarding any advertisement they have seen or heard.

## ■ STUDY AND EXAM TIPS

**1** Concentrate on the main services offered by advertising agencies and avoid presenting complicated organisational charts which are difficult to explain or understand.

**2** Be prepared to discuss the evaluation criteria which ought to be used by a client in selecting the most appropriate advertising agency and also the likely evaluation of a client by an agency. Remember that you are dealing with a two-way process.

**3** The main elements of a client's brief represent a vital information input to the total process. If an agency is briefed wrongly, then poor advertising campaigns are likely to result. Be prepared to identify and discuss the main areas of interest to be found in a client's brief.

**4** The main points of the Code of Advertising Practice are introduced here so that you can appreciate the need for honesty, truthfulness and professionalism. Allow for these issues in *all* your discussions on the topic rather than assuming that because advertising exists it must always be good for the public.

**5** Marketing journals often include reports on the operations and performance of advertising agencies. Use of practical examples will help you to highlight important points in the examination and will improve the depth of your answer, so do read such journals whenever possible. In the Practice of Marketing you should try to exhibit knowledge beyond this textbook and use your own commonsense when answering questions.

**6** Do *not* link advertising agencies only to advertising. Treat them as expert organisations which can help their clients with all aspects of marketing communications.

## ■ SELF ASSESSMENT QUESTIONS

Answer the following questions without reference to the text and then refer to the answers given at the end of the textbook to determine your score. Award yourself one mark for each complete question that you answer correctly. If you scored less than seven read the relevant parts of the chapter again.

**1** Do advertising agencies book space on behalf of clients or media owners?
   .................

**2** Major advertising agencies only book advertising space. True or false?
   .................

**3** The person in an advertising agency responsible for monitoring the circulation, readership and advertising charges of various media and for booking space/time is referred to as the ...................................................................................

**4** The person in the advertising agency responsible for liaison with the client and for co-ordinating the client's promotional needs within the agency is referred to as the
   .................

**5** Would every major advertising agency have the following specialists?
   a) Graphics Artist            YES ☐ NO ☐ (tick the appropriate box)
   b) Visualiser                 YES ☐ NO ☐
   c) Copy writer                YES ☐ NO ☐
   d) Media researcher           YES ☐ NO ☐

**6** When an agency makes its initial presentation to a client in order to obtain the client's account the process is referred to as the ....................................

**7** Advertising agencies always receive remuneration for the work they do in the form of commission. True or false? ....................................

**8** CAP stands for ........................................................... Committee.

**9** ASA stands for ....................................

**10** Complete the sentence. 'The British Code of Advertising Practice states, 'All advertising should be legal, decent, honest and .......................................................

---

# ■ PAST EXAMINATION QUESTIONS

### The Chartered Institute of Marketing

**1** Describe the role/s and function/s of an account executive in an advertising agency.

**2** You have invited three advertising agencies to submit their proposals and to make presentations for your account. Discuss the criteria you propose using to enable you to decide which agency will receive the business.

**3** Describe the functions performed by a full service advertising agency and say how it is organised to carry them out.

### Association of Business Executives – Advanced Diploma in Marketing (Advertising and Sales)

**4** What job would you like to have in an advertising agency? Give reasons for your choice. Describe the tasks you would expect to perform in your chosen advertising job.

# 6 Sales promotions, merchandising and public relations

*All promotions should be legal, decent, honest and truthful*

The previous two chapters concentrated on the most prominent form of communications used by modern marketing organisations, advertising. The value of advertising cannot be denied but a company cannot rely on it exclusively as it will not necessarily provide effective coverage or contact with the market.

The objective of this chapter is to examine two other forms of communication used to support or extend advertising campaigns. These are:

1 Sales promotions
2 Public relations.

They include a wide variety of techniques which can only be applied with reference to specific communication objectives. You are advised to consider sales promotions and public relations as distinct means of communicating to target markets and once you have a clear understanding of the key concepts you should then attempt to combine them with advertising. The key term to remember is the **'marketing communications mix'**, or **'promotional mix'**, which refers to the total collective communications undertaken by a company. Chapters 4, 6 and 7 deal with the individual elements of the promotional mix while Chapter 8 concentrates on how the elements should be combined into one meaningful, affordable and effective plan of action.

## ■ INTRODUCTION TO SALES PROMOTIONS

Definitions of marketing terms often fail to highlight all aspects of the topic under discussion but fortunately the definition of sales promotions is extremely informative and precise, as follows:

> *short term incentives offered to consumers, members of the trade or the company's sales staff in an effort to boost sales.*

This definition includes a number of key words which depict the nature of the topic. For example:

**Short term** As you saw earlier, advertisements can be used over an extended period of time in order to inform, remind, excite or attract potential customers to products, services or even companies. Sales promotions, on the other hand, must be used over short periods of time because they carry an element of marketing risk called **'product demeaning'**. If you, as the consumer, continually find a product carrying a special offer, it may be attractive initially but after a period of time you may feel that the product must be inferior, or is not popular among consumers, is overpriced or retailers are trying to selling it quickly, hence the special offer. Suspicions or worries of this nature may lead to loss of demand and it is essential, therefore, to use sales promotions selectively over short periods of time, and for a particular purpose, e.g.

a) To help with the introduction/launch of a new product.

b) To support flagging sales at certain times of the year.

c) At the decline period in a product life cycle to re-kindle sales or to clear stock of an old version ready for the introduction of a new one.

d) To support and highlight a short-term occurrence such as the company's presence at a trade fair or exhibition.

**Incentives** This almost tells you what promotions are all about: a series of attractions introduced to a product or service in order to increase its overall popularity. Not all consumers will respond to a particular incentive, so a number of sales promotions techniques are used. The actual techniques will be discussed later.

**Consumers, trade and sales staff.** This is possibly the most critical aspect of the definition. Consider the situation where a company wishes to attract consumers to their products. A number of incentives may be offered but the campaign is unlikely to succeed unless members of the trade are willing to stock the products at the right quantity levels. A number of incentives may have to be offered to the trade as well in order to guarantee effective distribution and subsequent consumer sales. Company sales staff will have to be motivated to approach as many distributors or product users as possible, so incentives will have to be offered to them.

A well-planned sales promotions campaign will have to relate to all three parties identified so that attractive levels of sales, distribution and consumption are achieved.

We can now examine the techniques used in relation to all the above and explain the considerations which lead to the correct application of the techniques.

## ■ COMMUNICATION TASKS PERFORMED BY SALES PROMOTIONS

All of us are exposed to sales promotions which attempt to encourage us to respond favourably to a product or service. How many times have you seen coupons offering a financial saving on a product or the chance to participate in competitions with attractive prizes? Every shop we visit exposes us to a variety of sales promotions, e.g. free product samples, free gifts, price discounted products or even refunds.

Like every other marketing activity, specific objectives must be introduced which link sales promotions with the remaining elements of the marketing mix, e.g. pricing, products and place so that the aims of the particular sales promotion fit in with the overall marketing strategy. Without these objectives there is no guarantee that any promotion will be effective.

Recent research suggests that a large part of the money spent on sales promotions is wasted and that consumers are increasingly sceptical, suspicious and even bored by many offers in stores. The main reason for this is that retailers tend to concentrate their promotional activity on price cuts which are easily imitated by competitors and have no element of novelty. It also leads to confusion and suspicion among shoppers who often find it difficult to remember the price of products and cannot judge the value of a discount offer. It is clear from research evidence on consumer attitudes to promotions that retailers must avoid an over-emphasis on 'me-too' price promotions where companies simply imitate competitors' sales promotions. An individual image must be developed if they hope to maintain loyalty among customers. Techniques like free gifts, competitions and genuine offers show dramatic increases in popularity.

It is odd that manufacturers who agonise over the selection or change of advertising agencies and demand detailed justification and pre-testing of their new advertising campaigns, will accept plans for spending larger sums of money on promotions without consulting expert advice from outside. It is now conventional wisdom that research can help in the advertising planning process and there is a strong case for planning promotional campaigns in the same way.

A number of objectives can be pursued through sales promotions and each objective will relate to a specific set of techniques. Table 6.1 provides a summary of typical promotional objectives and possible sales promotions needed to achieve them. Close examination of the recommended sales promotions activities is likely to present a number of problems because many techniques cannot be linked directly to the recommended objective. Use the above tables for general reference but concentrate on the practical applications of sales promotions discussed below. Remember that a well-planned sales promotion campaign should fit into the total marketing strategy and may be directed at consumers, the channels of distribution and possibly at a company's own sales force.

# ■ POPULAR SALES PROMOTIONS TECHNIQUES

## Competitions

The major objectives of competitions are to increase consumer awareness, increase the level of display at the point of sale and create enthusiasm among consumers. Over the years the number of competitions used has increased dramatically and it is becoming difficult to attract consumers' attention to one particular competition.

**Table 6.1** Sales promotions: a checklist

| Communication/ promotional objectives | Possible sales promotions activities |
| --- | --- |
| 1 To increase consumer awareness | In-store raffle/display; sweepstakes; free draws; competitions. |
| 2 To increase penetration of new or existing products | Free offers (within or on pack); money-off coupons or offers; sampling; refund offers; banded packs; reduced price offers. |
| 3 To improve repeat purchase | Competitions; free offers; on pack money-off coupons; reduced price offers; refund/buy back offers; self-liquidating premiums; re-usable container premiums. |
| 4 To increase consumer loyalty | Premium offers; money-off offers; personality promotions; coupons; buy one, get one free offers; twin packs; refund offers; re-usable containers. |
| 5 To increase purchase frequency or amount bought | Competitions; share-outs/giveaways; free offers; personality promotions; in-store promotions; banded packs; reduced price offers. |
| 6 To move high stocks out of stores | In-store raffles/competitions; free offers; in-store merchandising. |
| 7 To attract consumers to premises | Free gifts/trials; money-off coupons. |
| 8 Trading up to larger sizes | Consumer coupons; refund offers. |
| 9 To increase distribution | Trade competitions; salesperson's incentives; sample distribution; introductory discounts. |
| 10 To encourage display | On-pack premiums; banded packs; premium offers; heavy price cuts. |
| 11 To motivate sales staff | Bonuses; discounts on company products; attractive travelling allowances; effective sales leads; efficient training. |

The two golden rules when designing sales promotions are:

1 **Originality.** Consumers like to come across something different, unique and exciting. Too many competitions have concentrated on prizes like cars, houses, cash or household items. They may represent attractive prizes on paper but they are repetitive, boring and lacking novelty. It can work to the company's advantage if original prizes are introduced as part of promotions; consumers may treat them as a 'breath of fresh air' in an otherwise predictable market place.
2 **Amusing/interesting.** These factors can be treated as an extension to originality and add to the fun or interest in participating. Amusing offers can be linked to the purchase in question so consumers may be offered novelty products when they buy something less exciting like instant coffee, soft drinks or disposable nappies.

The validity of these rules can be highlighted by examining the way petrol companies relied on competitions over the years in order to attract motorists to their own petrol stations. In the 1960s most petrol companies promoted their products on the strength of their quality. Shell, for instance, claimed that their petrol offered good mileage. Esso gave you power, Mobil gave you economy. The result was that although motorists usually went to the garage that was most convenient there was brand loyalty. Then, in 1966 Shell introduced a major promotion called 'Make Money'. Motorists were given half a dummy banknote with each purchase of petrol. If they collected matching halves they won the sum of money printed on the note, which ranged from £1 to £100.

This was the first major petrol promotion run in Britain, and the response was outstanding. It became a major talking point, and people with half a mock £100 note even placed advertisements in *The Times* offering to buy the other half. Shell sales more than doubled during the promotion.

Competitors could not let this pass and they retaliated with coin promotions and a variety of other schemes. The high costs of these promotions forced the companies to reduce their advertising expenditure with the result that the leading petrol companies were concentrating on below-the-line promotional activities.

After a year or two the novelty wore off and brand shares settled down to close where they were to begin with. But there was a big difference. Research showed that the distinctive brand images had nearly disappeared. Motorists went from garage to garage looking for the latest promotion, having discovered that their cars performed the same on different brands of petrol.

Since then motorists have increasingly bought petrol on price alone. So the tactical advantages of highly successful sales promotions, at the cost of neglecting product advertising, destroyed the brand images which had been built up in the past.

In order to avoid major marketing problems, competitions should be clearly communicated to the public, for instance:

- The prizes to be offered must be identified.
- The requirements for entry into the competition must be clearly explained.
- Any limitations on the number of entries per person or per household should be explained.
- State the closing date of the competition.
- Explain the rules of the competition.
- Explain how participants can discover details of the winners.
- State the method of prize collection.
- If applicable, the solution of the competition and the judging criteria used in selecting the winner may be included.

It is pointless to rely on competitions as the ideal solution to sales growth but companies can learn by experience, reduce the number of failures and improve the effectiveness of future promotions they decide to introduce.

## Coupons

A brand carries a coupon redeemable against the consumer's next purchase of the same brand, for example, Maxwell House coffee 3p coupon on next purchase. The consumer tears the coupon off and its face value is deducted from a subsequent purchase of the same brand. Coupons are normally used as an alternative to the reduced price pack. They may also be used for recently launched products; consumers are offered coupons to be used for first time purchases.

The total number of manufacturers' coupons distributed each year is increasing and so is their value. In one year alone shoppers will be offered £600 million worth of coupons and will redeem £30 million of them.

Whereas theme advertisements create brand preference a coupon creates **brand insistence** and, as those involved in the product distribution – the sales force and the retailers – know, it creates **product insistence.** Most retailers redeem coupons fairly and honestly but in order to control any malredemption 'The Marketing Triangle Company' created a device known as the validation coupon (proof of purchase attached to the coupon).

The ability to change various aspects of a coupon within a campaign provides a unique facility to measure elements of existing advertising communication and motivation which are normally the subject of opinion and speculation. Many aspects of coupon design, layout, distribution or cost/value can have an effect on redemption.

## Personality promotions

The objective here is to link a well-known personality to a specific brand. For example, a personality may tour an area, calling upon a randomly selected sample of households. Those who can answer a simple question and have the appropriate brand on hand win a prize.

This method of promotion is appropriate for brands with high market shares because of high fixed costs in administration and possibly TV advertising support. It does, however, generate trade excitement and high display levels, which can significantly increase consumer sales. It does not require special packaging.

Other personality promotions may involve opening a new store in a region or endorsing a product by testing it in front of an audience.

## Cross couponing

Brand A carries a coupon, either on the label or inside the pack, redeemable against Brand B. The two brands may be from the same or different companies, for example: a 3p coupon for Robertson's jam on every packet of McDougalls' flour.

The advantages of this method are:
a) It is an inexpensive method of coupon distribution to potential customers.
b) It provides a selling point for the carrying brand at no cost.

c) It can increase consumer sales of the carrying brand if a high value coupon is included.

d) It can enable the couponed brand to reach a specific target group (e.g. slimmers, if the carrying brand is also aimed at slimmers).

## Refund offers

Refund offers request consumers to send the company a specified number of proofs of purchase in return for a fixed amount of money (the refund). It represents a reward for loyal purchase and use of the company's products. It therefore sustains loyalty among existing customers. It can also be introduced fairly quickly and relies on cash, which enjoys universal appeal.

## Sampling

Sampling describes the promotional methods of getting potential consumers to try a product or service without having to pay for it. In the case of a new brand of instant coffee, consumers may be offered a free jar for trial purposes or a freshly made cup of coffee at the point of sale to enable them to evaluate the product before they buy it.

In the case of industrial products, complex consumer products or services, the company may make them available to potential customers for a limited period of time to allow for trial and evaluation under real life conditions (car test drives, free use of a photocopier for two weeks, free hairdressing on a specific day or free consultancy service to new customers).

## Free offers

These are promotions where the purchaser receives a free gift as a result of buying a company's product. Free offers can be used in consumer markets but they can also form an essential element of promotional activities aimed at members of the trade. There will be differences, however, in the methods in which the gifts are presented and distributed:

a) **With-pack premiums** are taken by or given to the consumer when he or she makes a purchase but the item is not connected to the product in any way, e.g. for consumer promotions: glasses with petrol, plastic flowers with detergent, feed with day-old chicks; and for trade promotions: gifts for retailers in cash and carry wholesalers, to buyers in a garment showroom.

b) **In-pack premiums** are inside the packaging and frequently cannot be seen by the purchaser at the time of purchase, e.g. consumer promotions: toys in cereal packs, dishes in a refrigerator; and trade promotions: a ready reckoner inside a package. The purchaser is informed on the pack of the free object inside.

c) **On-pack premiums** may be attached either to the product or its packaging, though they may also be used to contain the product. Container premiums are more likely to be in-store-self liquidators. The on-pack gift may be an item, or the right to a sample of another product, or it may be a voucher or coupon giving the consumer a price incentive either off the next purchase of the same product or off the purchase of another product.

## Banded packs

This is a term which has assumed a number of different meanings over the years and represents one of the best known promotional activities. As implied, products are banded together, offering consumers an extra quantity or an extra product. Banded packs can take the following forms:

a) **Two for the price of one.** Consumers are offered two products for the price of one. It is ideal for trial purposes and encourages consumer loyalty.

b) **X per cent extra quantity for the price of one.** Consumers are offered an extra quantity free of charge, e.g. a 2 litre bottle of coke for the price of a 1½ litre bottle.

c) **A product and a gift.** Many companies offer an additional product to consumers as an incentive to try, or buy regularly, the main product. A new brand of toothpaste, for instance, may carry a free toothbrush as a gift. The two products are usually complementary and consumers may look at the gift as an attractive incentive to buy the toothpaste. Success will depend on the relevance, perceived value and popularity of the 'gift' offered: a low quality gift can destroy the image of the main product.

## Display at the point of sale

Point of sale, or POS, is one of those phrases which seems to have a different meaning and scope to everyone using it. If we take the most literal meaning we have the widest scope: POS is the place where the product can be purchased. Usually – but not exclusively – it is found in a retail outlet, but the retail outlet can have a multitude of sites for display such as: in the window, on the door, in a display cabinet, on the wall, on a counter, on a shelf or on the ceiling.

Because POS is concerned with 'sale' as much as display it is necessary to be as concerned with the product as with the display itself. Naturally this can overlap into the physical merchandising of the product itself, e.g.:

- Material to be sited near the product
- Display material, e.g. a card, with the product inserted in it
- Display and merchandiser unit carrying packs of the product
- Display to be sited with the product.

The creative decisions for POS are different from other forms of consumer communication. For example, the amount of time you can reasonably expect to have a consumer's attention is relatively short. Impact and clarity of proposition are all important. Indeed, where the POS is used in a promotion then it is the incentive/promotional message that should be stressed, not the standard product proposition.

The promotional material used for in-store displays includes: display units, signs, posters, leaflets, brochures, neon lights and more recently Q-TV (Queue-TV), a TV set on which adverts relating to the products or services being offered are screened. Q-TV is ideal where queues develop or some waiting is involved, as it attracts customer attention and helps in controlling the levels of frustration which result from having to wait. Major banks, post offices, department stores and certain supermarkets have introduced Q-TV in their premises.

While we have concentrated on POS aimed at consumers it must be remembered that POS may be applied in the retail markets. For example, suppliers often send to the offices of buyers calendars, pens, directories, diaries and other such gifts carrying the product or supplier's name, reminding the buyer and his/her visitors of the product.

## Re-usable containers

Many products may be packaged in a container which the consumers can use after they have consumed the contents of the package, e.g. drinking glasses, storage jars, toys, etc. The emphasis is on encouraging consumers to collect a number of re-usable containers because it is unlikely that individuals will be satisfied with one glass or one toy. The need to collect will encourage repeat purchasing and the collected containers will serve as constant reminders of the product and its benefits.

## Sales force incentives

This area of promotions is often neglected by marketing organisations which tend to concentrate exclusively on consumers or members of the trade. It must always be borne in mind that products, promotions and benefits must be delivered to the consumers (if direct marketing is possible) or to the trade customers, in particular, and this task is often accomplished by sales staff. Chapter 7 examines personal selling and the activities of sales personnel are also looked at later, but we must touch now on the techniques used by companies to motivate their sales forces during intensive promotional campaigns. Monetary rewards, such as special bonuses, extra commissions and competitive selling expenses, must be supported by non-monetary incentives like proper guidance, effective management/administration support, recognition of sales staff efforts as well as accurate identification of the most likely targets to be approached. Companies should avoid concentrating solely on monetary incentives because they cannot be relied upon as the sole motivator.

# ■ SALES PROMOTIONS CODE OF PRACTICE

The following basic principles apply to all sales promotions, and should be taken as the basis for determining good practice where no precedent exists.

1 **Legality** All sales promotions should be legal. The Code is designed to complement legal controls, not to usurp or replace them.
2 **Spirit of the Code** The Code is to be applied in the spirit as well as in the letter with the aim of eliminating practices which might lead sales promotion into disrepute.
3 **Fair competition** All sales promotions should adhere to the principles of fair competition as generally accepted in business.
4 **Consumer interest** All sales promotions should deal fairly and honourably with consumers and should be seen to do so. No promoter, or other person engaged in the conduct of a sales promotion, should abuse the trust of consumers or exploit their lack of experience or knowledge.
5 **Consumer satisfaction** Sales promotions should be designed and conducted so they do not cause avoidable disappointment.
6 **Fairness** The terms and conduct of promotions should be equitable to all affected by them.
7 **The public interest** Neither the design nor the conduct of a promotion should conflict with the public interest. In particular, promotions should not contain anything likely to provoke, or appear to condone, violent or anti-social behaviour, damage to property or the causing of nuisance or injury to any member of the public.
8 **Truthful presentation** The presentation of a promotion should be clear and honest and should not be likely to mislead those who are addressed, or those to whose attention such material is likely to come.
9 **Substantiation** When called upon by the Advertising Standards Authority or the CAP Committee, promoters should be ready to present such evidence or argument as may be necessary to establish the compliance of their promotion with this Code and of any advertising material with the British Code of Advertising Practice (CAP) (see pages 86–7).
10 **Limitations** Any factor which is likely to affect a decision whether or not to participate in a promotion should be communicated clearly so that the consumer can take it into account before being committed to any purchase which may be necessary for participation.
11 **Suitability of promotion to those reached by it** Promoters should take reasonable steps to ensure that neither advertising nor promotional material reaches those for whom the promotion concerned may be inappropriate.
12 **Administration** The administration of promotions should be prompt and efficient, so that consumers are given no grounds for justified complaint.
13 **Responsibility** The prime responsibility for all aspects of a promotion always rests with the promoter. Agents and intermediaries share responsibility to the extent of their involvement in the promotion in question.

There are companies which will seek to avoid the constraints of such codes in order to make sales, e.g. by unduly influencing children to purchase. While they may gain sales, however, they may also lose them through offending the audience. They may also lose the respect and morale of their own staff. The point is that good marketing should be clean marketing and if you compromise your better principles in order to make sales your own integrity and skill as a marketer is in doubt.

# ■ MERCHANDISING

Consider the information you accumulate every time you visit a supermarket, a department store, a chemist or even your local butcher, greengrocer or baker. You are exposed to a variety of signs, leaflets, posters, etc., designed to inform, encourage you to try or convince you to buy on a regular basis, which are designed by the store rather than manufacturers, e.g. signs saying 'special price today to clear stock' or posters telling you of the special services of the retailer. All these relate to a specialist area of promotions known as merchandising, which can be defined as:

> *an effort to achieve maximum persuasion at the point-of-sale without the help of personal selling.*

Point of sale (POS) refers to the point at which a product is sold. In the case of merchandising this concept is broadened to include the place in which the product is sold. Every retail outlet for example, must develop its own identity, reputation, attractions, etc.

A simple example highlights the dimensions of merchandising: consider the shop you favour for the purchase of specific products. Why do you go there? Possible answers to this question might be the variety of products sold, the friendly service, competitive prices, convenient location and opening times, a good reputation, etc. The job of the retailer is to emphasise to the target market the value of the services supplied so that potential customers will be attracted and retained. Merchandising, therefore, concentrates on attracting consumers to specific shops, in order to satisfy specific needs, through specific products or services. The major objective of any merchandising effort by stores is fast stock turnover, i.e. rapid sales, which will depend on:

- Predominantly stocking and displaying products which are in high demand
- Allocating shelf space relating directly to the amount of sales achieved for particular products
- Maximising the information given to potential customers of a retail outlet on products sold, the image of the store, special purchase opportunities, customer service availability, etc.

Merchandising would also take into account slow turnover stocks that return high profits or products that encourage customers into the store where they may purchase other products.

Merchandising activities can be divided into four areas of effort:

1 Efficient staff
2 Stock control
3 Store layout
4 Store promotions.

These are considered in detail below.

## 1 Efficient service provided by staff

A shopping expedition represents a minor social event which most of us face regularly. When consumers visit a retail outlet they tend to expect the following services:

a) Friendly, polite and professional advice on products offered within the shop
b) Familiarity of staff with company's promotions, features of different products, likely application of products and benefits consumers can derive from their purchases
c) Ability to inform of products' whereabouts within the store as well as efficient stock control of different product lines
d) Willingness to listen to complaints which may arise and ability to recommend solutions to the problems being faced
e) Generation of a feeling of professionalism and trust which can improve the overall relationship between customer and retailer, wholesaler or other type of distributor.

## 2 Effective stock handling and control

The heart of a shop's operations is the stock of products it has to offer to the customers. Offering the wrong products or inadequate supplies of the right products is detrimental to the overall operation. How often have you become frustrated with shops which never seem to stock the products you want?

This element of merchandising has grown in importance as a result of the growth of supermarket/self-service selling and an increased consumer awareness of alternative products available. Success in this area of merchandising will depend on:

a) Stocking and displaying effectively high-demand items/product lines
b) Allocating adequate shelf space in direct relation to the rate of product sales
c) Effective shelf filling during the course of a day's trading as empty shelves look unattractive, lose sales and may discourage customers from returning in the future
d) Careful re-ordering so that excess supply or stockouts of popular products are avoided
e) Careful positioning of products within the store. Impulse buys, e.g. chocolates and sweets, should be near checkout points where customers may be tempted to buy them while they are queuing. Products needing adequate

protection – frozen foods, meat, fish, etc. – must be placed in clearly identified areas, in freezers or open fridges with easy access and product protection.

Major retailers or wholesalers employ specialist staff for efficient handling of the stock of products they supply and new technology used increasingly in this area includes computerised stock control systems, new packaging materials, advanced refrigeration facilities, etc. The manufacturers of products often undertake this element of merchandising themselves or jointly with the store(s). Manufacturers may also employ sales staff who specialise in merchandising in order to advise distributors on the display required for the product, the nature of protection which must be offered, the different sizes or versions of specific products, the delivery policies as well as the promotional activities the company will be introducing. They may also carry out promotional activity in a store, e.g. in-store product demonstrations. The closer manufacturers and distributors work with each other, the more effective the marketing of products at POS is likely to be.

## 3 Attractive store layout

The point of sale, whether it is a shop, a warehouse or a showroom, must permit maximum customer flow, provide a relaxing, informative and professional selling environment and facilitate the identification, handling, trial (whenever necessary) and carriage of products. Consider a supermarket. The critical aspects of its layout are likely to be:

a)   Spacious aisles between shelves to allow for an easy flow of customers
b)   Adequate space to allow for efficient presentation of numerous products of interest to the customers
c)   Availability of shopping baskets, trolleys, scales, etc., in good working order
d)   Provision of numerous checkout points in order to minimise delays caused by queues
e)   Provision of clean and well-lit display units which can allow customers to evaluate the products in a relaxed manner
f)   Careful product segregation in order to avoid confusion or time consuming searches throughout the point of sale
g)   Clear signs informing customers of exits, lifts, checkout points, location of products, customer services, etc.
h)   Siting of essential products to the back of the store so that customers pass by other products on the way to their essential purchases
i)   Pleasing colours and music in keeping with the particular type of shop.

Consider other types of outlets like restaurants, cafeterias, clothes boutiques or shoe shops and suitable facilities can easily be identified: adequate sitting areas, clean lavatories, play areas for children, smoking and non-smoking areas and many other relevant layout aspects. The easier it is for the customer to consider, relax, and enjoy the experience of purchasing products the higher the chances of further sales in the future.

# 4 Effective store and product promotions

Store and product promotions are designed to project an attractive image to the residents of nearby communities or members of a company's target market.

There are numerous promotional activities undertaken for this purpose and they can be divided into three areas:

## a) IN-STORE PROMOTIONS

- Special offers relating to specific product lines
- Personalities invited to attend at specific times to attract customers to the premises
- Consumer competitions offering attractive prizes
- Provision of exciting gifts to purchasers of specific products or to customers visiting the premises at specific times (free balloons, pens, T-shirts, etc. carrying the company's name) as well as provision of free product samples introducing customers to new products
- Plastic bags, boxes or presentation cases to facilitate product carriage and to maintain the company's name in front of the public eye as long and as often as possible
- Use of Q-TV where customers congregate, to remind customers of the services offered by the retailer, announce special promotions or inform them of future developments
- Provision of adequate promotional literature in the form of leaflets, brochures, signs and coupons.

## b) IN-STORE ADVERTISING

- Posters on the wall with the name of the store and its central advertising message to customers
- Staff uniforms and customer receipts carrying the name of the store
- Posters designed to promote specific products or services available within the store
- Special counters where customers can be informed of products or services offered.

## c) OUT-OF-STORE ADVERTISING CAMPAIGNS

These are likely to concentrate on the unique selling points offered by a store and may include:

- Products offered; 'A wide variety to satisfy your needs'
- Competitive prices; 'Better value for your money'
- Attractive location
- Attractive peripheral service, e.g. free parking, late opening, Sunday trading, etc.
- Introduction of special events, e.g. personality visits, 'open days', half-price days', etc.

- Expertise of the company and the quality of the service offered by the staff
- Other themes of relevance to the operations of a specific store.

Stores cannot survive without customers, customers will suffer if stores do not operate effectively and manufacturers will find it very difficult to reach consumers without the help of retailers and wholesalers. Merchandising attempts to relate to all three interested parties and is gaining in sophistication and importance within the marketing mix. Effective combining of all or many of the elements identified provides a good platform for success.

Although we have concentrated on retail outlets to explain merchandising, it should be pointed out that it is rapidly gaining in popularity in other areas of business. Films today often have considerable merchandising undertaken to promote them: posters of the star, for sale in a setting associated with the film, T-shirts with the name of the film on, postcards, badges, etc. Finally, it is worth remembering that merchandising is also making its mark in industrial and user markets as explained earlier in this chapter.

## ■ PUBLIC RELATIONS (PR)

*Effective public relations requires believability and to be continuously believed we must constantly exhibit a high level of integrity.*

This area of communication represents one of the oldest methods of seeking to obtain a favourable response from a selected group of people. It should not be related to business organisations alone; all of us indulge in some form of PR on a social or professional basis. How many times, during a crisis or a problem period, have you resorted to a box of chocolates, a bunch of flowers, taking somebody out for lunch or dinner or giving a gift in order to obtain a favourable response? Thus, words, actions or gifts are used when you want people to think of you in a certain way, do something for you or sustain your relationship through an apology when you have offended.

A definition of public relations in the business context will give you an idea of the width and breadth of its applications:

*the planned actions designed to gain and keep the goodwill of every section of the public with which the company comes into contact.*

The term 'public' has enormous significance because it can include:

a) The company's customers
b) Shareholders, potential shareholders, financiers or bankers
c) Employees or potential employees
d) Suppliers and distributors
e) Other companies in the same industry or in industries which relate to a company's operations
f) Members of the community within which the company operates
g) Members of the general public.

The scope of public relations in the business world is far greater than when used by an individual but the ultimate objective remains the same: improve the relationships of an organisation or individual with relevant members of the public. The following diagram illustrates the relationship between the PR function within a company and the company's public.

Figure 6.1

The objective of this part of the chapter is to explain the role of public relations within marketing, to discuss the main techniques used by individuals or companies and to highlight the relationship of PR with the other elements of the communication/promotions mix.

Like all other elements of marketing PR has had its time as a luxury or a novelty marketing tool and must now be taken seriously, recognised as a distinct area of expertise, and treated with the same caution with which we treat advertising, pricing or selling. It must also be considered as a vital management function within the organisation.

The Institute of Public Relations presents PR as being:

*The deliberate, planned and sustained effort to establish and maintain mutual understanding between an organisation and its public.*

The words 'planned and sustained effort' should encourage all people involved in PR to proceed with caution, plan carefully, select the most appropriate techniques and use PR as a means of achieving well-defined objectives.

## Communication tasks performed by public relations

The immediate responsibility of advertising and sales promotions, as highlighted in earlier chapters, is to develop an 'environment' which leads to sales. Public relations on the other hand involves the presentation of all aspects of a company's operations to establish long-term relationships within the market/s. The emphasis is on presenting or creating a favourable image in order to enhance relationships with consumers. This may ultimately result in higher sales, but in the short term a reputation may need to be developed.

In general terms, the major tasks of public relations within companies could be summarised as follows:

a) To attract good quality personnel to the company
b) To encourage shareholders to invest
c) To build a favourable image over a period of time
d) To inform of changes relating to the product, company structure, ownership, acquisitions, mergers, etc.
e) To improve or maintain working relationships with suppliers or distributors of the company's products
f) To motivate employees or reinforce their beliefs or confidence in the company
g) To handle customer complaints
h) To maintain good working relationships with members of the media
i) To protect the company's or product's reputation in periods of adverse trading conditions or unfair criticisms
j) To develop relationships with influential bodies, e.g. the Government, companies overseas, opinion leaders, consumer pressure groups, institutes and associations
k) To generate favourable publicity surrounding the company and its products
l) To act on behalf of the company in trying to ensure that people are treated fairly who are adversely affected, directly or indirectly, by a company action.

Publicity must not be confused with public relations: publicity usually represents a reward for effective PR. Publicity can be defined as **'third party communications relating to newsworthy events'** and it implies that the company's own promotions are supported or contradicted by somebody else's – such as a journalist's – statements, opinions, beliefs or presentations. A company promoting, for instance, a new brand of powdered milk for infants may gear its communications towards the development of a good reputation for the product. It is also possible to meet adverse criticisms from medical associations, consumer watchdogs, doctors or the mass media if the product is considered to be unsafe or of poor quality. The criticisms represent 'third party' communications which will affect consumers' opinions on the product, the company and its promotions.

The tasks performed by PR cover all aspects of a company's operations and it is pointless to examine PR as one general marketing entity. Each task must be accomplished through the application of specific techniques which, for ease of memory and identification, may be grouped into the following types of PR:

a) Customer relations
b) Sponsorship
c) Media relations
d) Community relations
e) Internal public relations

As you examine in detail the techniques used you are encouraged to consider PR efforts you may be familiar with in relation to the theories and examples presented.

# ■ PUBLIC RELATIONS TECHNIQUES

## Customer relations

How often have you been unhappy with a product, a service, the behaviour of a sales assistant, the prices, or with delays or queues faced in shops? The resulting dissatisfaction affects people in different ways; research reveals that people tend to react in the following ways:

- They reduce their volume of business with the offending company.
- They complain to a sales assistant or a manager.
- They stop all purchases of the product.
- They complain to their friends, relatives, neighbours, etc.
- They complain formally in writing.

The common factor of all the above is dissatisfaction which can only be detrimental to a company's operations in the short, medium and long term. Complaints are obviously a problem but if they are treated positively they may help in revealing the following:

1 Areas of product, service or company weakness
2 Areas of likely improvement which can eliminate complaints
3 Performance and professionalism of the company's employees dealing directly with customers
4 Acceptance or response of consumers to the company's marketing mix
5 Degree of marketing orientation of the company
6 Ability to retain customers or seek to obtain new ones
7 Overall company or product reputation in the eyes of the consumers.

When you know what you are doing wrong – as well as right – how customers perceive your products and services and their attitude towards the aspects of the company with which they come in contact, you can then formulate procedures for staff that will improve customer relationships. Marketing managers must view complaints as a form of 'free research' or a means of 'self assessment'. Complaints – though not encouraged – can represent an opportunity to improve and a number of public relations techniques can be employed to ensure improvement, such as:

1 Letters of apology
2 Offers to refund money in full to dissatisfied customers
3 Replacing faulty or damaged products with quality products
4 Promising to eliminate problems by improving service standards, reviewing prices, re-briefing personnel, improving product performance, improving the speed of delivery or any other problem area identified
5 Introducing a complaints department specialising in customer requests or complaints
6 Apologising to the public for inconvenience caused or problems created
7 Warning people of any dangers associated with the product or service and encouraging them to seek advice

8 Compensating any affected parties
9 Offering free goods with the compliments of the company as a gesture of goodwill
10 Organising 'open days' which allow current or potential customers to visit the company's premises
11 Arranging personal contact with affected parties in order to discuss problems or complaints in detail.

PR may be used for a positive improvement in sales through such actions as staging special events that improve the image of the product. For example, using a well-known racing driver to illustrate the stability of a new car to motoring correspondents or cleaning a historical monument with the company's cleaning equipment to illustrate how safe and effective it is.

The nature of a complaint will dictate the selection of the 'right' method of response and it is necessary therefore, for PR staff to strive to be people oriented rather than sales or product oriented.

## Sponsorship

Financial sponsoring of activities is an attractive medium used by a company to maintain its name in the public eye. It represents a vehicle for a variety of marketing activities including direct consumer contact, sampling, dealer motivations, consumer promotions, etc., and provides an ideal opportunity for product displays and business negotiations. Sponsoring can be related to national or international:

a) Personalities
b) Events
c) Organisations
d) Competitions.

Sponsoring has proved particularly popular among international marketers because it can benefit the company or its products by:

- Breaking through national boundaries
- Obtaining media exposure overseas
- Serving as an efficient reminder of the company or product names
- Entering media where products are banned
- Associating the name with successful events, personalities, etc.
- Presenting the company as 'caring', 'successful', 'international', 'ethical', etc.

For many multinational brands, sponsorship in Grand Prix racing has proved extremely valuable because it provides a total 'marketing package' of personalities, competitions, events and participating organisations. There is a global following for the sport and it can accommodate most of the benefits already identified.

In the 1980s, 75 per cent of sports being screened were sponsored and television companies throughout the world found it far cheaper to televise sport than to create their own productions (a two hour documentary may cost a TV company £250 000, while televising a sponsored event is unlikely to cost more than £25 000). Sponsors finance the event (it is allowable against tax) and media owners pay for exclusive coverage of the event.

Success in sponsorship is not automatic and any involvement should be supported by:

- Adequate public relations back-up
- Continuous assessment of the progress, popularity and success of the personality, event, or organisation being sponsored
- Negotiations to obtain satisfactory media coverage
- Own advertising campaigns enhancing the basic theme of sponsorship agreements
- National or international exposure of the parties involved
- Avoidance of over-exposure which could lead to boredom
- The remainder of the marketing mix.

Public relations activities do not guarantee results, so any commitment to sponsorship must be a specific marketing goal. For example, sponsoring a special opera in order to influence a particular set of people within society.

Personal preferences, biased assessments, aimless promotions and infrequent evaluations are the basic ingredients for disaster. Objective thinking should be employed and the marketing philosophy should filter through all aspects of sponsorship.

## Media relations

Public relations must not be considered in isolation from the remainder of the promotion mix; an effective PR campaign provides a company and its products with much needed publicity. This is a period of uncertainty in terms of manufacturing processes, environmental decay and growing consumer power. The public requires information, reassurance and positive recommendation which, if provided, can generate demand. Media relations activities concentrate on providing media representatives with relevant, newsworthy, honest and accurate information to be passed on to the general public.

How would you react to a report on a new pharmaceutical product or a new cosmetics product which is favourably presented in the media? If you consider the media to be creditworthy, the likely reaction will be that of acceptance of the information and of the product. If you are a potential user you may buy it, if you are a current user you will continue buying it and if you are not personally interested you may recommend it to somebody who needs such a product. Media relations can take many different forms but the most widely used techniques include:

- Conferences involving representatives of the media, relevant to the audiences you are ultimately seeking to reach – this may include trade as well as consumer media representatives, TV and/or radio journalists

- Social events involving representatives of the media
- Personal visits to influencers in the media
- Press releases – one or two hundred words sent to the media regarding information the company considers newsworthy
- Special invitations to media representatives to examine, try or discuss the product or service under consideration
- Presentation of testimonials from satisfied customers or case histories which prove the true qualities of the product or service
- Release of specialist information – such as an independent scientific report – which can be used by expert parties for their assessment of what is being offered.

You must not forget that many media offering publicity may also be used for advertising by the company. Continuity and consistency between advertising and PR is, therefore, essential and the following issues must be closely considered by marketing management.

1  Make sure your advertising agency (if your company uses one) and PR consultants meet regularly on a professional basis and, if possible, socially.

2  Discuss your advertising strategy with your PR consultancy (if external consultants are used).

3  Ask your PR consultant to include 'implications for advertising' in his proposals to you, and conversely make your agency include any 'PR implications' in their proposals.

4  Make sure your PR consultancy keeps an eye open for public relations events which may have implications for your advertising, e.g. new Government legislation, environmental meetings, exhibitions and seminars.

5  Examine regularly the client/agency/PR company working structure to see if it is geared to sudden more intensive effort.

6  Encourage your different advisers to attend conferences on the others' subjects.

7  Try to bridge the media gap – by co-ordinating effort on special features, supplements, editorial/advertising.

8  Encourage the sharing of support services (statistical information, telex monitors, Parliamentary questions, press cuttings, etc.).

9  Make sure the client, the company's agency and the PR consultancy all agree on common objectives (define any separate objectives carefully).

10  Make sure new legislative information is passed on by your PR consultancy.

11  Prepare and test hypothetical emergency briefs with your advisory groups and keep them up to date so that the company can capitalise on unexpected opportunities or protect itself from adverse publicity.

12  Make sure you have the financial and manpower resources to deal with a crisis as well as on-going situations.

# Community relations

This area of public relations encourages marketing management to examine, maintain or improve the working relationships which ought to exist between the company and the immediate community within which it operates. Failure to consider marketing activities in this context may lead to the following paradox. Local consumer dining needs may be satisfied by a local restaurant which offers good food, excellent service, attractive environment, reasonable prices, etc. At the same time local needs may be adversely affected by other aspects of the restaurant's operations, i.e. pollution of the environment, loud music late at night, parking problems created by clients, etc. It is obvious that this imbalance will eventually affect the company's operations, the community may be divided, petitions or other means of complaint may be used and loss of revenue may be the inevitable penalty to pay for ignoring certain aspects of a community's life. Every company should try to be accepted by its immediate neighbours and should be seen as a valuable member of its community, contributing to its improvement, protecting its overall trading image and, at the same time, satisfying the needs of its customers.

A number of public relations activities are available to companies for community relations purposes with the more widely used techniques including:

1 Donations to local charitable causes which can benefit sections of the community

2 Development of good relationships with local media owners

3 Introduction of services or products needed by the local community

4 Introduction of special events or 'special days' where the local community can be exposed to the operations of the company (open days, social events, etc.)

5 Compensation to individuals who have been adversely affected by any aspect of the company's operations

6 Participation in local sponsorship (see page 108)

7 Provision of employment to members of the community (reducing local unemployment levels and contributing to the overall social and economic stability of the community)

8 Avoiding any actions which will adversely affect the reputation of the community

9 Making favourable contacts with the local council and chamber of commerce.

Selection of the nature and intensity of community relations to be used will also depend on the type of company operating in the community. A small bakery is unlikely to involve itself with extensive public relations activities while a major departmental store competing for business with other operators in the 'high street' will be strongly advised to seek a direct commitment to the community's activities and long-term interests.

## Internal public relations

The final category of public relations activities is devoted exclusively to a company's major asset: the human resource. How can a company expect to grow, or at least survive, in a highly competitive market when its own employees are neglected, suffer from low morale and believe that they are not fully appreciated by their employer? Heavy expenditure on external promotional activities with no thought of the employees who will service the increased demand raises doubts in employees' minds as to the care of the management and may even lead to hostility and demotivation. The extent and nature of internal PR will be guided by the size, dispersion, complexity and nature of a company's operations but the following activities lend themselves to most situations:

1 Introducing suggestion boxes/schemes
2 Introducing a house journal or any other form of democratic internal communication amongst employers and employees
3 Arranging social events involving employees and their families
4 Introducing incentive schemes designed to reward productivity, loyalty, good behaviour, etc.
5 Offering special discounts or free products or services to employees
6 Providing effective training and career advancement opportunities
7 Providing opportunities for employee participation in decision making
8 Taking adequate measures to protect the health and general well-being of employees – if this is not done by a personnel department
9 Helping to develop a fair, effective and enjoyable working environment which allows employees to contribute effectively to the development of the company.

Failure to recognise the importance of all forms of public relations limits the company's ability to respond to environmental changes and reduces the overall effectiveness of its promotional programmes.

PR is not to be associated simply with large companies and PR departments; it is pertinent to any size of organisation and most employees within an organisation. A sales manager may have to find a way to make amends to a large customer who has been poorly treated by the company's service or a hotel receptionist may use PR methods as part of his/her customer care when resolving any problems guests may have encountered at the hotel.

The objective of this part of the textbook was to introduce popular promotional activities and the topics of sales promotions, merchandising and public relations were presented for that purpose. Some techniques deal directly with the consumer, others with the trade, while some concentrate on 'third parties' to provide adequate promotional back-up.

All the issues discussed here must be linked to the spirit of the marketing philosophy and the long-term commitment to the satisfaction of consumer needs and the protection of consumer welfare. Marketing must develop. It does not need to change but rather it needs to come out of its shell and grow. If it is true that the purpose of marketing is to respond to consumer needs then the consumerist movement should be welcomed as a complete new volume of insights into what those needs are. Thus, what at first sight looks like a whole series of new problems, from a slightly different angle becomes a set of bright new opportunities. 'Pollution' care is restricting and costly at first sight but it is also a challenge and possibly an opportunity for profit, as the immediate desires that motivate customers to buy are satisfied. Above all, it is the duty of everyone – not just organisations – to attempt to make a better environment and social atmosphere in which to live.

## Summary

When answering questions on promotions you must be selective. If you are organising promotions in a company you will have a budget (set amount of funds) in which promotions for expansion must be planned. To obtain the best return on the money spent you will have to think carefully about all ways of promotion – not just advertising or personal selling.

Never sell yourself an idea because you are besotted by its creative aspects and always make an advertising agency you use justify the ideas it is putting forward in relation to concrete results.

## ■ STUDY AND EXAM TIPS

1 Distinguish clearly between public relations and publicity. The former is a controllable variable, while the latter is non-controllable.

2 There are numerous sales promotions techniques which are used in order to achieve specific communication objectives. Link the 'right' technique to the 'relevant' promotional objectives.

3 Avoid discussing public relations in a general manner. Be specific about the type of PR a company might need (consumer relations, sponsorship, etc.).

4 Always use examples to highlight the techniques you are discussing.

5 Do not forget the fact that PR and sales promotions are only two of the elements of the marketing communications mix. They may need to support or be supported by advertising and/or personal selling.

6 Your own experiences or observations should be used in order to highlight your exam answers.

■ **PAST EXAMINATION QUESTIONS**

*The Chartered Institute of Marketing*

**1** As a sales manager you have received a letter from a valued customer complaining about aspects of your company's service. Describe what you would do to resolve the situation.

**2** Describe and comment upon the use of the following forms of sales promotion:
   a) Banded offers
   b) Competitions
   c) Coupons

**3** Which marketing communication goals is sales promotion best able to help achieve?

**4** What is the normal purpose of public relations? Describe two marketing communications problems and say how public relations might help to solve them.

*The Association of Business Executives – Advanced Diploma in Marketing*

**5** What are the opportunities and problems in the use of sales promotion? Give an example of appropriate sales promotions for a bank wanting to attract new customers.

**6** What sales promotions might be used by a company launching a new instant tea? What are the dangers a sales promotion campaign should attempt to avoid?

■ **SELF ASSESSMENT QUESTIONS**

Answer the following questions and award yourself one mark for every complete question you answer correctly. If you score seven or less re-read the Chapters. Answers are given on page 238.

**1** One form of banded pack is 'a product plus gift'. Name two more.
   a) ....................................................................................................................
   b) ....................................................................................................................

**2** One sales promotion activity aimed at improving and/or repeating purchases is the use of 're-usable' containers. Name four more.

a) ................     b) ................     c) ................     d) ................

**3** One rule to obey when devising a consumer competition is that it must be 'amusing'.
Name another. ...............................................................................................

**4** Complete the sentence: 'Publicity may be defined as 'Third party communications relating to ...............................................................................................
...............................................................................................

**5** One form of PR is 'customer relations'. Name three more.
a) ...............................................................................................
b) ...............................................................................................
c) ...............................................................................................

**6** List three popular techniques of customer relations apart from 'personal consultation'.
a) ................     b) ................     c) ................

**7** Complete the sentence: 'Sponsorship agreements can involve personalities, organisations, competitions or...........................................................'

**8** Complete the following sentence: 'The marketing 'communication mix' involves sales promotions and merchandising, public relations, ................ and ................

**9** What is the alternative term used for the communication mix?
...............................................................................................

**10** What is POS? ...............................................................................................

**11** Complete the sentence: 'Sales promotions may be defined as, 'short term incentives offered to consumers ...............................................................................................

# 7 Sales management and personal selling

*The only things we have to sell is benefits. Benefits to those who purchase our company's products or services.*

## ■ INTRODUCTION

Selling, like advertising, is a marketing activity most of us come across each day. Every time you go to a shop you expect to get a friendly, professional and speedy service from the people working there. You want the milkman to deliver the milk on time and you expect to get detailed information on products or services from people if they are to convince you to buy something new. This is only a small sample of the different selling situations encountered but highlights the personal nature of this marketing activity.

Many people confuse marketing with selling, therefore it is essential to briefly outline the interrelationship of the two as follows:

1 Marketing, as a business philosophy, first identifies the needs of a potential market and subsequently concentrates on satisfying those needs and wants at a profit. Part of the satisfaction is the actual delivery of products to shops, door-to-door or to the places where people work. This does not happen by itself; it is often the result of the efforts of the company's sales force.

2 Consumers need to collect information relating to products or services to enable them to decide in a rational manner. Sales staff with adequate product knowledge can act as information providers and can help consumers select suitable products or services.

3 Daily shopping is to a degree a social event and it represents a large proportion of our lives. Sales assistants can develop an enjoyable and relaxing environment which contributes further to overall consumer satisfaction.

4 Marketing decision-making must be based on information from the market. Conventional research is obviously necessary, but sales staff can also provide further facts accumulated from their daily contacts with consumers or organisations in the market place.

5 A quality product, attractively priced, which can satisfy consumer needs, is useless unless the company possesses the necessary skills to sell the product to

116

interested parties. Sales staff regularly act as front-line troops for organisations – particularly those which supply industrial and/or retail customers and therefore represent a vital dimension of the marketing operations.

# ■ SELLING BENEFITS

The need for the company to be marketing orientated is essential if it is to properly support the efforts of its sales team. Selling can be enjoyable, interesting and rewarding but is made difficult if the company is not producing something really needed by a segment of the market and if it does not appreciate the value of features of the product in terms of benefits to potential customers. All the sales force can sell are **benefits** because people do not buy products, **they buy what products or services can do for them.** You do not buy a television: you buy entertainment for your home. That is why many people are willing to purchase satellite dish aerials to receive *more* entertainment through the medium of television. Even the value of entertainment received through television is different for different people. One person prefers watching classical concerts and opera while others prefer chat and quiz shows, soap operas and sports. It is the salesperson's job to be able to turn features of a product into the particular benefits different customers are seeking. To do this he or she will first ask customers questions and from their answers deduce what benefits are sought. Consider, for instance, two customers entering a hi-fi shop each with the intention of buying a hi-fi system to suit their needs. The experienced sales assistant would not instantly try to sell a particular system because he may appear untrustworthy and pushy to the customer or even embarrass the customer. Instead he will ask questions regarding the sort of music the customer likes to listen to, e.g. pop or classical, whether the customer needs a portable unit, how much the customer would like to spend, etc. By listening carefully to the replies of each customer and then giving professional advice in relation to their particular needs he is more likely to make sales to both.

# ■ PERSONAL SELLING AS AN ELEMENT OF THE COMMUNICATION MIX

Personal selling can be defined as:

> the oral presentation of a company's products, or services to one or more prospective purchasers for the purpose of making a sale.

It represents one of the personal channels of communication which consumers are exposed to and is especially useful when the potential purchase is seen as risky, complex, expensive or is of a significantly social, as opposed to private, character. Thus salespeople are particularly important in shops where a variety of complex equipment is sold and consumers require detailed information, and where a company sells to industrial customers who may ask many technical questions and purchase in large quantities.

Three main types of personal communication channels can be considered:

1 **Expert channels** Consultants, teachers, authors, advisors, doctors, etc., used by consumers in order to solve a problem they are facing
2 **Word of mouth** Friends, family members, colleagues at work, neighbours, etc., used by consumers as a means of acquiring the information required for decision making purposes
3 **Advocate channels** An advocate is a person with authority to present messages, cases, etc. a company's sales representative seeking to explain all relevant issues to current or prospective purchasers.

Public relations and advertising campaigns are developed in a way which maximises the creation of word of mouth and offers the opportunity to obtain favourable comments or 'publicity' from expert channels. Advocate channels, on the other hand, represent the priority area of this section and can assume many different forms.

1 **Field sales staff** seek to sell products or services on a door-to-door basis or through visiting companies. In other words they travel out from their companies to make sales.
2 **Retail sales staff** in shops handling the provision of information, trial of products and actual sales.
3 **Maintenance sales staff** specialise in the provision of after sales service necessary for technical products (repairs, replacements, conventional maintenance, etc.).
4 **Merchandising sales staff** employed to advise members of the trade on the promotion of products at the point of sale. They are involved in the positioning of display units, signs, posters, free samples, etc., which the company might have to use in order to maximise the level of awareness among shoppers.
5 **Delivery personnel** handle the physical distribution of products, responsible for punctual and accurate deliveries to specified locations.

Although there are numerous examples of specific types of sales people employed by companies, for the purpose of this textbook, field sales staff are referred to. Collectively, all the different individuals employed under the common theme of 'the field sales force' will be expected to make the following contributions to the company's communication efforts:

1 **Act as an ambassador for the company.** The behaviour of the salesperson must not negatively affect the company's reputation.
2 **Be a competent and helpful advisor** to present and potential customers. Providing customers with major information regarding a product's usefulness and answering customers' questions helps them to make a decision regarding the purchase of the product.
3 **Plan the most profitable use of his or her time** in order to minimise unnecessary travelling and visits to individuals who are not likely to buy.
4 **Compile a record system** to facilitate forward planning of sales to potential customers and keep a record of dealings with customers for continuity ensuring an effective service in the future.

5 **Act as a two-way communicator** between the customers and the company. Sales staff can provide the company with up-to-date information on market and/or customer developments and attitudes towards the company.
6 **Achieve sales targets set at budgeted sales costs,** or less. It is pointless to concentrate on achieving sales which do not offer the necessary profit to the company's future growth.
7 **Develop personal and professional skills** so that job and career ambitions are achieved. Salesmanship is not static so every individual involved in this field must try to expand his or her knowledge, ability, selling and social skills.
8 **Become an effective organiser and administrator** of all clerical, statistical and correspondence procedures.
9 **Show initiative** and take both preventive and remedial action when problems become evident.
10 **Liaise with customers** on behalf of the company to resolve complaints customers may have and to provide them with the latest information on the company and its products.

Having considered the contributions sales staff are expected to make to the marketing effort in the course of their work we are now in a position to group their activities under the following headings.

## 1 Actual selling

- Contact existing, new or potential customers
- Prepare presentations which will suit the expectations of the potential customers to be visited
- Develop trust by being truthful, honest, professional and informative
- Present selling propositions effectively by offering clear presentations to prospective buyers, by maintaining their interest and by explaining the benefits they may enjoy from the purchase
- Overcome objections by using points of relevance to the customer, the purchase and the nature of the objection
- Close the sale by getting agreement on quantity, method of payment, timing of delivery, etc.

## 2 Customer relations

- Problem solving
- Familiarisation with merchandising campaigns of distributors stocking the company's product
- Handling customer complaints or referring the complaints to the sales manager or sales supervisor
- Developing working relations with customers, e.g. friendship, trust and reliability

- Organising 'goodwill' visits to ensure that customers are satisfied with the products they have purchased, the quality of service received and to develop future 'sales leads'.

## 3  Product knowledge

This is an essential area of selling because if a salesperson is not fully familiar with the product/s he or she is expected to sell, success is unlikely. Sales staff should be aware of:

- Products or services offered
- Qualities of product or service offered by their company
- Benefits to the buyers
- Applications
- Prices charged
- Sale terms offered
- Competitors' products, so that comparisons are facilitated
- Technology used, in order to justify the benefits and qualities of the products/services for sale.

## 4  Administration

Sales staff should be trained to handle:

- Order forms
- Paperwork required once an order is received or generated by a salesperson
- Returns from dissatisfied customers
- Sales reports
- Correspondence with customers
- Follow-up enquiries
- Response to requests for sales literature, samples, posters, etc.

## 5  Intelligence

- Routine information and statistical data on products, competitors, the industry, other related industries, etc.
- Competitors' activities
- Market changes and needs of current or potential customers
- Co-operation with other sales staff
- Preparation of reports to superiors
- Interviewing customers and/or distributors in order to assess levels of satisfaction or even dissatisfaction
- Maintaining up-to-date records which can provide a clear picture of what has been achieved over a specific period of time.

Looking at the activities of sales staff you can see that it is an exciting, rewarding and demanding profession which will have a direct effect on the company's and/or product's success in the market place.

# ■ ROLE OF THE SALES MANAGER

The sales manager is responsible for all personal selling undertaken by a company or department and he or she is expected to perform the following duties:

1 Set clearly understood objectives designed to guide individual sales staff to contribute positively to the overall marketing objectives of the company
2 Be involved in the recruitment, selection, training and development of sales staff so that an effective team is created to achieve the objectives set
3 Devise competitive methods of remuneration to attract and maintain quality sales staff
4 Co-ordinate the activities of sales staff by advising on number of customers to be visited, length of time to be allocated to each visit, allocate them to areas, detailing types of customers to visit, products to sell or emphasise and by controlling the overall expenditure (budget) of the sales force
5 Co-ordinating sales force activities with the aims of advertising, public relations and sales promotions campaigns implemented by the company so that an effective communication mix is achieved
6 Be responsible for the administration of the sales department, acting as a 'link pin' between production, accounts, marketing, personnel and training and purchasing departments. This is a critical aspect of sales management with the prime tasks including:

- To create and implement motivational schemes for the sales force, so that marketing targets are met and company policy observed
- To distribute sales literature concerning the company's products or service to current or potential customers
- To devise, develop, implement and control a rational documentation system
- To receive customer complaints/inquiries and to follow them through
- To liaise between the customer and the company by progressing orders and occasionally visiting major customers
- To receive feedback from sales staff, to conduct strategic scanning from all sources and to disseminate the information.

The above functions, amongst others, should be carried out with a view to maximising profits. They may be carried out on either an international, national, or regional basis, depending upon the nature of the company.

For example, Rolls-Royce PLC have a sales force scattered around the world. These people require competent back-up, and the sales department must be effectively geared towards handling the orders they generate.

# ■ TASKS OF THE SALES MANAGER

The major management functions of sales managers are: planning, action and control. These elements are outlined below.

## The planning function

As part of the sales manager's planning function in a company, he or she is expected to:

1 Provide short-term, intermediate and long-term forecasts, in relation to company marketing targets
2 Plan sales campaigns in accordance with marketing objectives
3 Plan to achieve a profit of X per cent on sales
4 Estimate costs for budget purposes
5 Analyse markets by the use of the sales staff to identify new uses for existing products and new product prospects
6 Plan the overall activity of area managers, sales supervisors and sales staff in the areas, or regions
7 Plan and organise the sales office according to the expected workload – this may be for home as well as export customers, depending on the trading characteristics of the company
8 Plan and assign territories for effective coverage
9 Set standards of performance and conduct for all sales staff, both internal and external
10 Plan own time
11 Plan regular sales meetings
12 Plan for the general development and promotion of sales staff
13 Plan to use available headquarter services, such as direct mail facilities, PR, etc., where applicable
14 Assist with or control the planning of trade fairs and/or exhibitions.

## The action function

The action function within the sales manager's job involves him or her in:

1 Recruiting quality sales staff with future potential
2 Training new and experienced sales staff in selling skills and attitude, knowledge and interpretation of company policy
3 Motivating and developing each salesperson to his or her full potential
4 Considering dismissals, recommending promotions, demotions, and transfers
5 Keeping sales staff informed of sales developments and ensuring that enquiries related to their area are forwarded to them
6 Directing activities of area managers, regional managers, sales supervisors, sales staff, and sales office staff
7 Directing the application of sales programmes to support advertising and promotion programmes
8 Consulting sales staff and major customers on problems of service and delivery
9 Maintaining discipline
10 Encouraging sales staff, especially after failure, providing incentives, and recognition for a job well done

11 Liaising with heads of other departments, e.g. production, finance, accounts, design and personnel
12 Working in conjunction with the marketing manager and the heads of other marketing functions – advertising and sales promotion, market research, and distribution.

## The control function

The control function of the sales manager's job means he or she is expected to:
1 Maintain standards of performance and conduct
2 Establish frequency of calls on each class or type of customer, and adjust the frequency when necessary
3 Maintain an efficient record system to provide a quick analysis of performance for each product, area and salesperson
4 Periodically and systematically evaluate the performance of individual sales staff, and overall performance
5 Determine in what areas performance is progressing according to plan
6 Investigate causes of lack of progress against plans and take remedial action
7 Control costs as per budget.

Thus while the sales manager has specialised functions to perform in relation to personal selling he or she, like other managers, must be responsible for fulfilling these functions, e.g. plan, set objectives, direct, co-ordinate, control, motivate and monitor – through observing and maintaining good records.

## ■ THE ORDER PROCESS

The order process can be explained by examining the major steps which are involved when a new customer is obtained. These are:

1 Enquiry
2 Quotation
3 Order
4 Delivery
5 Invoice
6 Collection
7 Follow-up.

Every step involves a series of distinct activities which merit individual examination:

1 Enquiries may be verbal or arrive by hand, mail, fax, telephone, telegram, or telex. It is imperative that details of all serious enquiries from which an order may follow are recorded for future analysis. A simple listing may suffice depending upon the size and nature of the operation.

Promotional brochures and/or a written confirmation of the enquiry and a friendly letter should be despatched to the enquirer, with a copy to the salesperson. Arrangements should be put in hand to ensure that the salesperson follows through, or an appointment for a visit by the salesperson may be made at the time of the enquiry.

2 Quotations confirm to the customer the price he or she will finally pay and the terms under which the company will supply. Quotations should be well presented, informed, detailed, recorded and a copy placed in the pending file. If it is a standard production item then the price may be immediately given to the customer.

3 The customer's order should be carefully checked on receipt – ensuring that it has been signed by a person with the appropriate authority such as the commercial or sales office manager. Acknowledge the order – if necessary implement credit ratings or make preliminary arrangements for finance. Inform the customer on the 'Order Acknowledgement' form of any changes to the order: for example, the customer may have ordered 200 tonnes of potatoes but due to stocks you may only be able to deliver immediately 190 tonnes.

4 The delivery requires liaison between production, stock control (i.e. the warehouse), transport and sales staff. Advise the customer and update the order file.

5 The invoice is the form sent to the customer asking for payment within the terms agreed. It is usually multi-copied so that copies can be kept by the sales office and accounts (credit control). (*NB* Export orders require special treatment.) Consumer shoppers usually obtain a receipt only. In the case of industrial and/or retail customers the salesperson may also receive a copy or some other evidence of the sale for his or her own records.

6 Collection: industrial and retail customers usually make payment with a cheque while consumers use cash, cheque or credit card. The sum received should be checked against records to make sure that it is correct. Records should be up-dated, the cheque banked and payment acknowledged. The salesperson should be informed and the purchase file can then be closed.

7 Follow-up: as a matter of courtesy, the salesperson should be encouraged to call back on the customer to ensure satisfaction and to discover if there is the possibility of another order.

## ■ SALES PLANNING

Sales managers are expected to develop plans of action which summarise the activities of the sales force. A sales plan is a detailed document which establishes short, medium and long-term objectives for the sales function. The sales plan details the personal selling role in achieving the company's future sales objectives. Basically the plan defines the target for the future, how it will be achieved and the role each person will play in fulfilling the plan. It contributes to translating marketing objectives into selling sub-objectives and it outlines specific selling strategies and tactics. It is either part of the marketing plan (see pages 193–5) or a separate document developed by individual sales managers. The actual contents of a sales plan will vary from company to company but certain decision areas are likely to be similar across most sales forces. A typical sales plan will consist of the following:

- A summary of the environment within which the company and its sales staff are expected to operate
- Corporate objectives over a specified period
- Marketing objectives over a specified period
- Target markets to be reached by the sales force
- Number and nature of salespeople employed
- Area, product or customer allocation of sales staff
- Sales quotas per area, customer group or product group – quotas may also be set for shop sales staff if it is a retail sales operation
- Expected **strike ratios** (number of new customers generated compared with the number of sales calls actually made)
- Sales tactics and strategy to be used including the best sales techniques to employ
- Expected average order sizes
- Direct costs of the field sales force
- Direct costs of telephone selling (if used)
- Sales office and administrative costs (targets may also be set for the sales office in terms of increased efficiency)
- Cost and nature of support activities (sales aids, samples, exhibitions, etc.)
- Cost of any physical distribution of goods undertaken by sales staff
- Promotional support to be offered to sales staff
- Sales approaches to be used
- Evaluation criteria to be implemented in order to assess the performance and progress of sales staff.

## Controlling progress of sales staff

The last element of the sales plan highlights the need to examine the various **controls** which sales managers use in order to monitor the progress made by the sales function. Key controls include:

- Sales per area/product group/customer group
- Sales per sales period (quarterly/monthly/yearly, etc.)
- Number of new customers and current customers retained per area
- Time taken to cover territories – this gives the sales manager some idea of the best journey route to follow and if the salesperson is planning his/her workload wisely
- Actual costs faced in supporting sales activities, e.g. sales literature, slides, videos used in sales presentations as well as travelling and car costs

- Percentage of call quotas achieved – this enables the sales manager to relate and compare performance of sales staff
- Number of new accounts being opened
- Miles actually travelled
- Average cost per call
- Bad debt to sales ratios
- Number of accounts being lost and why
- Number and nature of complaints received
- Type of new customers being obtained and their profit value
- Qualitative standards achieved by sales staff, e.g. improved presentation, interaction with sales office personnel, etc.
- Actual strike ratios. 'Strike' in this context refers to a successful call, in other words a sales call which leads to a sale. If, for instance, a salesperson enjoys a 1 : 5 strike ratio, it means that five visits are made before an order is obtained. Strike ratios should not be treated as the only evaluation criterion because they can be misleading due to seasonal factors, area potential, special offers used or even luck.

# ■ SALES FORCE COMMUNICATION

Sales staff exist to transfer the company's philosophy to the marketplace, communicate important issues to selected audiences, protect and enhance a company's reputation, collect information, solve problems, remove anxieties and finally sell.

Their work is very personal and sensitive. Allowances must be made therefore for specific situations, types of products and companies, variety of personalities involved and changing expectations. As explained earlier, personal selling comes in many different forms (field selling, retail selling, delivery personnel, etc.) and can be used for the following purposes:

1 Creating awareness
2 Arousing interest
3 Developing product preference
4 Explaining technology
5 Increasing position in the stock market
6 Building enthusiasm
7 Inducing trial
8 Obtaining repeat orders
9 Discovering new sales leads
10 Offering reassurance to potential purchasers or current users.

Selling brings pressure on sales people. Perhaps this is why they often receive high salaries but they still cannot be expected to perform all their duties at an acceptable level unless they are given the necessary support and encouragement by sales management.

Provision of adequate information is a major key to success in this area and *sales manuals* are one of the first documents used when a salesperson starts with a company. A sales manual is, in effect, a job specification and a book of reference on the company's selling matters. It helps sales staff to improve their sales techniques and provides sales management with information on which to base sales bulletins, newsletters, sales training, etc. A sales manual should contain the following information:

## 1  Information on the company

- How it started
- Products and services provided
- Activities in other fields
- Overseas interests
- Future prospects
- Company structure
- Performance levels achieved, etc.

## 2  Personal information for the salesperson

- Salary
- Expenses allowed
- Position regarding absence from work
- Commissions
- Responsibility for company property used
- Holidays
- Bonuses
- Overnight allowances, etc.

## 3  Information on customers

- Terms of sale to be offered
- Collection of payment
- Procedure for slow or late payment
- Lapsed accounts, bounced cheques, etc.
- Daily cash sheet
- New account procedure.

## 4  Information on orders

- Completion of the procedure concerning pre-printed order forms and daily reports needed
- Posting or delivery of orders
- Urgent order procedure.

## 5  Territory coverage

- Journey plans
- Journey advice forms for management of journeys
- Routing plans
- Targets to be achieved
- Frequency of calls
- Information on other sales staff operating in the same area, e.g. one salesperson may be selling the company's X range of products while another is selling the Y range within the same geographical area.

## 6  Miscellaneous

- Correspondence
- Trade incentive schemes (special deliveries, merchandising support, special packaging arrangements, etc.)
- Role in preparing or helping to staff the company's stand at trade fairs and exhibitions
- Samples of products
- Explanatory notes on information provided
- Other contingencies which apply to a specific company's sales force activities.

The sales manual is favoured by sales managers as a means of communication and instruction and regular additions are introduced in order to ensure that it stays up to date and is a useful guide to all members of the sales force. There are other communication channels which the company and the sales staff can use to communicate with each other, some of which are considered in the suggested answer to the examination question on page 137.

## ■  RECRUITMENT, SELECTION, TRAINING AND MOTIVATION OF SALES STAFF

### Recruitment and selection

The recruitment of new sales staff is an important part of any organisation's range of activities, representing a costly and often time-consuming exercise. There is, however, a saying in industry to the effect that, 'it all starts with good recruitment and selection'. Therefore, any necessary time and effort spent on the selection process is worthwhile; the wrong choice can cost you much more in the long run.

Company policy normally sets certain guidelines within which recruitment takes place and expertise from the company's personnel and training department and/or external recruitment organisations is invariably used by the experienced sales manager.

Recruitment of quality sales people requires the following essential actions:

## 1 PREPARATION OF A 'JOB DESCRIPTION'

This is a description of the post or job to be filled and includes the job title, the responsibilities (tasks) involved, the skills required, the level of training and experience expected and possibly formal academic qualifications of relevance to the position.

## 2 PREPARATION OF 'PERSON SPECIFICATION'

A 'person' profile is a list of characteristics of the right applicant to fit the job description. It includes: age, health, past experience, qualifications, previous achievement levels (i.e. track record), etc.

## 3 MAKING THE POSITION KNOWN

As many sources of 'supply' as possible should be considered. Companies usually concentrate on:

- The company itself, i.e. internal staff
- 'Head-hunting' in universities, colleges, schools, etc, and amongst sales people employed by competitors
- Professional bodies, trade associations, etc. The professional body may keep a register of sales staff seeking a change or have a journal in which an advert may be placed
- Advertising in the media
- Recommendations from existing sales staff
- Government offices
- Employment agencies/consultants.

## 4 ISSUE APPLICATION FORMS

Application forms are issued by many companies for candidates to complete. They may be asked to write in first or provide a CV (curriculum vitae) which offers information on their working life, qualifications and personal details. The forms should be designed in a way which maximises information generation from the applicants and should be used as a method of elimination (screen out) of applicants who do not meet the criteria set.

## 5 SELECTION

Applicants who pass this first screening are invited to attend a series of interviews and/or tests used by the company to evaluate their abilities at first hand including their personal attire, presentability and skills in handling a discussion/interview. The applicant should be attempting to sell himself or herself as a professional salesperson.

Good selection techniques help in identifying competent individuals, produce a highly skilled sales force, reduce labour turnover, reduce training costs, increase sales volume and profitability and, of course, improve morale. The selector must try to predict the applicant's level of performance in selling. To accomplish this the following selection process is recommended though it must be adapted to different companies' policies.

a) **The initial interview.** The candidate should be encouraged to talk freely about him or herself, a relaxed atmosphere should be created, important issues on the application form should be thoroughly discussed and an overall assessment of the individual should be made.

Trained interviewers and/or a sales manager trained in interviewing techniques are useful during this stage in order to avoid making the following common errors in assessing the personal qualities of sales people.

i) Over confidence. Everyday experience gives most people plenty of practice in assessing the personal qualities of their social contacts. Some become over-confident of their ability in this respect, are too quick to judge and are biased in their views. There may be no 'great divide' between the candidate who has all the necessary qualities and the one who has not. It is often easy to pick out the outstanding candidates but only very careful consideration of the available evidence will permit proper assessment of those considered to be 'marginal'. A large sales force may regularly be seeking new staff, and making professional evaluations when selecting, therefore, becomes very important.

ii) Snap judgements. First impressions are notoriously unreliable and should be avoided. Careful, unprejudiced evaluation of the evidence obtained at an efficient interview, and observing the candidate in any exercise situations, ensures that snap judgements are not made.

iii) Over-simplification. The most elaborate personal case-history cannot give a complete analysis of a person's character. Briefer, more selective, records are bound to be even less useful. Common everyday characterisations, mentioning only one or two of an individual's central qualities are also of limited value. Care is needed to avoid being misled by one's own characterisations and well-turned phrases which often create a false impression or wrong decision.

iv) 'Halo effect' or 'global impression'. The cause of the 'halo effect' lies in emotional prejudice of various kinds. Nearly all analyses of personality assessments show the effect of one outstandingly 'good' or 'bad' quality in a person, which reflects on all judgements relating to him or her. A good example is the common belief that healthy, neat individuals with smiling faces are likely to be intelligent. This is not always true so every effort should be made to be more objective and professional in the assessment of job applicants.

Systematic evaluation is essential in order to avoid the errors mentioned above. There is no general agreement among psychologists about the true indications of personal qualities but interviewers should examine and decide on the following three key areas:

i) **Personality.** A good personality is one important requirement in a salesperson. The ability to inspire rather than to drive is mainly derived from these traits. On the other hand far too many people assume that personality reflects character and temperament or base their judgements purely on personality. A 'good' personality may disguise a confidence trickster; a dour personality may hide an impressive character. It is, therefore, necessary to penetrate below the personality veneer. Some of the more important personality traits are:

- Appearance and bearing
- Manner
- Composure
- Power of expression
- Self-confidence
- Sense of humour
- Enthusiasm.

ii) **Character.** The traits that make up a person's character are of utmost importance in the search for potential sales staff, and are difficult to develop in training. It is, therefore, doubly important that they should be recognised and correctly assessed during selection. The most important traits under this heading are:

- Integrity
- Determination
- Assertiveness
- Initiative
- Decisiveness
- Conscientiousness
- Sense of responsibility.

Integrity is the most difficult of these to assess. Evidence to support assessment of the traits must be pieced together from the many facets of a candidate's background and from his or her performance in practical exercises.

iii) **Temperament.** An individual's temperament governs his or her reactions to new situations and environments. It is necessary to forecast how well a candidate is likely to settle down and how adaptable he or she is likely to be in meeting the various challenges of the job. Traits of particular interest are:

- Imagination
- Judgement
- Co-operation
- Loyalty
- Clarity and logic in thinking
- Flexibility
- Consideration for others
- Breadth of outlook.

These are also difficult traits to assess during an interview but most of them can be identified in role playing, practical exercises or psychological tests.

b) **Psychological tests.** Tests are sometimes introduced by companies in order to assess the applicant's ability, achievement, aptitude, interest and motivation. They assume great importance during the selection of sales staff due to the nature of the duties and responsibilities discussed earlier in this chapter.

c) **Physical examination.** A healthy mind needs to be supported by a healthy body. Applicants are often asked to submit medical reports or are expected to attend a medical examination in order to assess overall state of health.

Physical examinations are becoming increasingly important in the selection process and many companies have made them compulsory for both new and existing members of the company.

## 6  FINAL INTERVIEW

The previous stages will enable the selector/s to eliminate unsuitable candidates and prepare a shortlist of likely candidates.

Applicants shortlisted are invited to a final interview so that additional information perhaps overlooked in the initial interview, can be collected and a final assessment made. To ensure that there is accuracy when interviewing most interviewers devise a standard interviewing procedure so that questions similar in form are asked of all candidates. In this way fair comparisons can be made.

## 7  PREPARATION OF PROFILE CHARTS

Using the data collected in the previous stages, the selector constructs a profile chart on each applicant shortlisted covering certain vital aspects, e.g. impact on others, natural abilities, motivation, adaptability, suitability for position. Each applicant should be graded according to the evaluation criteria used and the final selection can then be made.

## 8  OBTAINING APPLICANTS' REFERENCES

Character or professional references represent additional evaluation criteria and serve as a means of checking the consistency of information provided by the applicant. Opinions and/or recommendations by third parties can prove extremely valuable but should not be used to replace own assessment and evaluation. Most applicants currently in a post cannot allow a prospective employer to contact current employers until they have obtained the new post. To cover against the possibility of a subsequent bad reference the new employer may operate a probationary period.

# Training and development

As products become more complex, purchasing officers more professional, and consumers more demanding, the need for effective sales staff is greater than ever before and thus the need for training. In formula terms we can define the amount of training needed by a salesperson (the training gap) as follows:

*The training gap (need) = The skills and knowledge needed to do the job – the current skills and knowledge of the potential trainee.*

Training is not achieved by simply sending sales staff on training courses, it is the result of a continuous, well-devised process designed to:

- Generate in the trainee the wish to improve
- Enable sales staff to achieve a higher standard of performance and quality of salesmanship
- Improve performance of 'non-selling' tasks
- Reduce the amount of supervision required
- Lead to increased earnings and higher job satisfaction or promotion
- Reduce selling costs.

The issue of sales training is concerned with the learning process which sales staff must be taken through and it must be treated as an activity which covers four basic concepts: drive, stimulus, response and incentive:

1 **Drive** – for the activity to take place, e.g. ambition, the desire to do one's job as well as possible, higher pay, etc.
2 **Stimulus** – to provoke the drive into operation. For example, if you increase the quality of your job performance sufficiently, we will promote you or give you a pay rise.
3 **Response** – to the stimulation, i.e. some kind of reaction. For example, a negative response on possible promotion may indicate that the training or promotion is not of any value to the potential trainee, or 'When can I start on the training scheme, I really want that promotion', in which case there is a strong desire to learn.
4 **Incentive** – some reinforcement of the response. For example, praise or compliments, cash bonus or pay rise. There may be negative incentive, e.g. 'dismissal from the job' or the slowing down of promotion if response is not positive or adequate.

Lack of efficient training will lead to a general malfunction in the sales force; the signs that indicate training may be needed include:

- Sales staff are becoming order-takers and are failing to develop new accounts.
- Limited or no prospecting is carried out which subsequently leads to problems with sales growth.
- Higher costs of selling are witnessed.
- Customers are dissatisfied with approach, presentation, handling of complaints and product knowledge shown by sales staff.
- Discontent among sales staff, high staff turnover and low morale.

The actual needs of the sales force must be identified through regular discussions between sales managers and sales staff (individually or in groups), observation of selling situations, evaluation of job descriptions and discussions with major clients. Once training needs are clearly identified the training programme should be designed to take account of some or all of these factors:

- Evaluation of existing experience
- Definition of standards (or qualities), both:
  a) quantitative and
  b) qualitative.
- Analysis of the job in terms of:
  a) knowledge (products/areas/industry/company's policy/competition, etc.)
  b) skills (prospecting, making successful contacts, presenting the sales proposition, demonstrating products, using visual aids, obtaining the order, etc.).
- How training should take place, i.e.
  a) demonstration
  b) lecture
  c) role playing
  d) discussions.
- Field practice, i.e. before actual or potential customers.
- Feedback – an important reinforcer for trainees. Knowledge of progress or praise which is merited are essential motivators and may be derived from:
  a) subjective assessment: personal observations or assessments, or
  b) objective assessment: observations on progress actually made, objective tests, etc.
- Evaluation of standards achieved either while training is taking place or subsequently, by assessing any improvement in actual job performance following the training programme.

The sales manager, and possibly his or her superiors, may contribute positively to the effective development of the sales staff by:

1 Holding discussions with sales staff individually and/or in groups)
2 Carrying out observations of selling situations
3 Checking job descriptions against what sales staff are actually doing
4 'Designing' selling situations
5 Introducing up-to-date sales manuals
6 Setting attainable and practicable sales targets
7 Accompanying sales staff in the market
8 Demonstrating sales approaches
9 Introducing a positive management philosophy which can accommodate general organisational and personal needs
10 Holding regular sales reviews
11 Providing sales staff with adequate market and product information
12 Regularly evaluating individual performance
13 Regularly evaluating staff for promotion.

Generally speaking, training is an activity that needs to be well-planned and understood by both trainers and trainees. It is not a process applied only to new employees; it is also a means of improving the efficiency of existing sales staff. If it proves a success then a more effective sales team has been developed or a new, competent salesperson is ready to pursue the tasks for which he or she has been trained.

# Motivation

Many managers make the fundamental mistake of assuming that attractive rates of pay and continuous training provide sales staff with the necessary motivation to work hard and achieve their sales targets. This could not be further from the truth because it represents a very one sided view of human motivation and ignores the personal expectations of people within the context of a job. Attractive financial rewards are obviously essential but sales staff must be given a feeling of achievement, belonging, opportunity to voice their own opinions as well as attractive working relationships.

People care about what has to be done, how it must be accomplished, the timing of the achievement, the implications of success and failure and the value of the task. Money only relates to the implications of success or failure and can only be relied upon as a short-term motivating force. Boredom, dissatisfaction, depression, stress and confusion are standard human feelings which sales managers must attempt to consider when seeking to motivate sales staff. Highly paid sales people who are bored with the job or do not feel valued may do just enough to hold the job rather than perform at their best.

This aspect of staff management is not going to be evaluated by examining well-known motivation theories but some years of experience and numerous research findings have repeatedly shown that the motivation of a company's sales force will depend on some of the following factors:

1 Competitive and fair remuneration
2 Attractive travelling expenses
3 Opportunities to gain promotion through achievement
4 Opportunity to attend company sponsored academic courses or tailor-made training courses designed to expand the personal and professional skills of sales staff and thus their job prospects
5 A democratic management style allowing sales staff to express themselves in the field of selling with clear guidelines laid down by the company
6 Frequent consultation with sales staff in order to discuss sales targets set, problems faced in the market, personal opinions, means of improving overall performance, etc. – in other words management by consensus
7 Praising individuals who have contributed positively to the company's ambitions and objectives (praise should not be limited to selling achievements as sales staff also perform a number of non-selling tasks)
8 Efficient advertising and promotional support designed to provide the sales force with adequate back-up
9 Competitions among sales staff designed to create healthy challenges rather than destructive rivalries
10 Provision of up-to-date market information covering competition, products,

technological developments, implications of new legislation, opportunities for making extra sales, etc.
11  Maintenance of a good company reputation which can give sales staff a sense of pride to be part of a respected and growing organisation
12  Introduction of social events for sales staff and their families
13  Provision of attractive health care, pension and life insurance packages
14  Respect for salespeople's beliefs, achievements and personal goals
15  Constantly attempting to produce goods or services that people really want, thus reducing the need for over-persuasive selling techniques.

It should be clear that the relative importance attached to the above 'motivators' will vary from person to person but every sales manager must seek to understand the needs and expectations of the sales force in order to use the most appropriate methods of motivation. It is often easy to attract or develop a good salesperson but keeping him or her in the company may present the hardest task. The final word should be a message to all prospective sales people or sales managers: '*A demotivated salesperson will not sell*'.

## ■ STUDY AND EXAM TIPS

1  Do not refer to sales staff as people devoted solely to selling. Remember all the other non-selling duties which are also important to the overall success of a sales force.

2  Be prepared to identify and discuss the different types of sales staff identified in this section.

3  Remember, personal selling is an element of the promotions mix and, therefore, must be effectively combined with advertising, public relations and sales promotions.

4  Sales force recruitment, selection and training are very popular examination topics so careful preparation is strongly advised.

5  Do not forget that personal selling is an essential element of marketing. All recommendations must allow for the fact that consumer satisfaction is the key to long-term success.

6  Questions on this topic tend to be specific so avoid long and meaningless discussions on sales staff in general and concentrate on the topic the examiner expects you to discuss.

## ■ PAST EXAMINATION QUESTIONS

### The Chartered Institute of Marketing

1 A sales representative is a very expensive marketing resource. As a marketing manager what might you do to improve the effectiveness of the field sales force?

2 What is the role of a sales force in relation to merchandising and to promotion?

3 The primary task of a sales representative is to sell his/her company's products or services. What additional tasks could the sales representatives be expected to undertake and how may they affect their selling role?

4 How can sales management help a salesman to improve his performance?

5 What channels of communication would you introduce or use in order to ensure that the company's sales force is fully informed as to what is required of them by the company?

## ■ SUGGESTED ANSWER TO QUESTION 5

The main cause of a sales person's frustration is possibly the lack of information supplied to him regarding the company and how it affects what he does or is expected to do.

This lack of communication occurs particularly in large companies and is bad for the company and its sales force. It is necessary, therefore, to set up certain lines of communication between the company and its sales force. These should not simply be 'one way' channels of information from the company or its senior managers to the sales force. All channels of communication should have built into them the facility for feedback of information and healthy criticisms made by the sales force.

When designing such lines of communication, one must first consider what has to be communicated to sales people. All information, be its sales instruction, new targets or quotas, or general interest information such as new appointments within the organisation, should reach sales staff as soon as possible. They should not hear of changes second-hand or receive unclear or ambiguous messages.

The main organs of communication open to any company are the sales manager, senior salesperson, area managers, or whoever is directly responsible for the sales force within a region. Meetings should be called by the sales manager whenever there are important matters to discuss or instructions to be issued to the sales force – a change in sales policy for instance – and sales staff should have the opportunity to voice their views in the knowledge that major concerns they raise will be attended to. If the information to be communicated is complex and designed to improve sales presentations then training sessions may be the best format.

Newsletters are an effective means of communication, as they can be used to inspire as well as instruct. A regular newsletter should be part of every large company's line of communication, although it has a 'one-way communication' disadvantage – unless sales staff are encouraged to write in with their opinions regarding the articles to be included or the major issues to be covered.

One of the best means of two-way communication is the sales conference away from the daily working environment at which the marketing and/or sales manager and staff can talk directly to the sales force, and vice versa, in an informal setting, e.g. at meal times or relaxing in the evening. Although this is a relatively expensive operation, it should be a regular part of the sales force programme. Sales conferences are an ideal way to direct and inspire sales staff to greater efforts and provide them with general encouragement.

Most sales managers consider the sales manual an ideal means of communication and instruction, and may regularly add to it, ensuring it is kept off the shelf and out of the glove compartment.

There are a number of ways of communicating with a sales force in the field but the importance of feedback cannot be stressed enough. The sales force should submit regular reports on sales, customer satisfaction, competitors' activities and new product development. It is apparent, therefore, that an efficient company will rely on two-way communication systems and not simply on telling its sales staff what it wants.

In order to summarise the communication channels which can be used we can refer to useful outward communications (manager to salesperson) and inward communications (salesperson to company):

| **Outwards** | **Inwards** |
|---|---|
| bulletins | letters |
| letters | house journal |
| circulars | complaints/suggestions |
| house journal | reports |
| additions to sales manual | special reports, e.g. forecasts |
| phone calls |    or marketing intelligence |
| meetings | phone calls |
| visits/'observation' | meetings |
| continuous training | conferences |
| sales aids | continuous training |

Having considered formal and semi-formal methods it must always be remembered that communication must not be an *ad hoc* process. A sales manager should not fear the individuals who comprise the sales force but should take every opportunity to follow an open door policy, speaking with sales people individually to make them feel valued and genuinely listening to their grievances so that each is seen as an individual and not simply a pawn of management.

# ■ SELF ASSESSMENT QUESTIONS

Answer the following questions without reference to the text and then refer to the answers given at the end of the book to determine your score. Award yourself one mark for each complete question that you answered correctly. If you scored seven or more you are reading efficiently. If you answered questions incorrectly read the chapter again to see what the answer should have been.

**1** Complete the sentence: Personal selling can be defined as 'the oral presentation of a company's products or services to ...................................................................................

..............................................................................................................................

**2** Complete the sentence: 'The only things we have to sell are ................................. .

**3** Complete the missing entry: We can group the activities of sales staff into five major activities, namely
a) Actual selling
b) Customer relations
c) ................
d) Administration
e) Intelligence

**4** Complete the entries missing in the following 'order process' relating to industrial and retail buyers.
a) Enquiry
b) Quotation
c) Order
d) Delivery
e) ................
f) ................
g) Follow-up

**5** The work of the sales manager relates to three functions, one of which is the planning function. Identify the other two.
a) ................
b) ................

**6** Complete the following equation:
The training gap =

**7** Recruitment and selection represents an eight step process. Identify the eighth part.
a) Preparation of a job description
b) Preparation of a person specification
c) Making the position known

d) Issue of application forms
e) Selection
f) Final interview
g) Preparation of profile charts
h) ................................................................................................................

**8** Complete the following sentence: Standards (or qualities) of a salesman may be quantitative or ................................................................................................................

**9** Three types of personal communication exist, one of which is expert channels. Name the other two.
a) ................................................................................................................
b) ................................................................................................................

# 8 Promotional planning

*A written plan is only as good as the thinking that goes into it.*

Part 2 of this textbook has concentrated exclusively on the promotional output of marketing, examining the four elements of the marketing promotions mix. It is now possible to summarise these elements under one management activity called **promotional planning** or **marketing communication planning**. You will rarely find a marketing person concentrating on only one element of the promotional mix because, as the word **mix** implies, a combination of two or more elements relevant to the individual company's marketing needs is the key to successful promotion.

This chapter looks at:

1 The steps to be followed in developing the marketing communication plan, and
2 Approaches that may be adopted, using two mini case studies.

## ■ THE PROMOTIONAL PLAN

The promotional plan (or the marketing communication plan) identifies the communication activities to be undertaken by a company over a specified period of time, in order to achieve clearly established objectives. Like all forms of planning, it represents decisions in response to a specific business situation and provides a detailed account as to how these responses will be implemented.

The development of the plan depends on the implementation of a procedure that provides justifications for various elements of the promotions mix to be used. Consider, for instance, a situation where a company has a small budget but it needs to reach a large, geographically dispersed target market. The need for national advertising media like TV, newspapers or possibly magazines may be the first consideration but the financial means necessary to use such media may not be available. Promotions planners will need to find the most attractive options within the constraints of the budget, e.g. direct mail. The two key words to emerge from this scenario are **constraints** and **responses.** With these in mind we can proceed to the **steps** to be followed when developing a marketing promotions plan:

1 Identification of constraints

141

2  Definition of target market to be reached
3  Nature of appeals to be used
4  Promotional objectives
5  Promotional-mix necessary to achieve the objectives set
6  Allocation of the promotional budget.

It is vital to follow the sequence as presented above because, as you will see, decisions made at one point of the sequence will directly affect decisions reached later.

# ■ IDENTIFICATION OF CONSTRAINTS

All marketing decisions are made within the boundaries of the business environment/s within which companies find themselves. You cannot justify marketing communication decisions before you identify, explain or summarise four important constraints, considered below.

## 1  Positional analysis (SWOT analysis)

SWOT refers to the identification of the major 'strengths' and 'weaknesses' internal to the company in relation to external 'opportunities' available and 'threats' which the company faces – or may face if it changes its marketing approach. A SWOT analysis of the company provides a means of understanding the situation within which decisions must be made.

A case study may include a wide variety of often conflicting facts which must be summarised into a meaningful total which the reader of the plan or the report can use in order to relate to the situation being faced. Imagine you are submitting your plan of action to a third party who is not familiar with the overall situation. A summary will prepare the reader and will enable him or her to assess the quality of the recommendations to be made.

During examinations, do not waste time writing long and detailed SWOT analyses; try to keep them short, informative and precise in order to provide yourselves with enough time to attempt all the examination questions.

## 2  Time available

Marketing promotions campaigns do not run continuously over many years; they tend to concentrate on specific periods which are considered to be the best times to reach selected target markets with particular promotional messages. Some products may be aimed at the Christmas market, e.g. home decorations, others may be linked to summer holidays overseas, while a large number of products or services are in demand throughout the year (e.g. newspapers, food items, shoes). Alternatively, a campaign may be to establish a new product in the marketplace. The time constraint implies that the period which promotions will be expected to cover must be clearly specified in order to facilitate media selection, budget allocation and effective combination of the elements of the promotions mix.

## 3  Budget available

Marketing managers – or their advertising agency – are often full of creative ideas as to how to promote their products or services, but they are constrained by the finances available to them.

Students often complain that it is pointless to even consider marketing communications if the budget allowed is extremely small, say £3000. However, many small businesses do manage to promote effectively with very limited budgets.

## 4  Marketing objectives

Marketing promotions represent only one element of the marketing mix, but they must make a positive and quantifiable contribution to the achievement of overall marketing objectives. Informing consumers about a new product or service does not necessarily create sales nor does it generate a good reputation for the company's operations. The other elements of the marketing mix – price, product, place – will have to make their own contributions.

Identifying the marketing objectives will provide promotions planners with reference points needed for the achievement of consistency between marketing and promotional activities.

Constraints can be summarised as follows:

- **Reasons** for response – Determined via positional (SWOT) analysis
- **Period** of response – Time constraint
- **Cost** of response – Budget available
- **Framework** of response – Marketing objectives.

## ■  DEFINITION OF TARGET MARKET

Identification of the constraints will help a promotions planner to select the 'right' target markets for the company's promotions because they will identify problems, expectations, available financial resources and timing of the campaigns. Target markets must be defined in very precise terms by using demographic, geographic, psychographic, usage rate or organisational descriptions, taking account of constraints such as finances, competitor responses, etc.

A promotional campaign aimed at women is a useless description unless the age, location, socio-economic grouping and usage rates associated with women targeted are clearly identified. Precise descriptions of the target audiences will facilitate the selection of advertising media, sales promotion techniques or public relations activities which are the most suitable to reach the audiences selected and are cost-effective. In addition, the information needs of different target markets may vary, so clear identification of **who** is to be reached will also serve as a guide to the presentations which must be made in order to get a favourable response.

## ■ NATURE OF APPEALS TO BE MADE

Many people feel that once the target market has been defined, marketers can proceed to the selection of the elements of the promotions mix to be used. This line of thinking ignores one of the most fundamental aspects of effective promotions which is to encourage planners to 'consider the content and length of the message first' before they select the 'means of communication to be used'. This is a valid point in that, the creative dimensions associated with different advertising media or sales promotion techniques vary widely. It is possible to find that the best means of communicating an extensive technical message is by relying on sales staff who can explain face-to-face all the benefits of a product or service, rather than using advertisements which are relatively short.

Promotional appeals (or messages) can be divided into:

1 **Functional appeals.** Presentations or statements designed to highlight or explain the functions associated with a product or service, such as a vacuum cleaner providing the user with a clean carpet.
2 **Emotional appeals.** Presentations designed to generate reactions like: surprise, happiness, greed, excitement, etc. Consider advertisements that inform the audience of the prizes which can be won by entering a competition for the users of a company's products. The prizes represent an emotional appeal because they may convince consumers to buy the product in the hope of winning a holiday, a car or a cash prize. Likewise, adverts encouraging you to donate to a charity may include a picture of a person suffering from a particular physical condition, and so appealing to your emotions.
3 **Moral appeals.** Presentations designed to make audiences feel guilty, ashamed, careful, etc. They concentrate on what is socially acceptable and decent and encourage audiences to respond accordingly. Advertisements by health authorities in many countries warn about the dangers of smoking cigarettes, being exposed to too much sunlight or using certain chemicals or dangerous goods. There is often a thin dividing line between moral and emotional appeals and care should be taken when selecting examples to explain the two types of appeals.

## ■ PROMOTIONAL OBJECTIVES

At this critical part of the plan **directives** must be set in relation to the constraints identified, target markets selected and the nature of appeals to be made to the audiences. Promotional objectives should take account of the need to:

a)  Be as precise as possible provided the message to be communicated is not lost
b)  Be consistent with marketing objectives
c)  Be informative – this may not always be possible through media advertising due to cost, but may be possible with promotional literature appearing on the product/pack
d)  Allow for a logical build-up of objectives – for example, it may be necessary to promote to distributors before consumers at a planned pace in defined areas, so that products are in the shops when consumers go to buy
e)  Ensure that objectives are attainable and affordable
f)  Be positive and creative.

# ■ PROMOTIONAL MIX NECESSARY TO ACHIEVE OBJECTIVES

In the previous chapters of this textbook you learnt about the elements of the promotions mix and identified the **promotional tasks** which they can perform. During this part of promotional planning, marketers must reconcile the promotional objectives to be achieved with these tasks. The marketing manager may decide, for instance, that a large national audience needs to be informed quickly about a company's special offer. Television advertising may be costly, advertising space may not be readily available and the creation of an advert for TV may be considered too time-consuming. Newspapers or point-of-sale promotions may prove to be better solutions for the initial part of the campaign launch and a plan can be developed accordingly.

A brief justification behind the selection of the mix to be used may be necessary but do not hesitate to defend your decisions by using the facts and the constraints surrounding them.

# ■ ALLOCATION OF THE PROMOTIONAL BUDGET

The budget has been identified as one of the major indicators of what a company can afford in a specific period of time. This constraint influences the selection of the mix to be used and the plan should be completed by showing clearly how the budget has been allocated.

Costing of activities recommended should take account of frequency of use, timing of use, size of advertising space used and nature of the media or activities used. A good planner should also allow for certain contingencies in case communications need to be intensified or altered during the campaign period. A contingency figure of 10 per cent of the total budget may be recommended in order to enjoy much needed flexibility. It is pointless spending the full budget in advance because many variables may be unknown or unclear at the time of planning.

Keeping a small percentage aside provides security against counter promotions by competitors and allows for any corrective action deemed necessary.

# ■ REPORT WRITING

Before you attempt to apply the theory to practical situations, it is important to consider the need to present a promotional plan in a neat report format to the company's directors, colleagues, teachers or examiners.

For our purposes a 'Report' may be defined as a document in which a given problem is examined for the purpose of:

- Conveying information
- Reporting findings
- Putting forward ideas
- Making recommendations.

Three **rules** of report writing are:

1 Accuracy
2 Brevity
3 Clarity.

A report writer must constantly strive to make the reader's task as easy as the subject matter permits.

Some common faults are:

1 The reader is frequently required to retrace the long and weary investigations of the author.
2 In many cases, facts, conclusions and recommendations are neither clearly drawn nor presented in logical order.
3 Sentences tend to be too long and paragraphs long-winded.
4 Points are stated and re-stated too often.
5 In some cases the author surveys either too much or too little, or misses the purpose altogether.
6 Complicated formulas and extensive statistics appear in the text instead of being placed in an appendix for the reader to refer to if he or she wishes.

The purpose of a report is to place facts and ideas in perspective and to weigh arguments carefully. If the report is to be effective and to get results it must:

1 **Carry impact:** gain and hold the reader's attention
2 **Convey meaning:** it must explain clearly what the writer is attempting to communicate
3 **Stimulate:** it must achieve the desired response – or at least a response – or action from the reader.

Basically, a report should highlight:

- What the current and past facts mean.
- What problems they present.
- What changes are called for.
- What action should be taken.
- What course/s of action do you support.
- Why you support such courses of action.
- What other things could be done.

This check-list and the following guidelines on facts, presentation and style may help you to correct errors of fact, presentation and style.

## 1  Fact

Beware of:

a) Mis-statement, exaggeration, misinterpretation or omission of facts
b) Failure to distinguish between fact and opinion
c) Contradictions and inconsistencies
d) Conclusions unwarranted by the evidence
e) Vague descriptions where accurate (or approximate) figures could be used.

## 2  Presentation

Beware of:

a)  Omission of matters important to the chain of thought
b)  Inclusion of material in wrong section or paragraph
c)  Inconsistency in layout and presentation
d)  Failure to open each paragraph with a sentence clearly related to the theme of the paragraph
e)  Inclusion of irrelevant or tedious details
f)  Failure to distinguish between new knowledge and what is already well-known.

## 3  Style

Beware of:

a) Long sentences (more, say, than 18–20 words or two or three lines), long paragraphs and complicated grammar
b) Writing in too flowery or too factual a style. The reader should enjoy reading the report and yet feel throughout that it is written for reading by someone in business
c) Having opened each section with a telling comment or observation list what will be covered in the section and at the end of the section summarise the thrust of what has been covered so that the main messages are reinforced in the reader's mind.

# ■ MINI CASE STUDY

## The Chemicon Group

'Believe me, I am fully aware of the nature and size of the job I am giving you and I am also unlikely to forget the difficulty I had in getting the Board to agree to my plan. My fellow directors were very quick to tell me of the problems and commercial dangers of changing established company names and corporate images.' Robert Preston, Chairman of the Engineering Division of the Chemicon Group, was talking to Jenny Langton, Group Communications Advisor. He had just outlined his proposals, which he now had Board agreement to implement, for restructuring the operating companies in his division to bring them together under a single new company name.

In presenting his plan to the Board, Preston had argued that although the Chemicon Group had worldwide sales of some £300 million, no effort had ever been made to develop a corporate image. As a result the Group was almost unknown to the public and, more particularly, to the City and financial institutions whose support was needed in providing capital to fund the vigorous programme of expansion and acquisition which Preston was masterminding in the Engineering Division. Instead, the policy had been to rely on the creation of a good reputation for quality, service and technical expertise by the individual operating companies who, because the Group had been put together by acquisition, traded semi-autonomously under separate names. As a result the Group lacked a clear and consistent identity, and was known only through the ten or so operating subsidiaries who would, if they remembered, state on their stationery or packaging that they were 'a Chemicon Group Company'.

Preston, an energetic and ambitious man, felt that this was unsatisfactory and unlikely to help achieve the objectives he had set for himself in the Engineering Division, one of the three divisions of the Group. He had analysed the Group's present situation and found that sales and profits for the Group as a whole had been stale in real terms for some years and there was little prospect of substantial growth in the near future. However, this disguised the fact that the share of Group turnover accounted for by his division had risen from 15 per cent to 65 per cent in six years. The less encouraging Group picture was due to a rapid decline in sales to traditional markets in which long term secular decline had accelerated dramatically in the recession. His own success had been brought about by the correct identification of new high technology markets, sustained product development and acquisition and great effort in export markets. Anxious to exploit this successful foundation by moving into new markets, Preston reasoned that because of the disappointing performance of the Group as a whole it would be unwise to attempt, at this time, to build on what little Group image existed to improve communications to markets and create awareness. Moreover, because the operating companies ranged from household names to specialised services to industrial markets it would be difficult, time-consuming, expensive and perhaps impossible to create one, sharply focussed, corporate image. He had not been impressed by the corporate image campaigns undertaken in the 'quality' press in recent years. He had, therefore, proposed and won agreement that, as a first step towards greater integration at Group level, within the Engineering Division, the four operating companies should cease trading as separate entities and become part of a new company: Chemtech International Limited, which would be the trading name of the Group's Engineering Division. The name had been carefully chosen to retain a link with Chemicon, to emphasise a modern concern with new technology and to reflect the worldwide nature of the markets served.

Preston concluded his meeting with Jenny Langton by saying, 'I want you to draw up a detailed plan for implementing these changes in respect of marketing communications. You will obviously need to consider basic things such as a 'house style' for letterheads, packaging, visiting cards, promotional literature, etc. and suggest how the design work should be carried out. I envisage the preparation of a visual standards manual, to be used by the companies during the transitional phase and you should think about how we are going to ensure that those standards are adhered to. But I also want your recommendations on all aspects of marketing communications. Perhaps we should have a corporate brochure or you may feel that our PR effort needs to be stepped up. In which case, I would like to know how.

'Also the question of advertising needs to be considered. As you know the separate companies have been used to doing a certain amount of advertising themselves. Naturally I shall want proposals with bugetary estimates and a timetable for the changeover although I shall want a lot of persuading that the cost should exceed £50 000. Finally, you will be all too well aware of the need to 'sell' your recommendations to people in the new integrated company. Managers will have lost a great deal of autonomy and hence status under the new arrangements. I anticipate that you will be subject to a lot of hostility from the Marketing Services Manager of the old subsidiaries. After all, if this move goes well, they will be doing little more than progress-chasing.'

Students should use this case study to practise the techniques and frameworks presented in the analyses so far. Students are encouraged to follow the guidelines presented and to allow themselves 90 minutes maximum to analyse the case and complete the three tasks below.

**Tasks**
1 Identify prime marketing objectives and define target markets that need to be reached if the objectives set are to be achieved.
2 Decide upon the nature of appeals that need to be made, set communication objectives and clearly identify the tactical resources used.
3 Decide the budget needed to carry out recommendations. Since a budget is given, students are encouraged to present a detailed breakdown. If you are in disagreement with the budget set, introduce your premise, present your rationale, alter the budget figure and present the breakdown according to the new premise set.

*Note:*

If you are a student of the Chartered Institute of Marketing you are reminded that answers are only required in extensive note form. The examiner (in Practice of Marketing) is checking to see if you can go to the heart of the matter quickly and cover the main issues, providing concrete suggestions to the company as if you were a marketing consultant.

While part of your answer will be based on facts and inferences arising in the case some of the ideas in the answer are expected to be suggestions of the examinee, e.g. timing of work involved, budget amount and allocation, etc.

# ■ SUGGESTED ANSWER TO CASE STUDY

The tasks relating to the case study cover all the steps associated with a promotional plan already discussed.

1 a) Positional (SWOT) Analysis. To identify internal strengths and weaknesses in relation to external opportunities and threats so that the marketing objectives below are set against a realistic backcloth:
   - Rapid growth of Engineering Division
   - Appears to be a good range of products as a result of new product development processes
   - Chemicon is a well-established company
   - Technical expertise is a major source of strength
   - Aggressive leadership
   - Lack of identity
   - Other divisions of the Group are losing their share
   - Many semi-autonomous units implying lack of integrated effort
   - Internal communication problems
   - There seem to be market opportunities at home and overseas
   - Opportunity to establish identity within the market
   - Recession and frequent technology changes represent a major threat
   b) Time
   - First three months – planning and briefing period
   - Three to six months – implementation period.

(The activities to be undertaken during these time periods are discussed in detail on page 152.)

   c) Budget: maximum £50 000

   d) Marketing objectives:
   - Integrate effort of Engineering Division
   - Seek synergy of marketing effort
   - Establish a new, clear, consistent and progressive identity that will unify the separate parts of the organisation so that all divisions may benefit from corporate promotion
   - Sustain profit levels and maintain growth trends already established
   - Provide a platform for long-term expansion and corporate growth through acquisitions
   - Enter into hi-tech markets.

2 Definition of target markets – you must consider both internal and external audiences; the main audiences of interest include:
   - Managers of semi-autonomous units
   - Staff of operating units
   - Operating subsidiaries
   - Company directors
   - Directors/managers of other divisions

- City and financial institutions
- Suppliers of Division
- Government
- General public
- Existing customers of division
- Shareholders.

3  Nature of appeals
- Explain reasons for change
- Clarify positions of all involved or affected
- Quality of service will be continued
- Explanations about the actual change
- Benefits to be derived from integrated approach to marketing
- Change of identity will facilitate growth
- Define how 'Chemtech' implies modern, hi-tech, traditional company with progressive attitude.

4  Communication objectives
- Reach target audiences selected
- Inform of changes
- Seek agreement to changes
- Improve internal efficiency
- Introduce new name
- Reassure target audiences
- Maintain and enhance existing company–market relationships
- Facilitate Chemicon Group identity-building under the new name.

5  Communication mix to be used
   a) First three months
- Meetings with managers of units to explain plans, discuss their concerns and seek further ideas
- Preparation of letters and technical literature
- Announcement to staff (letters, notice boards, etc.)
- Letters to suppliers and customers
- Amend Memorandum of Association (legal requirement)
- Amend Articles of Association (legal requirement)
- External consultant for design for fresh view on proposed changes of:
    - brochure
    - letterheads
    - visiting cards
    - packaging
    - house journal
- Upon completion of all the above a **formal announcement** must be made using press releases, press conferences, company meetings, staff announcements, etc.

b)  Three to six months
- Press conferences seeking to generate editorials in technical publications or quality press, highlighting reasons for the change and Engineering Division's excellent growth
- Press releases
- Advertising in quality press to announce the change
- Advertising in professional publications and technical press
- Direct mail
- Brochures to key targets (refer to definition of target market)
- Reports to shareholders
- Reports to company's own sales force
- House journal or newsheet.

The above communication activities will be extended and supported by additional communication campaigns designed to promote and sell the company's products. Reminders of the name, products, technology, success, etc. will take place over a period of 12 months so the changes become clear in audiences' minds.

**6** Budget allocation

| | |
|---|---:|
| • External consultant fee (design only) | £3 000 |
| • Allowances for internal meetings | 2 000 |
| • Registration and administration costs of new name | 1 000 |
| • Visits to key customers and suppliers (PR) | 3 000 |
| • Allowances for press conferences and other activities aimed at media representatives | 4 000 |
| • Quality press (advertising) five days × three publications × £1000 (⅛ page) | 15 000 |
| • Professional/trade publications three months × two publications × twice a month × £800 | 9 600 |
| • Production costs of advertisements used | 1 000 |
| • Allowance for direct mail | 1 000 |
| • Reports (sales staff, shareholders, managers, key accounts, etc.) | 2 000 |
| | 41 600 |
| Contingency | 8 400 |
| **Total** | **£50 000** |

Technical literature, brochures, visiting cards, letterheads and other elements of the company's promotional material will be prepared for the transitional period only. It will form a part of product and company promotions and be covered by the individual budgets allocated to specific promotional campaigns.

# ■ MINI CASE STUDY 2

## Greenash School

### Chartered Institute of Marketing

The annual Whitsun fête, organised and run jointly by the teachers and pupils of Greenash school, had for many years been a popular occasion in Ashton. It was, by tradition, the 'done thing' to support the event. Many townspeople had attended the school or had connections with it and the fête had always proved in the past to be a successful fund-raising event. Ashton is a prosperous commuter town in the Home Counties with a population of 20 000. Like many such towns it has grown rapidly in recent years and established residents have been known to say that it has lost its character in the process.

'People seem to lack any feeling of identity with the town and, therefore, with the school. Frankly, many of the new people do not have any commitment to community service in a town where they have no ties and see no need to work for the school. They feel that if they pay their taxes that is the 'end of their responsibility.' Mike Hemmings, the newly elected Chairman of Greenash School Parents' Association, was speaking at a Committee meeting called to plan this year's fête. The subject under discussion was, as usual, money and a catastrophic drop in attendance at the previous fête, which had meant that the event had barely broken even. Since the fête was the major fund-raising event of the year for the school, continued poor attendance would be very serious, especially as Government cuts in public expenditure had meant that the school was more reliant than ever on successful fund-raising for essential books and equipment.

Analysing possible reasons for the sudden drop in popularity of an established event, the Committee had noted that, in addition to the changing character of the community and its inhabitants, people's taste in entertainment generally had become much more sophisticated in recent years. They concluded that the undisputed 'good cause' which the fête represented was no longer sufficient to attract attendance if the stalls only sold home-made jam and the side shows were hoop-las and coconut shies.

The decision had, therefore, been taken to spend several hundred pounds on the Royal Air Force 'Red Devils' parachute display team as a big attraction which would revive interest in the event and persuade people to come along. In addition, the fête would be opened, not by the mayor, but by a TV personality, whose fee would also be substantial.

Mike Hemmings was acutely conscious that if this investment was going to pay off more money would have to be spent on publicity than ever before and new ways found to raise the money to meet the bills with a healthy surplus left over for the school. He was, therefore, greatly relieved that Frank Bird, a marketing communications consultant with children at the school, had recently joined the Committee. 'Frank,' he said, 'I want to hand over the whole of the communications task to you, while the rest of us get on with organising the fête itself. I know you agree that a few posters in shop windows and children selling rather poorly designed and printed programmes to their parents and friends are not going to raise enough money and bring back the crowds. Please propose objectives, a budget, a timetable and a plan. If you can think of any other promotional devices such as competitions or sponsorships which might generate media interest and revenue from people who do not even attend the fête, so much the better. All aspects of our communications, even down to a 'house style', should be looked at. Above all our approach must be exciting and original, though of course, realistic with respect to the funds we are likely to have available. Our revenue target is £8000–£10 000 and you have a key role in helping us reach it.'

**Questions**
**1** a)  What marketing communications objectives should Frank Bird set for himself?
(*10 marks*)
b)  Prepare a detailed promotional plan to achieve these objectives.     (*25 marks*)
**2**  Comment on any aspect of the communications task that interests you. (*15 marks*)


# ■ SUGGESTED ANSWER TO CASE STUDY 2

The examiner has not asked for a detailed analysis, therefore useful suggestions, in note form, are justified. Bear in mind that schools do not have much surplus money for preparing such events and rely considerably on the efforts of the children, their parents, teachers and other volunteers.

Your answer must be structured in the way described in this chapter (see pages 142–5).

1  a)  Marketing communications objectives
   - Announce and remind community members of the school fête
   - Explain the importance of the fête to the survival of the school
   - Present the fête as a vital means of preserving educational standards
   - Present the main attractions (see later part of the suggested answer on attractions)
   - Seek to obtain free publicity by attracting the attention of media owners
   - Seek maximum exposure within the community
   - Present the fête as part of the community's tradition – particularly personal values and character – while emphasising the forward looking nature of the school
   - Create interest and build enthusiasm
   - Inform of date and times
   - Protect the school's credibility while attempting to maximise attendance
   - Reach revenue targets set within the budget (see (iv) below)
   - Establish an effective platform for future fêtes of similar nature.
   b)  Promotional plan
      (i)  Target audiences which they must try to influence
      – local press; editorials and free publicity will inform, encourage and possibly stimulate members of the community into attending or participating in the fund-raising activities of the school
      – local radio (see above).
      – local or regional TV

– all members of the community
– local businesses; i.e. craft shops – may provide free products for competitions or prize draws and/or participate in the fête
– local celebrities must be invited to attend or encourage others to attend
– members of staff
– parents' association    } can be involved in the activities leading up to the fête as well as during the fête
– school pupils
– past pupils

(ii) Appeals – promotional message/themes

– 'Help the school in meeting demands of the future' – particularly technical and educational
– 'Red Devils come to town'
– 'A day out full of fun'
– present the fête entertainment 'package'
– celebrity opening
– runs/walks or treasure hunts, involving pupils
– parents' events
– teachers' events
– prizes/draws
– canteen
– excellent and unusual children's entertainment and activities – including team events between classes
– picnic areas
– open day (people attending the fête will have the opportunity to see school facilities)
– displays of past and current work and photos of old and current pupils
– short school play
– tasty food and drink for all ages at attractive prices
– events in the open and under cover in case of poor weather.

(iii) Promotional mix

– billboard posters around the school informing pedestrians and motorists of the event
– advertisement cards/posters in libraries, supermarkets, etc.
– lively letters to parents informing them of the value of their attendance
– letters to addresses of previous pupils who may now be adults – stressing the nostalgic aspects of the day and the desire to see them again
– using parents who are helping with the fête to spread the word to their friends and encourage others to attend
– using a raffle through pupils and/or their parents to generate interest and commitment to attend
– prizes from local businesses
– editorials in local press
– radio announcements
– free space for posters obtained from local businesses – particularly retail premises

- parents place posters in their windows
- leaflet distribution by pupils
- ticket sales by pupils, teachers, parents and other interested parties
- local celebrities should be encouraged to be supportive and to attend (no fee involved).
- events on the day will not involve any fees being paid to event organisers, e.g. karate, American football displays, traditional dance displays, etc.

(iv) Budget

| | |
|---|---:|
| - leaflets – production cost only 10 000 at £35 per 1000 | £350 |
| - posters (say 500) production cost only | 200 |
| - competitions – cost of literature and tickets | 100 |
| - public relations (travelling and personal expenses for committee members/teachers – most parents involved will do this for nothing) | 100 |
| - Red Devils (parachute display) | 400 |
| - contingency | 250 |
| | £1400 |

*Note*: If air displays and parachuting are not possible an alternative such as helicopter trips or horse rides may be arranged.

Avoid cash donations – unless for specific equipment, facilities, etc. – as they may demean the school. Prizes should be preferred so that they can be used for competitions/raffles.

2 The question relates to communication tasks which could interest Frank Bird. The nature of the problem being faced should encourage the examinee to concentrate on public relations activities which could generate enough interest in the school fête.

Main areas of interest could include:

a) Parent relations
b) Community relations
c) Media relations
d) Sponsorships
e) Generation of free publicity
f) Press releases
g) Negotiations for advertising space
h) Free prizes for competitions prior to and during the fête.

You should discuss the above and explain the communication tasks related to (a) and (h) as explained in earlier chapters – in particular, public relations (see Chapter 6). Remember that £1400 is a high expenditure for most state schools and, therefore, obtaining funds prior to the event via raffles, donations or conversely by reducing costs through free printing/photocopying services all help.

# PART 3

# Marketing planning

# 9 Sales forecasting and test marketing

The third part of this textbook attempts to collate all the theories covered in the previous parts into one meaningful total, the 'marketing plan'. This document summarises all the decisions relating to the company's planned marketing objectives, strategies and tactics and is a vital guide for everybody working within the organisation.

The objective of this chapter is to identify the information marketing management requires for planning and control purposes and for developing the marketing plan. Two major areas where information will be needed are future sales, and the acceptability of the company's current and/or new products to the market. This chapter examines sales forecasting and test marketing as part of developing a marketing plan.

## ■ SALES FORECASTING

*Any method of forecasting is better than none at all.*

The word **forecast** possibly represents one of the most misused terms in marketing; it is linked to wild estimates, personal expectations, complicated mathematical calculations often of little meaning, or even simple guesses based on past information which are of little use to a future situation or event. Three terms used in relation to forecasts are: projections, predictions and forecasts.

### Projections

Projections describe the activity of extending a series of past data into a future period, based solely on established trends revealed by the data. Assuming, for instance, that the sales revenue of a company has grown from £10 million three years ago, to £11 million last year and to £12.1 million this year, there is an underlying trend of 10 per cent growth per year over the three year period. A projection into next year will automatically offer a figure of £13.31 million, extending the 10 per cent growth. However, at least six sets of past data are usually required to be able to extend (extrapolate) past data into the future with any accuracy.

## Predictions

Predictions, as opposed to projections based on past events imply an element of guesswork or subjectivity. These factors may, however, have some relevance when determining future outcomes. For example, if there is an expected downturn in the economy, possible loss of a major customer account or an anticipated increase in the supply of materials for production then it would be reasonable to assume that any prediction should be modified to take account of these aspects.

## Forecasts

The term forecasts is used more widely in marketing and brings together the elements of projections and predictions based on the knowledge and experience of people involved in the day-to-day marketing effort. Marketing sales forecasts are:

> *estimates in numerical form of the expected future sales of products or services of a company or an industry nationally, internationally or within a defined market segment.*

This definition is extremely important as past information cannot be totally relied on to determine what the future may hold. Economic, technological, social, political and internal changes are inevitable, and affect companies and products in an unpredictable manner. The activity of sales forecasting encourages detailed examination of past and present and consideration of the future to obtain a reasonable numerical estimate.

## ■ USE OF SALES FORECASTS

Sales forecasts must be viewed from the marketing viewpoint rather than as an activity designed to simply predict sales. The heart of the marketing philosophy is the ability of a company to predict or respond to business environmental changes in a way which maximises profitability through customer satisfaction. Profits from satisfying customers is not automatic; it is the reward of careful planning, continuous monitoring of needs and wants evident within markets, and the selection or adaption of the most appropriate products and marketing approach to maximise the degree of 'satisfaction' offered. Sales forecasting will *not* guarantee perfect prediction of future events, but by forcing marketing management to look into the past, the present and the future, it can be an aid in the selection of the most attractive marketing mix. As forecasts are so important in the planning of future activities, it is necessary to identify and evaluate the most popular forecasting techniques in order to appreciate the value, complexity and limitations of sales forecasting as a marketing activity.

# ■ FORECASTING TECHNIQUES

Forecasting involves both past data and people's knowledge, so the most widely used forecasting techniques may be divided into two main approaches, namely:

1 **Qualitative techniques**, which rely on people's opinions, expectations, perceptions, value judgements or educated guesses. Some researchers dismiss them as personal, subjective or even highly emotional, but before rejecting them one must consider another valuable asset, experience. Company executives, sales staff or retailers with many years' experience are often better judges of a situation than statisticians relying on numbers to prove their case. Inaccuracies or mistakes are inevitable but their estimates are significant in terms of forecasting techniques, and of particular use are:

a) Sales force estimates,
b) Buyers' estimates,
c) Executive opinions.

2 **Quantitative techniques** rely on statistical analysis for the construction of a forecast. They are objective but lack the value judgements of 'experts'. The most widely used techniques are:

a) Moving averages
b) Correlations
c) Exponential smoothing.

Both quantitative and qualitative techniques will be examined in more detail but in order to safeguard the relative accuracy of the forecasts developed, one must always remember to:

a) Be objective
b) Use valid numerical data wherever possible
c) Involve skilled people whose knowledge of the market, product or industry under examination is established
d) Be cautious of bias resulting from using people's opinions or faulty statistical procedures.

# ■ QUALITATIVE TECHNIQUES

## Sales force estimates

It is often assumed that the people closest to the market, such as the sales force, know best how the market will behave in the future. Their knowledge is used as follows:

a) Individual sales staff estimate the number of units they expect to sell during the forecast period.

b) The area sales manager consolidates these estimates and adjusts them on the basis of past experience. Usually, each salesperson's estimate is compared with actual sales in previous years and in the case of a new salesperson the area manager may have to evaluate how well he or she will sell in the forthcoming period.

c) The area estimates are then sent to the sales manager, who combines all the area estimates and may also make slight adjustments to develop the sales force estimate. Sales staff may underestimate to ensure they can reach future targets or overestimate to illustrate their ability and this will have to be considered when determining the final forecast. The salesperson's lack of knowledge of the total market situation is a drawback to this method. However, in small companies where there is inadequate past sales data to project into the future or where sales are erratic, this method may represent an attractive option.

## Buyers' estimates

A representative sample of all buyers in the market are requested to estimate sales or purchases for the forthcoming year. The advantage of this is that the company is not depending solely on the opinions of its own sales force, and a more unbiased estimate may be obtained. The disadvantages are that collection of buyers' opinions is time-consuming, any recent environmental changes cannot always be accommodated, and buyers may not always be totally honest. Regular research at set intervals is needed so that comparisons can be made. Sales representatives may be asked to complete a questionnaire with the buyers they visit, to obtain the opinions of current customers who will form a major element of the company's future sales.

## Executive opinions

This technique utilises the opinions of high ranking managers and executives within the organisation, with the actual forecast being derived from the averaging of these opinions. If, say, ten people are used, ten different figures may be obtained, which may be divided into 'optimistic' (i.e. the three highest figures), 'pessimistic' (i.e. the three lowest figures) or 'likely' (i.e. middle four figures). The average of the middle group is determined and the executives/managers used are then asked to respond or discuss the figures submitted, until a general opinion is formed. This technique is ideal when sales or market statistics are missing or are incomplete, or in situations where other methods have yet to be accepted or understood. Subjective judgement is, however, a major problem with this method and total dependence on it would be risky.

# ■ QUANTITATIVE TECHNIQUES

## Moving averages (MAs)

One quantitative method of forecasting is to forecast by extrapolating (projecting forwards) the moving average as a trend. By averaging out the sales figures the erratic and seasonal nature of sales is eliminated and it is possible to identify the underlying trend. The monthly sales for a particular period are added together and divided by the number of months, as illustrated in Table 9.1:

**Table 9.1**

| Year | Quarter 1 | Quarter 2 | Quarter 3 | Quarter 4 |
|------|-----------|-----------|-----------|-----------|
| A | — | — | 300 | 320 |
| B | 360 | 260 | 300 | 320 |
| C | 370 | 280 | 280 | 326 |
| D | 360 | 270 | — | — |
| TOTALS | 1090 | 810 | 880 | 966 |
| Averages for the particular quarter | 363.33 | 270 | 293.33 | 322 |

The average sales for each quarter and the approximate degree by which each quarter's actual sales deviated from the average sales figure can be seen in the table. If the average figures are used as a trend, they can be extended into the forthcoming period, an averaged actual sales deviation from the trend can be added and the result is the actual forecast for the forthcoming period. This is illustrated in Figure 9.1 (page 164) and in the key below it. If sales figures are curving significantly then a curvilinear 'line of best fit' can be statistically determined for extrapolating the MA trend into the future, as illustrated in Figure 9.2 (a and b). The examples used are simplistic – to provide you with a general idea of how the quantitative method works.

### ADVANTAGES

1 MAs work on past data so optimistic or pessimistic predictions of management are eliminated; moving averages solely consider the past performance of the company in forecasting the future position.
2 The method is objective, relying solely on actual figures and statistical formulas.
3 It irons out fluctuations in sales enabling managers to evaluate why actual

Figure 9.1

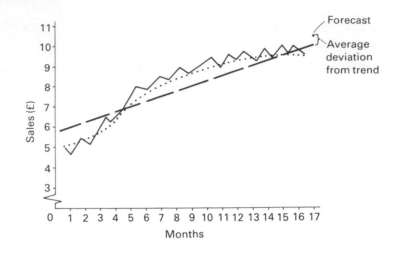

**Key:**

—— Actual sales (AS)

···· Moving average indicating the underlying trend

— — Approximate line of best fit drawn through the moving average line to take the general trend into the future

} Average seasonal deviation between the moving average and actual sales added back (or subtracted where necessary) to obtain forecast

Figure 9.2

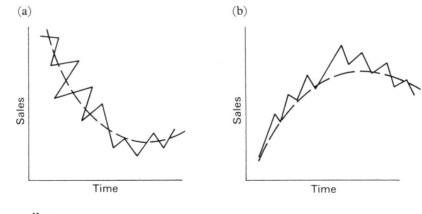

**Key:**

—— Actual sales

— — Curvilinear line of best fit

sales for a particular period deviated from the trend (which constitutes deseasonalised data).

4 Figures as forecast can be plotted on the same graph as actual sales figures which is not always possible with other methods.

## DISADVANTAGES

1 Little allowance is made for the most recent performance of the company as figures are evened out.

2 It relies on past performance and data which when averaged may be several months old. Averaged sales figures are graphed between the actual sales figures as they are an average of the actuals. Therefore, the more figures used to average e.g. 12 months, the more likely the averaged figures will be out of date. The 'moving' part of the term 'moving averages' in fact arises because as time goes by we are constantly re-evaluating the averages (for a particular number of months, quarters, etc.) and therefore all figures for sales and the trend move forward.

3 It takes no account of other actual facts that may exist that have affected, or will affect, sales, e.g. the direct correlation between sales of a company and some external or internal factor (see Correlation below).

# Correlation

This is another statistical method that determines the degree of relationship between two activities or events. If there is a strong and useful relationship between a company's sales and some other activity or event it may be possible to use this knowledge to forecast future sales. For example, if historically an increase in the purchase of cars by 5 per cent has always meant an approximate increase in steel purchases from a company of 4 per cent you may assume that there is a strong correlation (relationship) between car sales and the company's steel sales figures. The degree of strength of the relationship may be determined by a statistical formula (coefficient of correlation); calculators and computers are likely to be used for this purpose. The method however, does rest on the assumption that there is a relationship between sales of the product in question and some other activity, and that the relationship is significant enough to be useful for forecasting. This may be the case with regard to sales resulting from advertising, i.e. as advertising increases so do sales, but it may be difficult to find other external factors that will correlate – or should – with the company's sales.

It is important that you appreciate when correlation may or may not be used. You cannot, for instance, use correlation simply because two activities have a strong similarity. For example, the sales of pigs in Germany may continuously and perfectly correlate with the sales of televisions in America but common sense tells us that the sale of one does not affect the other; thus, a correlation for useful purposes is not possible. It should also be recognised that a positive relationship between two activities is not always necessary for correlation to exist. It may be, for instance, that an upward turn in one activity causes a downward (rather than upward) movement in another business activity, e.g. an increase in the production of a plastic item will mean less sales of the same item made in metal.

### ADVANTAGES

1 Using correlation enables management to evaluate the effect of other activities on their own company's activities and the degree of any effect.
2 May be more accurate than the company's internal forecasts; e.g. a national strike by a large group of electrical engineers will cause an immediate downturn in the sales of electrical equipment manufactured. Other events that may affect a company's forecast may be an oncoming recession, foreign competition, use of alternative products by consumers/users, etc.

### DISADVANTAGES

1 Spurious correlations may be heeded which, when closely analysed, have little affect on the company's performance.
2 Management may adopt a passive posture believing that their personal efforts can have little affect on the company's fortunes as the company's activities depend on the performance of another industry.
3 Management may begin to ignore the limitations of the correlation. With correlation there must be a variable that is independent of the other and yet effects the other. For example, advertising expenditure may be considered independent of sales and yet affect sales, but for how long? Continually spending extra on advertising will not mean that sales continue to expand at the same rate. Therefore, the correlation takes place within limitations.

## Exponential smoothing

A forecasting method becoming increasingly popular is exponential smoothing which involves attaching a weighting to current sales figures in order to forecast the sales expected in the forthcoming period. The weighting given – which is between 0 and 1 and is referred to as the **smoothing constant** – takes account of past performance while giving more credence to current performance. Multiplied by recent sales figures a projected figure emerges which evens out some of the erratic movements that can take place when forecasting only with actual sales figures. This is somewhat analogous to attaching a counterweight to a pendulum to stop it swinging too erratically. The smoothing constant keeps the forecasted sales on an even footing.

### ADVANTAGES

1 The company can be selective in choosing only what it considers to be relevant past sales figures to obtain a smooth constant which is particularly pertinent to the current nature of the company's sales.
2 Once the smoothing constant is determined the method is easily applied and

thus it is useful for companies needing to forecast sales for many products with widely different sales patterns.

3  The method is ideal for rapid short-term forecasting in order to control stocks. Many companies use this form of sales forecasting and link it with controlling ordering, stocks and production. If a company knows what sales it expects over the next month to three month period it knows what it must order, produce and stock. This operation is usually computer-controlled.

4  The weighting can be adjusted quickly to meet recent changes without lengthy statistical workings.

## DISADVANTAGES

1  It does not exhibit the underlying trend.
2  If weighting is not handled properly over or under forecasting and ordering of stocks may take place at great cost to the company.
3  It is more appropriate for short-term forecasting.
4  Management may be over-cautious or optimistic when choosing actual figures to use.
5  Takes no account of factors that may be relevant, e.g. an anticipated recession.

# Combining qualitative and quantitative methods

### MODEL BUILDING

This again employs statistical methods but allows for the input of variables that are qualitative as well as quantitative. The object is to build a model for the major variables that affect sales such as price, seasonality, pattern of previous sales, etc., that attempts to simulate the real situation. The advantage is that assumptions may be made, a variable changed and then an estimate of future sales instantly predicted. Because such modelling is normally done on computer, the result can be seen immediately.

The problem is in determining the right variables to input the value of those variables. Nevertheless, this method is becoming more popular and does cause marketers to consider closely all the major factors that may affect sales.

### FORECASTING WITHOUT PREVIOUS DATA

If a new product is to be launched then clearly past data on sales on which to make a forecast of possible future sales is unlikely to exist. Yet a forecast must be made in order to know the quantities to produce.

For the large companies selling nationally to consumer markets the most accurate method is probably a **test market** (see pages 169–72) which tests the response of the market itself as well as all aspects of the marketing mix. However, for the smaller company or sole trader with limited finances this method is not feasible. A useful method for companies with many outlets is a **test shop.** A large chain of clothes shops may, for instance, sell a new range of clothes in only one of their shops initially. This shop will be in an area that roughly represents the buying behaviour of the national market. Once they see how the range sells over a period of time in the one shop the information can be used to forecast how much they may expect to sell nationally.

For many companies and sole traders a mixture of field and desk research may be necessary, using primary or secondary information or a mix of both. For example, a sample of target consumers may be asked to test/taste a product and would then be questioned to determine if they would buy it and what price they would expect to pay. The figures (proportion willing to buy) may then be related to the target market in which the product will be launched.

Sometimes the forecast will have to emanate from the company itself rather than from the market place. For example, the development of a new car has to be kept secret until the day it is launched for fear of competitors' activities in response to a new model. In this case the company must rely more on its executive experience and opinions, information gleaned from testing the product, comparing its qualities with competitors' products, by relating to sales for the old model and considering the state of the economy and current demand levels.

## COMBINATIONS

As already indicated all the forecasting techniques suffer from certain limitations and so a combination of methods is most popular. Selection of the combination to be used will depend on the following criteria:

1  Availability of relevant data
2  The cost of gathering and processing the data to be used
3  The overall purpose of the forecast (production, purchasing, sales planning or even general curiosity about the future)
4  Detail required
5  Accuracy expected – this will depend on the nature of operations; in the case of a company generating £100 million of sales per year a 10 per cent error is equivalent to £10 million while for a company reaching sales equal to £150 000, a 10 per cent error may be more acceptable
6  The frequency of the forecast – the more frequently the exercise is repeated, the easier it is to update data and identify errors already made
7  The skill and knowledge of the company's staff involved in forecasting.

## SUMMARY

There are no absolutes in sales forecasting but using a methodical approach will help, i.e.

1  Using a quantitative method first – if possible – and then adjust the forecast as a result of other information, e.g. a large customer recently acquired.
2  Always use as many methods as cost effectively as possible – even mixing qualitative and quantitative methods – so that they can operate as a cross-check on one another.
3  Choose the method(s) appropriate to the situation, e.g. for forecasting for an

unlaunched product, or for many products, or where there is plenty of past data, etc.

# ■ TEST MARKETING

Sales forecasting relies on numerical data and people's opinions to enable management to project figures into the future and assess the implications of any changes identified or expected. Test marketing represents an equally vital activity but has the advantage of using an actual market area and thus, actual market data is obtained. Test marketing represents:

*the launch of the product in a small but representative area of a national market in order to assess the level of success to be expected, under real-life conditions.*

In other words, before a company commits itself to the massive expenditure associated with a national launch a small test is undertaken in order to evaluate:

- Whether the product is acceptable to the targeted consumers and the members of the trade
- All the elements of the marketing mix which the company has opted for
- The level of sales which can be achieved and the level of profitability which can be reached
- Any areas of improvement which are necessary before the national launch (different package, lower or higher price, advertising theme used, etc.)

Test marketing is often referred to as a mini-launch because it is similar to a 'small' launch situation in a small segment of the total market. It must not be confused with the term 'market test' as a market test may simply be a market survey on one element of the marketing mix. Test marketing is a broader form of research covering all elements of the marketing mix, and attempting to reveal positive or negative relationships between these elements. The relatively low price, for instance, may be contradicted by the 'up-market' profile of the product; distributors may not accept the trade incentives offered; advertising campaigns used during the test may fail to maximise interest in or awareness of the new product.

Such a vital operation for many medium to large sized companies selling nationally must be carefully planned, implemented and controlled. The steps which follow are a guide to ensuring the successful outcome of a test market.

1 **Establish clear objectives relating to the test market operation.** Objectives may relate to expected sales revenues, profitability, assessment of consumer reactions, product positioning in the market or any other issue of interest to the company.
2 **Define criteria of success.** Test marketing is a means of assessing the risks associated with a new product about to be introduced into a highly competitive market. Risks do not always relate to revenue alone. For example, poor or inadequately tested products may have adverse effects on the company's reputation which in turn creates problems for the company's products already on the

market. Unfavourable publicity, retailers' dissatisfaction, complaints from consumers or high financial losses can all prove extremely problematic even to well-established companies. The company must decide in advance, therefore, what constitutes 'success' or 'failure' so that they can compare actual results to predefined expectations. Failure to reach these standards may lead to product withdrawal but at least such an action can be professionally justified.

3 **Select representative markets (test markets).** The characteristics of the market chosen for the test must closely resemble the characteristics of the product's target market. Consider the situation where a sample of consumers needs to be drawn for research purposes: membership of the sample must be representative of the total universe it is expected to represent. The same rule applies in the case of the test markets, but in this case geographical areas are used, which must satisfy the following criteria:

a) They must be large enough to be representative of a much larger national market.
b) They must have a distribution and retail outlet system similar to that nationally.
c) They must include all demographic groups in proportions similar to those evident nationally.
d) They must have all the necessary marketing communication services that are normally available nationally.
e) They must not be unusually affected by unemployment levels or seasonal factors (holiday resorts, etc.); any data collected in such markets may prove biased and untrustworthy.
f) They must be relatively isolated so that they are not strongly affected by passing or spasmodic purchasers.

4 **Decide upon the duration of the test.** No clear-cut guidelines are laid down here but the following factors must be considered:

a) Finance available for the test
b) Accuracy required – the more accurate the results required, the longer the duration of the test
c) Replacement cycle of the product – this refers to the product's useful life (replacement purchases made by consumers) and is an indicator of the number of likely opportunities given to consumers to purchase and, hopefully, repurchase. The higher the number of repurchases included in the data collected, the more reliable the information will be for forecasting sales for a national launch. No test market should be stopped until the level of re-purchasing is established, so that steady levels of national sales can be determined
d) Intensity of competition and ability to imitate the new product. Overtesting offers the opportunity for competitors to become aware of the new product, evaluate it, monitor the company's test marketing operations and prepare for any likely launch with counter strategies. A test market must be kept as confidential as possible and retail outlets must be monitored so that competitors cannot spoil the test, for example by buying up large amounts, or making

extraordinary sales efforts in the test area resulting in misleading test market findings.

e) Number of marketing variables being tested. As already indicated, all elements of the marketing mix may be included in the test marketing operation and the sheer number may delay the collection and evaluation of the necessary information.

Assuming the first four steps have been taken in the manner described and assuming all evaluation criteria have been finalised, the company is now ready to implement its test marketing operation and begin to evaluate its new product.

5 **Implementation and monitoring of test marketing operations.** This phase of the operation relates to the actual test and can be divided into a series of sub-phases:

a) Evaluate the overall situation of the market before the test actually begins. Consumer preferences, sales of competitors' brands, attitudes to the type of product to be tested and types of outlets preferred by consumers should be investigated and evaluated. Conventional research techniques, i.e. field and desk research, can help and information collected can be used for comparison purposes once the actual test market operation has started.

b) Implement the test marketing programme. Caution is needed at this stage, because many companies create a very biased situation by using marketing tactics which do not represent a truly normal situation. For instance, using the best sales people, launching intensive advertising campaigns, introducing unrepresentative merchandising or trade promotions and implementing extensive consumer promotions. If the programme used is not indicative of what might happen in a true market launch situation, the results of the test will be distorted by unrepresentative marketing activities. During the test, research should concentrate on monitoring market movements, consumer buying habits, reactions to the new product, sales actually achieved, degree of 'switching' from other brands, etc. Professionalism is necessary during this phase; professional research services are provided for companies contemplating a test market.

c) Once the test marketing operation is complete and the product is taken out of the test market, additional research must be undertaken in order to determine the 'after-effects' of the test. Trade and consumer representatives should be approached in order to obtain honest assessments of the test operation and comparisons must be carried out involving the 'before' and 'after' data collected.

Upon completion of these three phases, the company should evaluate all the facts collected and decide about the future of the product. Product elimination, product adjustments and marketing modifications are a few of the aspects that may be considered before decisions to launch nationally, how much to produce and the marketing mix to use, are taken.

An example of a product which enjoyed attractive test marketing results is a brand of instant coffee test marketed in the USA in the late 1960s. Test results were exceptional, a national launch was easily justified and everything pointed to an enormous success. Unfortunately, test marketing results did not repeat themselves nationally because the users of this new product were perceived to be lazy by their friends, relatives and associates. Sales suffered as a result and intensive advertising was undertaken to 'educate' consumers and eventually market acceptance was achieved. The brand was 'Nescafé'. The test marketing operation itself was excellent but could not accommodate competitors' counter-arguments (tactics) following Nescafé's launch.

It is sensible to conclude this section on test marketing by listing the key areas of advice in this field. The list below summarises the steps to test marketing as recommended by A. C. Nielsen, an international company specialising in marketing research.

### NIELSEN'S STEPS TO SUCCESSFUL TEST MARKETING

1   Decide on the primary purpose of the test
2   Base test targets on the overall marketing plan
3   Be realistic and objective in evaluation
4   Make comparative tests (a single test is not of any use)
5   Benefit from professional advice
6   Use appropriate research techniques during the test (retail audits are strongly recommended)
7   Study competitors' sales movements and market shares
8   Be prepared for competitive counter measures
9   Examine retailer co-operation and support
10  Study repeat sales following initial purchases (consumer panels may be useful here)
11  Seek co-ordination of advertising and sales promotions
12  Consider all factors influencing sales
13  Avoid change of plans once test is launched (may lead to bias, confusion, etc.)
14  Take into account all changes during the test
15  Let test run its course (duration varies according to replacement cycles, competitor activities, accuracy sought and cost).

Read the case study at the end of the chapter, and remember that forecasting is essential in the writing of a marketing plan.

## ■  STUDY AND EXAM TIPS

1  Sales forecasting tends to be a highly numerical subject dominated by complicated formulae. You are only expected to be familiar with the most popular techniques and to be in a position to discuss their relative advantages and limitations. Complex calculations are not necessary for the Practice of Marketing examination.

**2** Treat sales forecasting and test marketing as useful information inputs to a much wider topic: marketing planning.

**3** A broader view of sales forecasting can be achieved by referring to textbooks on business statistics or quantitative methods.

**4** Do not confuse test marketing with market tests which involve one specific marketing variable.

**5** Marketing magazines or quality newspapers often include articles or reports on current or past test marketing operations undertaken by well known companies. Refer to them, use them in examples in your examination and prove that you are up-to-date.

**6** Test marketing is one stage of the new product development process which is covered in detail as part of the Fundamentals of Marketing syllabus. The examiner will expect you to be familiar with this theory.

**7** Do not view test marketing as yet another research technique. It represents a complete research programme and it utilises a number of research techniques detailed in the first part of this textbook.

## ■ SELF ASSESSMENT QUESTIONS

Answer the following questions and award yourself one mark for each complete question that you answer correctly. If you achieve five marks or less, re-read the relevant parts of the chapter. The answers are on page 239.

**1** Sales forecasts bring together predictions and ...................................................

**2** One quantitative technique used for sales forecasting purposes is moving averages. Name two more.
a) ..........................................................................................................................
b) ..........................................................................................................................

**3** One qualitative technique used for sales forecasting purposes is executive opinions. Name two more
a) ..........................................................................................................................
b) ..........................................................................................................................

**4** Complete the sentence: Test marketing may be defined as, 'the launch of the product in a small but representative area ...............................................................
..........................................................................................................................

**5** Two criteria used in deciding upon the duration of a test marketing operation are 'finance available' and 'intensity of competition'. Name three more.

a) ......................................................................................................................

b) ......................................................................................................................

c) ......................................................................................................................

**6** Accuracy of forecasts depend on four critical issues, one of which is 'being objective'. Name three more.

a) ......................................................................................................................

b) ......................................................................................................................

c) ......................................................................................................................

**7** One criteria used in selecting the most appropriate sales forecasting method (or combination of methods) is, 'availability of relevant data'. Name four more.

a) ......................................................................................................................

b) ......................................................................................................................

c) ......................................................................................................................

d) ......................................................................................................................

---

# ■ PAST EXAMINATION QUESTIONS

### *Chartered Institute of Marketing*

**1** Evaluate three different sales forecasting methods and explain why so many different methods are used.

**2** Describe three main approaches to sales forecasting and show the strengths and weaknesses of each. Explain the type of forecasting problem to which each is appropriate.

**3** Why would it be dangerous to base marketing decisions upon statistical sales forecasts alone? What other information should be used to supplement such forecasts?

**4** Give an example of a successful test marketing operation. Describe the ingredients which ensured its success and state the criteria by which success in such an operation is judged.

# ■ MINI CASE STUDY

**Note to the reader**

You should, by now, be able to undertake the answering of a mini case on your own. However, to provide some further assistance we have provided some recommendations on the case which you are at liberty to accept or reject. As a marketing manager has to do, you must sift through all the information that you receive and determine which pieces of information you consider to be relevant and add your own ideas so that you can make reasoned suggestions to the marketing director on which a final decision can be made.

Before reading this case study, however, check with your tutor how your answer should be presented. Some examining bodies prefer answers in a listed form, while others prefer an extended essay style, concentrating more on analysis and quintessential aspects. Both approaches — or a mix — are valid, so check!

Bear in mind that absolute answers rarely exist in marketing; what matters is the quality of your suggestions. A company may, as a result of research, decide that it has three routes it may follow. However, when it chooses one it rarely has the opportunity to know what would have happened had it taken one of the other routes.

# Joy Chewing Gum

Miss Roberta Sharpless is the Marketing Manager of a leading confectionery company in the UK and she is currently facing a dilemma concerning the future of a new brand of chewing-gum called Joy.

The product was test marketed seven years ago, and even though the test proved a major success in terms of sales, it was not launched. The test was carried out in a representative city in Berkshire over a period of 17 weeks and monitoring concentrated on the appearance, taste, texture and shape of the new brand.

The product was aimed at children and young adults and it was supported by local newspaper and poster advertising as well as promotional efforts directed at the channels of distribution, e.g. local newsagents, confectionery shops and major supermarket chains.

There is a renewed interest in the product within the company and Miss Sharpless must now decide whether to launch the product or not. She must consider the following aspects of the situation:

a)  Can seven-year-old test marketing results still be valid, or is a new test market needed?

b)  Is the name right?

c)  The market is currently worth £200 million and has grown by 49 per cent over the last four years. Is there sufficient potential in the market to justify the launch of an additional brand?

d)  There is a growing trend towards sugar-free chewing gum. How will today's market respond to Joy, bearing in mind its high sugar content.

e)  Are changes in packaging and price needed?

f)  Can older adults be attracted to the new product?

g)  How will the product be launched?

h) Will the launch of a new product affect the sales performance of other brands marketed by the company in the same segment?

Roberta realises that she must discuss these issues with the marketing research expert of the company and attempt to reach joint decisions as to how to proceed.

**Question** As market researcher what advice would you offer Miss Sharpless on the research which must be undertaken in order to decide about launching Joy?

## Analysis and recommendations

You cannot make direct recommendations before you summarise the facts provided in the case study and consider the implications of these facts.

### TEST MARKET FOR JOY

Test marketing is designed to offer a 'real situation' idea of consumer's reactions to specific offers, concepts, pricing, etc., associated with a product. The problem identified in this case study is: can seven-year-old test marketing information be relied upon? These factors must be considered:

1 Consumer tastes change over time.
2 Other brands launched since the test marketing may have changed the structure of the market and overall consumer expectations.
3 Attitudes towards sugar content may have changed drastically.
4 Awareness and liking of advertising campaigns used by current brands are likely to make consumers biased.
5 The actual information collected during the test, even if it is treated as valid, presents certain problem areas, e.g.

a) The name was not tested fully. There is no information as to how consumers perceived and responded to the name.
b) Consumer test information concentrated on general appearance, shape, taste and texture. How did consumers respond to the price?
What were the prices of competitors' brands? Were current products available then? In other words the information collected was incomplete.
c) There is no information on the reaction of distributors to the product or pro-motional incentives they were offered.
d) The test concentrated on children and young adults and proved a great success. Miss Sharpless is currently considering the positioning of the product, but lacks information on the likely response from older adults.
e) No information is given as to the advertising theme used or consumer reactions towards the overall campaign.
f) The duration of the test (17 weeks) was satisfactory as the replacement cycle of chewing gum is very short. During the test, consumers would have had the opportunity to try, consider, reject or re-buy the product many times.
g) As indicated, the test was a great success, but the product was not launched; the reasons behind the no-launch decision are not identified in the case study but it is worth considering the following 'likely reasons':

- Possible lack of funds
- Risk of destroying any other brands the company may have launched in the same segment was considered to be too great
- Limited information was collected, so a launch could not be fully justified
- The market segment has grown very rapidly in the last few years and is currently worth £200 million including a total increase of 49 per cent over four years. If this trend is extended to cover the seven year period in question, the segment of the market was probably worth half its current value and it was possibly seen as too small. Consequently a launch was considered unattractive.
- One must also allow for the possibility of a genuine mistake or failure to identify and respond to a market opportunity.
- Possibly the company was over-committed in other areas of its business or was cutting back for financial reasons.

Does the above serves as adequate justification for having to re-test the product under today's market conditions in order to obtain the necessary information? Full-scale test marketing may ultimately be considered by the company but in the short-term information must be collected in relation to every element of Joy's marketing mix. Variables must be isolated and evaluated separately before the full marketing identity of the product is finalised.

## POSSIBLE RESEARCH NEEDED?
### 1 Research objectives
- Determine acceptance of the product by different age groups
- Assess responses to the product's appearance
- Obtain consumers' opinions on the proposed name
- Obtain information on taste
- Carry out comparative tests involving leading brands in the market segment
- Seek to assess reactions to the recommended price
- Concentrate on references, descriptions, reactions, etc., used by respondents which could prove helpful in devising an attractive 'theme' for the product
- Identify unique selling propositions associated with the product
- Be in a position to finalise Joy's marketing strategy, assuming product launch is justified.

### 2 Sample section
- As indicated all age groups should be considered
- Representatives of the trade must be included in the research
- Quota sampling should be recommended and justified
- Identify the criteria that will be used in finalising the sample size
- Consider the geographic spread of the target market and select samples to allow for geographic dispersion.

### 3 Research techniques to be used for the evaluation of the variables identified:

a) Package testing:
- Visual tests
- Group discussions

- In-depth interviews concentrating on the evaluation and rating of different elements: colour, shape, size, texture, information provision, memorability, attention getting, etc.

(b) Product testing. Home placement testing is ideal for this purpose and it can be supported with:
- Personal interviews
- Group discussions
- Blind tests.

c) Product comparative tests. Simple product comparisons are useless because the company must obtain a clear understanding of the following:
- Consumers' perceptions of different brands
- Consumers' perceived differences of brands
- Overall brand 'personalities'
- Individual consumer preference
- 'Joy's' standing in relation to existing brands
- Strength of competitors' USPs (unique selling propositions) and identification of Joy's USPs
- Nature of risk associated with the purchase of different brands
- Importance of major decision-making criteria, e.g. price, appearance, contents, name, manufacturer's reputation, personal profiles, etc.

**Motivation research** techniques represent the most attractive options for product comparison tests (see Chapter 3).

d) Public reaction to sugar content. A combination of users (consumers), trade representatives, dentists, general practitioners, pressure group representatives and health advisers must be considered here. Sugar content could prove a major bone of contention and public awareness of the dangers associated with sugar is likely to be much higher today than it was seven years ago when the product was test marketed.
Research here should involve:
- Evaluation of published reports on sugar and its effects
- Evaluation of medical press editorials on sugar
- Evaluation of consumer movements in taste and responses by the retail market
- Discussions with representatives of each group identified
- Discussions involving representatives of all groups, in order to examine reactions to arguments and counter-arguments.

### 4 Evaluation of information collected

Data should be grouped by type of respondent, variables considered, geographic location and method of information collection, and a series of correlations should be established. Significant results should be compared with the original test market results, in order to identify the extent of opinion change over a period of seven years.

Research findings rarely offer cast-iron guarantees for marketing decision-making and they often provide a wide variety of conflicting options. Any decisions reached on the strength of the information collected must be fully tested under real life market conditions and a repeat test marketing programme must be implemented before a launch is justified.

## Tip

Ask yourself the following questions before attempting the case study.
1 What would the risk be of launching Joy without any further research? If this is done, how should the launch initially take place – nationally or to a segment, etc?
2 Is other research justified before a launch decision takes place? If so, how much, and would it be cost-effective?
3 Is the only answer to undertake another test market? If so, in what form should the product and marketing mix now be?

Keeping such questions in mind will help you to concentrate on essential recommendations that relate to cost-effectiveness and marketing success.

# 10 The marketing plan

*If you know where you are going, all roads lead there.*

Theodore Levitt

A few years ago a student confused himself so much that he changed courses three times in a period of two weeks. The courses he chose were Business Studies, then Computing, before deciding that the best course for him was Marketing. The problem was brought to the attention of one of the authors who was the Management Studies Course Tutor at the time and after a lengthy interview with the student both parties agreed that the ideal option for the student was in fact a course in Banking. In the years that followed the student excelled in this field of study and is currently a prominent member of a well-known bank.

How can such confusion take place and how was the right choice made? It may seem very complicated but it was actually a straightforward evaluation process. The course tutor examined the student's previous academic record and discovered the main areas of strength and weakness and discussed with the student his character and future career aspirations. It seemed obvious at the time that the student had not evaluated his situation in detail. He was not fully aware of his own potential and career aspirations and thus was unable to select a suitable course for himself. This simple example highlights the basic dimensions of planning in general which can equally be applied to something more specific like Marketing Planning.

Companies operate within markets or environments which are constantly changing as a result of legal, economic, social or technological developments. They need to assess all changes in a logical and professional manner, discover opportunities which developments offer and seek to exploit them through the most efficient use of their **human, physical** and **financial resources.** Marketing research, marketing communications, distribution, pricing, product development, selling, etc., which involve these three resources play a prominent role in the attempt to take advantage of market opportunities through effective planning.

The purpose of this chapter is to highlight in detail the process of marketing planning, so bear in mind the information presented in previous chapters because, as you will soon discover, marketing planning covers all aspects of marketing activities.

# ■ INTRODUCTION

A written marketing plan:

*defines the trading position the company wishes to accomplish at some time in the future and how to get there*

Compiling a plan is not simply the writing down of ideas. A plan calls for logical marketing thinking and evaluation which in turn requires consideration of what has been and is happening and what will or could happen. Therefore, the activity of planning:

- Provokes managers into analysing what is happening and what should happen
- Encourages better management, e.g. setting of targets for individuals, co-ordination, control, measurement and assessment of what takes place
- Ensures the company re-evaluates its policies
- Helps to prepare staff for possible changes in trading conditions
- Encourages staff to feel that the efforts of the company are integrated, that management has planned and is prepared for the future
- A well thought out plan enables banks and investors to feel more confident when lending money or buying shares
- Affords management the opportunity to assess whether the necessary returns on investment will be achieved
- Provides senior management with a control document to refer to in order to check what should be taking place against what is taking place
- Helps keep monthly expenditure under control and related to planned costs and the revenue being generated
- Provides a framework for staff selection, development and training
- Helps to ensure that resources – physical, human and financial – are sufficient.

The list could go on but enough advantages have been expressed for any serious marketer to realise the value of planning and the writing of a plan to which all key managerial staff may relate.

The plan:

1 Examines the major problems in the business or marketing situation which a company is currently facing
2 Identifies the external opportunities and threats associated with the marketing of the company's goods and/or services
3 Reveals a company's internal strengths and weaknesses in order to assess the full variety of actions a company may have the ability to take
4 Establishes objectives to be pursued over a specified period of time, which take account of the internal Strengths and Weaknesses in relation to external Opportunities and Threats already identified (abbreviated as SWOT analysis)
5 Identifies specific marketing actions and activities associated with the objectives set
6 Clarifies what resources – physical, human and financial – are needed to fulfil

the plan and how they may be used – this may also include recommendations on staff training needed to meet forthcoming changes
7 Recommends the finance (the budget) required to support and implement the necessary marketing programmes.

Marketing plans will usually be required by the company at a specific time of each year but may also be required between such times in response to a fundamental change in market conditions. If, for instance, a company realises that many consumers are not familiar with the company's products or services and as a result their competitors are selling like products which are better known and are enjoying an attractive growth, the company may decide to prepare a total marketing plan with strategies to improve the awareness levels among members of the general public. Improved awareness may lead to better sales, higher profits and obviously a more competitive position within the market.

Planning is the function of the marketing plan activity which precedes the writing of the plan and its implementation, and can be considered as the:

*examination and evaluation of the past, present and future in order to decide on courses of action to be taken.*

A marketing manager with the ability and willingness to determine where he wants to go, **when** he wants to be there and **what** is the best **way** to get there is likely to be the one that proves to be successful in competitive markets. Unless these decisions are properly communicated to all concerned – against the back-cloth of a plan – they are likely to remain a collection of meaningless ideas, facts or proposals which cannot be converted into action. For an organisation to enjoy the full benefits of their marketing planning the following four **key ingredients** must be present in the plan:

1 **Specificity.** The facts and recommendations included in the Marketing Plan document must be clear, detailed and relevant to all. How many times have you been faced with proposals made to you by friends, relatives, employers or work colleagues which did not make any sense?
2 **Measurability.** As indicated, the marketing plan includes objectives to be pursued, actions to be taken and results required by the company. If these are not presented in acceptable measurable terms, failure is inevitable. How would you feel as a student if you did not know what is expected of you in terms of grades in order to pass an examination? Would your preparation be hindered?
3 **Flexibility.** It must be appreciated that all decisions made are reached at one specific point in time and are based on facts evident at that time. Unfortunately, markets change, consumer expectations differ and success of the plan is far from guaranteed. It is necessary, therefore, to make provisions for adjustments to the plan developed (contingencies) which can accommodate later facts about the market. The weatherman may forecast rain for the next three days and as a result we all carry an umbrella but this forecast does not mean that it will rain continuously nor does it mean that the rain will continue

for more than three days. Flexibility on our part is necessary and the same principle applies to the implementation of the final marketing plan.

4 **Accountability.** The marketing plan covers all aspects of marketing activity and it is, therefore, essential for communicating all decisions made to the people within the organisation responsible for different activities. These people are accountable to their superiors for the implementation and control of the activities recommended and collectively can provide the organisation with an effective platform for growth and profitability. Failure to recognise the importance of these ingredients to effective marketing planning limits or delays the company's response to market changes and may lead to substantial losses or even inability to survive.

The importance of the marketing plan having been examined, its development and its precise contents are now considered.

## ■  DEVELOPMENT OF A MARKETING PLAN

Like all forms of planning the key to success is the accumulation, evaluation and accurate implementation of relevant information. Figure 10.1 summarises the steps which should be taken in order to develop an effective plan. Each step is discussed separately so that you may appreciate all the necessary activities leading to a plan.

### Step 1  Environmental analysis

Every company exists in a certain environment. Some layers of that environment affect the firm closely, others more distantly. The firm must recognise the components of its environment so that it is prepared for changes within it. The major areas of the **marketing audit** are examined here before the three environments of organisations and the elements that may affect an organisation are defined.

The term 'marketing audit' is used to describe a:

*comprehensive, systematic examination and assessment of a company's marketing operation and environment with a view to providing facts regarding the company and its environment against which marketing planning decisions can be formulated.*

The marketing audit consists of examining and recording five major components of the company's marketing situation, which are:

1 The **marketing environment** audit, which analyses the major macro-environment forces that might have an impact on the company and major trends in the key components of the company's task environment: markets, customers, competitors, distributors, dealers and suppliers.

2 The **marketing strategy** audit, which reviews the company's marketing

Figure 10.1

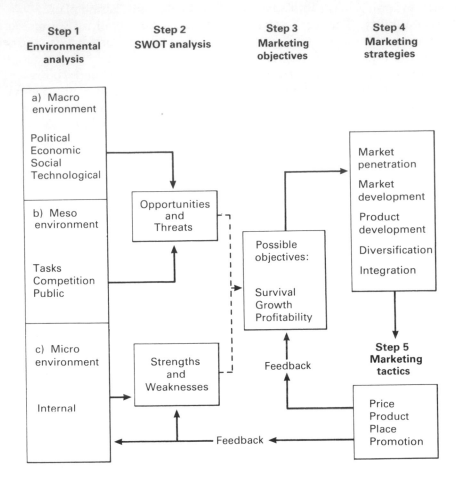

objectives and marketing strategy to appraise how well these are geared to the current and forecasted marketing environment.

3 The **marketing organisation** audit, which evaluates the marketing functions capability for developing and carrying out the necessary strategy for heading the forecasted environment to the benefit of the company.

4 The **marketing productivity** audit, which examines data on the profitability of different marketing efforts and on the cost-effectiveness of different marketing expenditures.

5 The **marketing function** audit, which involves carrying out in-depth evaluations of major marketing mix components, namely products, price, distribution, sales force, advertising, sales promotion and public relations.

The following checklist highlights the key areas of the three environments to be investigated as part of the marketing audit.

## MACRO ENVIRONMENT

The macro environment is the national environment in which a company operates; it generally has the least on-going effect on a company. Macro environment factors include:

- The economy – inflation/deflation, etc.
- Political, fiscal, legal situation
- Social, cultural setting
- General technological development.

## MESO ENVIRONMENT

The meso environment refers to the industry in which a company operates and the industry's markets, i.e.

- The market
- Total market – size, growth and trends (value/volume)
- Market characteristics – developments and trends: products, prices, physical distribution, distribution channels, customers/consumers, industry practices
- Competition – major competitors, size, market shares coverage, market standing and reputation, production capabilities, distribution policies, extent of diversification, personnel issues, international links, profitability.

## MICRO ENVIRONMENT

The micro environment is the company itself; the internal environment of which has an effect on the performance of the company and the formal and informal relationships that exist within the company. It also includes factors relating to the company's own market share:

- Sales (total, by geographical location, by industrial type, by customer, by product)
- Market shares
- Profit margins
- Marketing procedures
- Marketing organisation
- Sales/marketing control data
- Marketing mix variables as follows:

| | |
|---|---|
| Market research | Samples |
| Product development | Exhibitions |
| Product range | Selling |
| Product quality | Sales aids |
| Unit of sale | Point of sale material |
| Stock levels | Advertising |
| Distribution | Sales promotion |
| Dealer support | Public relations |
| Pricing, discounts, credit | After sales service |
| Packaging | Training |

Number of employees        Financial resources
Physical resources         Production – capacity and variety

Each one of these headings should be examined with a view to isolating those factors that are considered critical to the company's performance. Initially, the auditor's task is to screen the enormous amount of information and data for validity and relevance. Some data and information will have to be re-organised into a more usable form and judgement used to decide what further data and information are necessary for the marketing director and his/her team to accurately identify and evaluate internal strengths and weaknesses.

## Step 2 SWOT analysis

As already indicated, any information collected in relation to the different environments must be classified into meaningful sections in order to enable marketing director/managers to appreciate the implications of their findings. External information will highlight **opportunities** open to the company and its products, or, **threats** to its existence, growth or profitability. Opportunities must be definable and it will be necessary therefore, to make a variety of sales forecasts for the market and then make assumptions regarding the percentage of the market the company – given its strengths and weaknesses – can achieve (i.e. an achievable sales forecast). Further forecasting continues throughout planning for all products until a realistic sales mix and forecast is made.

Internal information highlights areas of company **strengths** or problems and limitations which represent **weaknesses.** It is easy to refer to checklists or to inform people what is a strength or a weakness but the difficulty lies in obtaining comprehensive findings and evaluating the relevant issues to complete a SWOT analysis. In an effort to highlight this difficulty, the following mini case study, from the Chartered Institute of Marketing is reproduced here. Though the case is an old one, it illustrates the approach to a mini case involving a SWOT analysis.

## ■   MINI CASE STUDY

## Firndale Toys

Firndale Toys Limited was established in 1968 as a subsidiary of Firndale Plastics Limited, a manufacturer of plastic household goods. The objective was to diversify the product range while utilising existing production techniques derived from the manufacture of plastic goods. This approach had worked well and, despite the entry into totally new markets, Firndale Toys attained a £2.2 million turnover in 1976 and made net profits of 8 per cent. Although this turnover was the highest ever achieved, net profitability was actually down on previous years. Virtually the whole of the turnover was derived from UK sales; less than 10 per cent of revenue resulted from exporting through a London agent. At no stage had Firndale Toys sought direct representation in overseas markets.

Although of high quality, the toys which Firndale produce have a relatively small unit price, with 85 per cent of turnover being derived from products selling at under £5 each and 52 per cent at below £3. With increasing competition from the East, the company is faced with considerable difficulty in maintaining its market share. Margins are being increasingly squeezed through rising costs with no opportunity to raise prices without losing sales and profits.

Having seen the results for 1976, Group Managing Director, Charles Green, has asked the Managing Director of Firndale Toys, John Caxton, to prepare plans either to revitalise existing operations and profitability or identify an alternative strategy that would restore growth and a higher return than that currently achieved. Within Firndale Toys two schools of thought have emerged. Peter Greaves, the Production Director, is firmly convinced that the products are highly saleable and of good quality. He argues that more effort is required in the market-place, including more serious attention to overseas opportunities. Charles Smart, the Marketing Director, has plenty of experience of the UK toy market and his efforts were fundamental to the earlier successes of the operation. He does not, however, have past experience of export markets. His recommendations in the present situation are to diversify the product range, particularly in the direction of larger and more expensive toys. This view is supported by the Finance Director, Tom Bradley, who wants to establish the feasibility of producing toys in materials other than plastics and in particular in wood.

Time is short, since Charles Green requires firm proposals within six weeks and to date there is no consensus of opinion as to the course of action that should be taken. Indeed, the near crisis has caused serious rifts between members of the Board. Caxton has never been a particularly forceful leader and is now undecided whether to re-organise his management team immediately or to find the solutions to the company's problems first and perhaps introduce fresh blood later.

By referring to the key evaluation criteria identified in Step 1 of the planning process we can now prepare a detailed SWOT analysis for Firndale Toys Limited by using the actual information provided.

## STRENGTHS
1 Firndale have experience in producing quality toys.
2 They can draw on the expertise in plastics of the parent company (Firndale Plastics).
3 They have established business contacts in the UK.
4 Sales turnover has reached a peak of £2.2 million which implies growth and success.
5 They are well established.
6 They have a reputation for a good quality product.

## WEAKNESSES
1 The Managing Director of Firndale Toys is not a decisive leader.
2 Too many conflicting views are evident within the organisation which imply lack of defined purpose and lack of co-ordination of effort within the senior management.
3 Staff motivation is questionable bearing in mind the unclear leadership identified in the case study and the trading difficulties of the company.

**4** The company is uncertain which of the market segments it should be servicing, i.e.
   a) 15 per cent of revenue from toys over £5
   b) 33 per cent of revenue from toys between £3–£5
   c) 52 per cent of revenue from toys under £3.
   There is an insufficient profit margin at 8 per cent net to be certain that profit will not disappear altogether if overseas competition continues or one or two key accounts are lost.

## OPPORTUNITIES

**1** To sell larger more profitable toys through their established reputation for quality
**2** To develop further overseas operations if company expertise in overseas marketing is obtained
**3** Expand current distribution network by capitalising on their good reputation and existing business contacts – a process Charles Smart has already started
**4** Maintain current major market (85 per cent under £5) through product development designed to reduce the cost of production
**5** Possible opportunities to allow prices on certain products to float up so that profit is maximised.

## THREATS

**1** Difficulties in protecting their market share
**2** Rising costs affecting profitability (reduced to 8 per cent)
**3** Increasing competition from eastern producers of plastic toys
**4** Market sensitivity to price which prevents price increases in their major market without the possibility of losing sales.

This example is a simple one. In the real life situation these SWOT factors would need closer scrutiny through a market audit to quantify many aspects. For instance, can the products be produced more cheaply without losing their quality image? Is quality the most important aspect of toys? After all, consumers are already purchasing overseas products that they may be seeing as equivalent. Where are the major increases in cost taking place, i.e. distribution, sales, production? Only when a careful and detailed audit is completed can marketing objectives be determined.

# Step 3 Marketing objectives

This is the stage when clearly identified aims are selected in order to guide the actions of all individuals involved in the marketing function of an organisation. Typical marketing objectives may include a set percentage increase in profitability and/or sales turnover, protection or improvement of the reputation of the company and its products, protection of market shares achieved and ultimately survival.

Many people underestimate the importance of survival as a valid marketing objective but you must consider the enormous financial commitments which are often made to complex marketing activities. Any heavy investments in risky projects could lead to liquidity problems, loss of morale, marketing problems and subsequent liquidation of the company or withdrawal of the product. The only possible guarantee to survival is efficient growth while safeguarding 'bread-and-butter' (essential) business already developed.

The most attractive objectives for a company depends on the situation and the best guideline is to seek to link the company's strengths to the market opportunities identified in Step 2. Look at the Firndale Toys case study once more and examine the options open to the company. Every option has certain advantages and disadvantages which must be closely evaluated before a decision is made.

## ALTERNATIVE COURSES OF ACTION OPEN TO FIRNDALE TOYS LTD
### 1 Wooden toys

*Advantages*
- Opportunity to enter a new market segment
- Opportunity to enhance profit margins, assuming that raw materials offer a higher profit potential
- Opportunity to introduce wooden ranges of toys without affecting plastic toys' sales.

*Disadvantages*
- Absence of technical and commercial 'know-how' on wood
- New skills are needed in order to accommodate the new material.
- Additional/new production facilities are needed.
- Entrance into the wooden toy market contradicts the 'reason for being' for Firndale Toys Ltd. They were set up in order to help the parent company diversify its plastics operations.
- Acceptance of proposal by Firndale Plastics Ltd may be either doubtful or only as a result of extensive research findings to justify it.
- Risky venture that may need financial support of parent company.

### 2 Concentration on overseas markets

*Advantages*
- Initial contact already made (low profile)
- Applications of products likely to be similar to UK's
- Proposal consistent with overall corporate objectives stated (they remain in the plastic toy markets)
- Possible to produce additional types of plastic toys related to the 'play culture' of children in other countries.

*Disadvantages*
- Cultural differences, nature and types of toys may need to be adapted to overseas requirements.
- Firndale Toys Ltd is a relatively small company. Current ability to support such course of action is questionable.
- There is limited international experience within Firndale Toys.

Note how disadvantages may also be seen as advantages depending on the strengths of the company and the characteristics of the market.

### 3  Introduction of larger, more expensive plastic toys

*Advantages*
- Technical and commercial 'know-how' is available.
- New line/s can supplement existing line/s (balanced product mix).
- New profit centre/s can be introduced; declining profit margins can be controlled.
- Proposal is consistent with overall corporate objectives stated.
- Toy market (UK) is growing.
- Plastic is flexible and can be used for a wide variety of toys.
- Transfer of technology from small to larger plastic toys is relatively easy.
- Quality image can be transferred to new line/s.

*Disadvantages*
- Limited profitability may force Firndale Toys Ltd to seek financial help from parent company (likely loss of flexibility and control of the project).
- Eastern competition may still be a problem in this segment of the market.
- Market is very price sensitive and this may affect the consumers' willingness to accept more expensive and larger versions of plastic toys.

The most attractive option seems to be the third one (introduction of larger, more expensive toys) and assuming the company decides to pursue it the following marketing objectives may be introduced:

- Develop new product lines for evaluation and market testing
- Finalise new product range by using research findings as justification or guidelines
- Introduce new products to the UK market within the next six months
- Seek acceptance of new range by 80 per cent of existing distributors
- Recover costs incurred in the development, testing and launch of the new product lines within 18 months, i.e. break-even
- Protect existing product range. Maintaining its natural sales growth would be the indicator that this has been achieved
- Protect the credibility of Firndale Toys as a quality toys manufacturer. Using consumer/retailer questionnaire to establish that this has been achieved
- Increase revenue by 30 per cent by the end of the first year.

The above objectives are based on findings from the case study. They are affordable because they do not involve any massive investment in new technologies or personnel. They can guide the efforts of everybody within the company and they provide the company with a sequence of aims to be achieved during the next 12 months. Any deviations or developments in the market place can be recognised and considered more easily once a thorough investigation has taken place, which will also facilitate the selection of the 'right' strategies and tactics needed for the achievement of the objectives.

Before proceeding to the next stage, a word of caution is necessary: the objectives identified do not represent typical objectives for all situations, they merely try to show the logical build-up required towards ultimate objectives applicable to one particular company. If any information inputs are changed, the decisions on objectives, strategies and tactics will change accordingly.

# Step 4  Marketing strategies

The term strategy refers to long-term courses of action undertaken by companies in order to achieve their objectives. Imagine that a company seeks to improve its profitability by, say, 30 per cent over a period of three years. A number of major actions must be taken over the three year period which collectively will represent the strategy which the management of the company considers to be the most appropriate. For example, it may be intended that the 30 per cent growth in profitability is to be obtained through a new pricing and distribution strategy. This overall strategy would then be broken down into quantifiable targets that key management personnel within the marketing function have to achieve. They in turn would determine targets for their staff to achieve.

Marketing growth strategies have been successfully summarised by I. Ansoff in his work involving the **product/market growth vector matrix** which examines the relationship between products and markets and identifies the strategies open to companies. This relationship is summarised in Table 10.1, and sub-strategies listed below the table.

**Table 10.1**  Product/market growth vector matrix

|  | **Current product** | **New product** |
|---|---|---|
| **Current market** | Market penetration | Product development |
| **New market** | Market development | Diversification |

The table suggests the company may achieve growth in four different ways:

1 **Market penetration.** Increasing sales of products in current markets through:

a)  Increasing present customers' rate usage by:
- increasing the unit of purchase
- increasing the rate of product obsolescence
- advertising other uses
- offering price incentives for increased purchases.

b)  Attracting competitors' customers by:
- establishing sharper brand differentiation
- increasing promotional effort.

c)  Attracting non-users by:
- inducing trial use through sampling, price inducements, etc
- pricing up or down
- advertising new uses.

2 **Market development.** Sell current products in new markets through:

a)  Entering additional geographical markets, i.e.
- regional expansion
- national expansion
- international expansion

b) Attracting other market segments by:
- developing product versions to appeal to other segments
- entering other channels of distribution
- advertising in other media.

### 3 Product development

a) Developing new product features for current markets:
- adapt (to other ideas, developments)
- modify (change colour, motion, sound, odour, form)
- magnify (stronger, longer, thicker, extra value)
- minify (smaller, shorter, lighter)
- substitute (other ingredients, process, power)
- rearrange (other patterns, layout, sequence, etc.
- reverse (inside out)
- combine (blend, alloy, assortment, ensemble, etc.).

b) Developing quality variations.

c) Developing additional models and sizes (product proliferation).

### 4 Diversification. New products for new markets, e.g.

a) Extension to related lines

b) Extension of company technology or know-how

c) Extension of plant utilisation

d) Financial development (investing in new markets)

e) Overseas markets adaption

f) Skill development

g) Extension to unrelated products or services.

### SELECTION CRITERIA TO BE USED

Identification of the main strategic options available to marketing management does not imply that all strategies can be applied at the same time. Selection of the most suitable strategy will, therefore, depend on the following criteria:

- Finance available
- Time required to implement each strategy; developing a new product, for instance, is time consuming and will delay the company's response to market changes/developments
- Recruitment or development of skills required before or during the implementation of each strategy
- Investment appraisal of all options
- Problems which may be encountered when switching from one strategy to another
- Adequacy of current organisational structure
- Consistency with marketing and corporate objectives
- Management confidence in the strategy recommended

- Estimates of expected results
- Ability to implement the necessary tactics to support the strategy preferred.

The last point leads to the next important issue of marketing planning and it serves as a final reminder that strategic decisions must be supported by day-to-day actions called **tactics.**

## Step 5  Marketing tactics

This step of the marketing planning process concentrates on selecting the most appropriate courses of action to be used in pursuit of the marketing strategies. Tactics represent short-term activities and may encompass every element of the marketing mix, namely price, product, promotion and place. It is critical to achieve an effective balance between these elements because any inconsistency usually has an adverse effect on how the market actually responds to what the company is offering. Imagine a quality plastic toy, distributed through prestigious distribution outlets and promoted in quality magazines, being set at a price which the market perceives to be far too low for what the product promises to be.

Test marketing provides a useful technique for measuring and evaluating the probable and actual performance of the marketing tactics under actual market conditions. It ensures that tactics are working and provides feedback to management on any unforseen problems occurring in the market which may necessitate a change of plan (for detailed examination of test marketing refer to Chapter 9). Where test marketing is impossible, alternative methods of determining on-going tactics may be necessary such as, testing tactics on a segment of the market before a national launch, or, if selling to an industrial market, testing on a few minor customers first.

## ■ THE WRITTEN PLAN

Once a final decision has been taken the plan may be written and should cover the following five areas:

- A short analysis of internal **strengths** and **weaknesses** in relation to **opportunities** and **threats** from the environments
- A preamble to the objectives justifying their selection and the strategies that will be used to achieve them
- An operations plan, defining the role of the departments and their activities in fulfilling the strategies, with timetables or schedules detailing prime events and activities
- Resources that will be needed and when
- A financial budget that will detail the areas of expenditure and amounts allocated for those areas so that monthly checks may be made on expenditure to see that efforts are remaining within the budget.

From the marketing plan individual plans will be determined for each department; everyone should be clear as to their department's targets, workload and expenditure in relation to the marketing plan of the company. From the departmental target the departmental managers will agree individual targets with those staff working within their departments.

# ■ CONTENTS OF A MARKETING PLAN

The following is a summary of the elements of the written marketing plan.

1 A summary of the total environment facing the company and the company's current strengths and weaknesses

2 Marketing objectives
   a) Short-term (one year)
   b) Medium-term (one to three years)
   c) Long-term (three to five years)
   Some companies may operate different short-, medium- and long-term periods depending on the nature of their business.

3 Proposed strategies and justification for strategy selection in relation to the results of the SWOT (positional) analysis

4 Tactical decisions covering:
   a) Pricing policy (including price/s, terms of sale, discounting, profit margins sought, etc.)
   b) Product decisions (design, packaging, variety to be offered, branding decisions, etc.)
   c) Distribution decisions (distributors to be used, territories to be covered, market penetration expected, etc.)
   d) Physical distribution decisions (warehousing, invoicing, transportation, stock handling, stock control, etc.)
   e) Promotion decisions (covering all elements of the communication mix covered in Part 2)
   f) Innovation decisions (new product development, commercialisation of new brands, screening procedures used, test marketing activities, etc.)
   g) Sales force decisions (number of sales staff, sales force structure, sales targets, recruitment, selection, training, remuneration, etc.)
   h) Budgets available to support all the above tactics.

5 Means of integration with all the other departments of the organisation; production, finance, personnel, research and development, purchasing, etc.

Whatever the plan, however, it must take into account one overriding factor – people. Even the finest plan is only as good as the people who have to make it work. Therefore, always make certain when compiling a plan that you have consulted other staff and considered how they will be organised, directed, co-ordinated, controlled and above all motivated into performing at their best.

Make sure that the plan is reviewed regularly by checking progress against previously agreed objectives, issue a monthly report on the progress actually made or the problems being encountered and always seek to be marketing-orientated in all decisions made. Unexpected changes in the environment may demand a complete re-think of the plan in which case the whole procedure must be gone through again to develop an alternative approach.

# ■ CONTRIBUTION AND BREAK-EVEN ANALYSIS

It is impossible to discuss marketing planning without considering the various costs which a company faces, their behaviour and their recovery through sales and profitability. Two valuable accounting techniques can help marketing managers in quantifying alternative decisions and assessing their profit potential namely; **contribution** and **break-even analysis.** Certain terms which must be used to explain these techniques are defined here.

**Fixed costs:** This describes all costs which do not vary directly with production or sales. They include rent, rates, electricity (lighting not power) and other company overheads which will have to be paid irrespective of the level of sales made.

**Variable costs:** This refers to those costs which vary directly with the operations of the company. Raw materials, cost of labour per unit, distribution cost per unit etc., will be affected by any increases – or decreases – in operations.

**Contribution:** This represents the difference between the selling price of one unit and the variable cost associated with that unit. The formula used to calculate contribution is, therefore:

Contribution per unit = Price per unit − Variable cost per unit.

For example: A company is facing annual fixed costs of £50 000. Each unit sold has a variable cost of £1 and the selling price is currently £2 per unit.

$$\text{Contribution (C)} = \underset{\substack{\text{(selling} \\ \text{price)}}}{£2} - \underset{\substack{\text{(variable} \\ \text{cost)}}}{£1} = £1$$

The implication is that every unit sold provides the company with £1 towards the recovery of its fixed costs. The remaining £1 is used to recover the variable costs. Can the company be profitable? Profitability depends on its ability to sell enough products to recover all its fixed costs, which brings you to the concept of **break-even (B/E).** This term described the point where the company makes no profit but at the same time suffers from no losses. In others words the total revenue is equal to the total costs faced.

Break-even (B/E) can be calculated by using the following formula:

$$\text{B/E point (in units)} = \frac{\text{Total fixed costs}}{\text{Contribution per unit}}$$

If we continue with our earlier example, we can now find the break-even point of the company which is equal to: 50 000 units

The company has to sell 50 000 units in order to recover all its costs to that point. Anything above this level of sales will result in profit while failure to reach this level within a given period will lead to a loss. In both cases the actual profit or loss can be calculated as follows:

(Actual level of sales − B/E in units) × Contributions per unit = Profit or Loss

Let us assume two scenarios, A & B.

A:  The company expects to sell 70 000 units.

B:  Due to recession the company does not feel that it can sell more than 40 000 units.

*Scenario A*

(70 000 units − 50 000 units) ×  £1         = £20 000

(Expected sales − B/E point) ×  C per unit   = Profit

*Scenario B*

(40 000 units − 50 000 units) ×  £1         = £10 000

(Expected sales − B/E point) ×  C per unit   = Loss

This position can be illustrated graphically by the construction of a simple contribution break-even chart, see Figure 10.2.

Figure 10.2

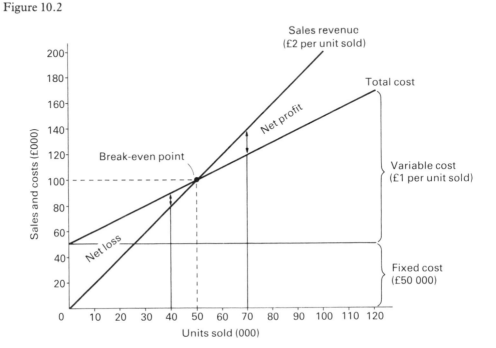

Marketing decisions can be made on the strength of these findings and companies may decide to:

- Accept short term losses in expectation of profits in the longer term
- Try to simply recover their costs before they embark on a more aggressive marketing programme
- Realise the profit potential of a market or product and implement plans of action immediately
- Seek to find ways of reducing internal fixed and variable costs in order to increase contribution or profitability
- Adjust pricing structure in an effort to achieve B/E with a lower quantity of sales
- Seek discounts from suppliers which will reduce some of the variable costs being faced – this may be linked to economies of scale which imply a reduction in cost per unit as output increases
- Delay product launches until costs being faced are more favourable
- Withdraw from the market altogether as a result of imminent losses or poor profits
- Seek to minimise losses so that overall liquidity is not affected
- Maximise profits by selling just above variable costs to obtain new orders but provided fixed costs have been or will be covered – e.g. an export order.
  Thus contribution costing may, in many cases, present opportunities for varying pricing strategies.

All these likely decisions can be facilitiated by contribution and break-even analysis which can be expanded in order to take a more global view of a situation. Consider the situation of a company currently offering five product lines to the market. Estimated demand for the products has exceeded the production capacity of the company and the marketing manager needs to decide on the product mix which will maximise the company's profitability. The data relating to the products is as follows:

| Product | Variable cost £ | Selling price £ | Estimated demand (units) |
| --- | --- | --- | --- |
| A | 20 | 30 | 1400 |
| B | 28 | 40 | 1900 |
| C | 52 | 85 | 300 |
| D | 15 | 30 | 1800 |
| E | 14 | 30 | 600 |

Total capacity of the company is 5200 units. For simplicity all product lines involve the same production time per unit, indicating that raw material and labour costs are much higher for some products. Finally, the total fixed costs for the year are equal to £50 000.

Contribution analysis encourages the identification of the product line offering the highest contribution per unit so that fixed costs may be recovered more easily (and hopefully faster) and every production hour is linked to the highest contribution possible. Analysis of the data provided will give the following mix, which will be a guide to maximising profits and identifying a profitable marketing strategy:

Product-mix ranking (contribution per unit basis)

| Product | Price − VC | = | Contribution per unit | Ranking |
|---------|------------|---|-----------------------|---------|
| A | £30 − £20 | = | £10 | 5th |
| B | £40 − £28 | = | £12 | 4th |
| C | £85 − £52 | = | £33 | 1st |
| D | £30 − £15 | = | £15 | 3rd |
| E | £30 − £14 | = | £16 | 2nd |

Production and marketing capacity can now be allocated to the products with the highest contribution, in order to obtain the following sales.

Allocation of production capacity

| Product | Estimated sales (units) | Capacity (units) |
|---------|-------------------------|------------------|
| C | 300 | 5200 |
| E | 600 | 4900 |
| D | 1800 | 4300 |
| B | 1900 | 2500 |
| A | 600 | 600 |
|   |     | 0 |

The market demand for product A is equal to 1400 units but due to capacity limitations the company may have to forego 800 units worth of demand.

The above combination will provide the highest possible profit which can be calculated as follows:

Determination of total contribution

| Product | Amount sold (units) | Contribution per unit | Total contribution |
|---------|---------------------|-----------------------|--------------------|
| C | 300 | £33 | £9 900 |
| E | 600 | 16 | 9 600 |
| D | 1800 | 15 | 27 000 |
| B | 1900 | 12 | 22 800 |
| A | 600 | 10 | 6 000 |
|   |     |    | Total £75 300 |

This total contribution will be used towards the recovery of the fixed costs resulting in profit equal to:

$$£75\ 300 \quad - \quad £50\ 00 \quad = \quad £25\ 300$$
$$\text{(total} \qquad \text{(total} \qquad \text{(total}$$
$$\text{contribution)} \qquad \text{fixed costs)} \qquad \text{profit)}$$

The value of contribution and break-even analyses cannot be disputed but like most accounting techniques they fail to allow for certain market realities which must be considered:

- Products with the highest contribution per unit may be declining as a result of loss of popularity or the introduction of better products by competitors.
- Certain products may be preferred to others because they carry greater prestige for the company. Contribution analysis does not consider this marketing issue.
- Products may suffer from low contribution per unit now but due to expected increase in sales, variable costs may be reduced and subsequently improve contribution per unit.
- There are cases of derived demand (demand for one product may depend on the demand for another). If such a product is withdrawn because of its contribution per unit, other products with greater contribution may also suffer.
- They do not allow for competitors' activities or consumer needs and expectations. This is very risky in terms of the marketing philosophy.
- They ignore the stages of the product life cycle and the marketing implications of each stage.

It is important to be aware of these limitations and use the techniques as references rather than solutions to problems. They can be very helpful during the internal marketing audit and can reveal a number of strengths or weaknesses associated with the production, selling, distribution, packaging or promotion of different products. They must always be supplemented with market information, manager's own intuition and with accurate 'yardsticks' as reference points. Failure to do this may lead to total dependence on internal accounting data which will not help a company seeking to achieve profit through customer satisfaction rather than through the satisfaction of the accounts department.

## ■ BUSINESS PORTFOLIO MATRIX (GROWTH SHARE MATRIX)

A very promising tool emerged a few years ago following the work carried out by the **Boston Consulting Group (BCG).** This tool is known today as the **product** or **business concept portfolio** and, like many effective tools of management, it is a very logical and simple concept to apply. The Boston Consulting Group analysed the relative performance of services or products and categorised them into four groups as described in the growth share matrix shown in Figure 10.3. Refer to this figure before reading the following.

Each quadrant of the diagram represents the relationship between the relative market share that the product and/or activity has achieved and the growth rate that the market itself enjoys. Both the market share level and the market growth rate have been divided into 'high' and 'low'. The theory is that most products and/or activities are capable of being slotted into one of the four boxes, depending

Figure 10.3 Growth share matrix

| | | Relative market share | |
|---|---|---|---|
| | | **High** | **Low** |
| **Market growth rate** | **High** | Stars | Problem children |
| | **Low** | Cash cows | Dogs |

10%

1

their performance in the market *vis-à-vis* the behaviour of the market itself.

When designating the terms 'high' and 'low' one can use quantifiable criteria for each of the dimensions. Thus 'low' market *share* could be defined as less than 1, and 'high' a figure above 1. Low market *growth* could be defined as less than 10 per cent, and high a figure above 10 per cent.

Before the mechanics of this planning tool are examined in detail the issues of **market share** and **market growth** must also be explained.

## Market share

The technique uses **'relative market share'** as an indicator of success or failure. The figure is calculated by applying the following simple formula:

$$\text{Relative market share} = \frac{\text{Own market share}}{\text{Leading competitor's share}}$$

For example: assuming that the market of disposable razor blades is dominated by four brands which have achieved the following market shares:

Brand A 40 per cent
Brand B 30 per cent
Brand C 20 per cent
Brand D 10 per cent

If the portfolio is developed for brand A then the calculation will be:

$$\frac{40\% \quad \text{Own brand share (A)}}{30\% \quad \text{Leading competitor's share (B)}} = 1.33$$

The answer is greater than 1 so the brand will be positioned in one of the high share quadrants. If the portfolio was developed for, say, brand C the calculation will be:

$$\frac{20\% \quad \text{Own share (C)}}{40\% \quad \text{Leading competitor's share (A)}} = 0.5$$

The answer is less than 1 so the brand will be positioned in one of the low share quadrants.

Relative market share is extremely important because it gives an indication of the product's overall position in the market, the likely economies of scale it may enjoy, the brands which present the most serious threat as well as the changes which may be witnessed over time.

## Market growth

Market growth is also used as a means of classification. Before its importance is explained consider the following questions:

a) Is high market growth attractive?
b) Would you be happy if your product or services sales revenue grew by 20 per cent every year?
c) Is market growth a source of competition?
d) Is market growth costly?

You may have answered these questions with a 'Yes', but the importance of market growth merits a closer examination of the implications of each question:

a) High market growth is not always attractive because it offers an opportunity to your competitors to grow faster than you and eventually overtake your company's product.
b) It depends on the rate of market growth. If the market is growing at a rate of up to 20 per cent then the product is doing well because it is keeping up with market growth. If on the other hand, the market is growing at a rate of, say, 40 per cent it means that one, some or all your competitors are growing faster than you. Problems could, therefore, be faced in the near future.
c) Market growth does attract competition. New brands are rarely launched into stagnant or declining markets and attractive rates of market growth breed new competitors because there is sufficient new demand in the market to accommodate any new entries.
d) It is basically an extension of the previous question and the answer is definitely, 'Yes'. Consider the following scenario:

| | |
|---|---|
| Current company sales: | 2 million units |
| Current market share: | 50 per cent |
| Current market growth: | 40 per cent |

This means that the current size of the market is 4 million units and it is expected to grow to 5.6 million units in the next year (40 per cent growth of 4 million units). If the company wishes to maintain its market share, it needs to achieve sales equal to 50 per cent of 5.6 million units (2.8 million units). If we compare this figure with current sales we can see that maintaining market share will involve the sale of an additional 800 000 units, assuming that the current level of sales can be continued into the future. Such an increase is not automatic; it will require additional marketing efforts by the company in the form of advertising, sales promotions, additional sales staff, public relations, wider distribution network, etc. All the above creates new cost centres for the company, evidence that growth can be a very costly development. Bearing in mind the importance of the two dimensions used for the development of the business portfolio matrix, we can now proceed.

The four quadrants that emerge are 'high'/'high', indicating products which have a high relative market share in a high growth market; 'high'/'low', where a high relative market share exists in a low growth market; 'low'/'high' where the relative market share is low but the market is growing fairly fast; and 'low'/'low' when both the relative market share and the market growth are low. The Boston Group gave memorable titles to the four groups, as indicated below:

| | |
|---|---|
| 'Stars' | high/highs |
| 'Cash cows' | high/lows |
| 'Dogs' | low/lows |
| 'Problem children' | low/highs |

(Two alternative terms to 'problem-children' are: *wildcats* or *question marks*. All three terms are acceptable to the various examiners but try to use only one when answering questions.)

**'Stars'** are relatively new products and are in the growth phase of the product life cycle. They enjoy high market shares and are today's breadwinners. At the same time they may require heavy investment to preserve their position in growing markets.

**'Cash cows'** are the products that have achieved high market shares but in markets that have ceased to grow. They are often yesterday's successful stars. Most probably they have reached the maturity phase and require limited investment and financial support. Alternatively 'cash cows' are very useful generators of cash, and are used in order to support other products within a company's product portfolio.

**'Problem children'** are products suffering the disadvantage of low market share yet operating in growth markets. They may be former 'stars' whose position has been eroded. They offer a useful potential for exploitation but require the addition of funds as well as marketing effort before they can enter or re-enter the star quadrant.

**'Dogs'** suffer a dual disadvantage. Not only do they have a low relative market share but they also operate in low-growth markets. Prospects are generally poor and a strong case for divestment exists. But if properly managed they can generate a positive cash flow while they are kept in the company's product portfolio.

This technique is simple and extremely helpful when devising a plan, especially in complex multi-product and multi-market environments. It enables the planner to allocate products, activities and subsidiaries into four distinct boxes, each of which has different managerial, marketing and financial needs. Such a classification can contribute to every aspect of the planning process.

The planner can attempt to calculate and quantify the cash that can be diverted from one quadrant to another. Cash acquired through 'cash cows' can go into research and development to improve the product mix and to improve the market share of the 'question marks' or 'stars' which may need additional financial support.

## Summary

- The technique suggests specific marketing strategies to achieve a balanced mix of products for the company to market.
- The competitive value of market share depends on the structure of competition and the stage of the PLC that the product is at.
- Market share is strongly and positively correlated with product profitability (BGC emphasises relative market share as the ratio of company's share to the share of the largest competitor).
- The present position of a product is defined by the relative share and market growth rate during a time period.
- The future position may be (a) a momentum forecast or (b) a forecast of the consequence of a change in strategy.

Developing a sound strategy requires a good understanding of the factors influencing long term costs and this planning tool attempts to guide marketing planners towards the most appropriate strategies for their products.

## ■ DEFINITION AND SCOPE OF CONTROL

Control may be described as

*the process of taking steps that attempt to bring desired and actual performance together.*

It is a vital marketing management activity because it is concerned with keeping events and activities on time and in line with plans and objectives – a major function of any manager.

Imagine a situation where a lot of time and possibly a large sum of money has been expended on setting objectives and developing plans of action, but then no action is taken to ensure that all activities are contributing towards the achievement of the objectives. Advertising campaigns may fail to maximise information provision to consumers, sales staff may not meet their targets, prices set for products may become very unattractive over a period of time and distributors may become dissatisfied with the service they receive. Such outcomes indicate inevitable failure and all efforts directed into effective planning become obsolete. An effective control procedure is summarised in the following steps.

## 1 Identification of desired performance

Standards are laid down for all levels in the organisation in accordance with the objectives and plans selected. They represent what is 'expected' with regard to marketing performance and identify the tasks each person or marketing unit is expected to perform.

## 2 Identification of actual performance

Upon implementation of plans of action, the on-going performance has to be closely monitored in order to ensure that the right direction is taken. It is very rare to find that all targets set have been achieved, but being in a position to measure actual performance enables marketing management to maintain a direct contact with the company's activities and environmental changes.

## 3 Comparison of actual performance against initial standards set

This is an activity which must be undertaken at regular time periods in order to identify any serious 'gaps' between actual and expected performance. Early recognition of problems will enable the company to respond more quickly, maintain its momentum and protect its overall competitive posture. For instance, if a salesman has failed to reach his first month target by 20–25 per cent then there are early signs of possibly having misunderstood the complexity and implications of specific environmental issues, of having set unrealistic targets or of having selected the wrong tactics in pursuit of these targets. Obtaining, collating, recording, monitoring and above all analysing the performance of each element of the marketing mix are essential activities of control.

## 4 Identification and analysis of deviations

The term deviation is used to describe the real difference between 'expected' and 'actual'. Differences identified can be quantitative (sales, market share, growth, profit, etc.) or qualitative (selling skills, handling of complaints, staff motivation etc.) and they must be isolated in order to identify likely causes behind the deviation. This is an area where many managers fail to respond correctly, simply because they cannot separate **cause** from **effect.**

Failing to reach a sales target by, say, 10 per cent is something that has happened and cannot be changed directly. Identifying the cause or reason for this failure, on the other hand, will provide management with an issue they can respond to, re-assess, change and hopefully improve.

## 5 Correcting deviations

The causes of the deviations identified provide marketing management with a new situation or 'environment' which they must consider in their planning. New or assessed plans are often necessary and the planning process discussed in this section may have to be reactivated in order to provide such a plan. Plans must be flexible enough to allow for adjustments and management must be positive in its thinking to accept the need for change or even to recognise any errors in assessment or decision-making; controls do not exist to check 'others', they are there in order to ensure that everybody is contributing in the most suitable and productive manner. This includes management.

# 6 Implementation of corrections (corrective measures)

The control process is completed once amended plans are put into action, all management functions are briefed accordingly, external audiences are informed of any relevant changes and an amended set of tactics become operational. This represents the same point discussed in step 5 of the marketing planning process but it now includes more up-to-date information which hopefully improves the overall quality of the plan. It is also the point when controls are re-introduced in order to assess the progress of the amended tactics and the whole process of control starts again.

The controls identified in Table 10.2 provide a general reference to the variety of quantitative and qualitative factors which must be considered for performance

**Table 10.2** Marketing controls

| Area of interest | Popular controls |
| --- | --- |
| Sales analysis | • Sales by area<br>• Sales by product line or product version<br>• Sales trends<br>• Seasonal peaks or lows<br>• Sales by type of outlets used, etc. |
| Stock analysis | • Stock levels held by the company<br>• Stock turnover<br>• Stock condition<br>• Average order sizes<br>• Buffer (safety stocks), etc. |
| Distribution analysis | • Number of deliveries per period<br>• Number and nature of complaints received<br>• Quantity of returned goods<br>• Cost of deliveries<br>• Journey times<br>• Vehicle maintenance<br>• Efficiency of staff<br>• Accuracy of invoicing, etc. |
| Sales force analysis | • Number of sales calls per period under evaluation<br>• Number of orders obtained<br>• Performance of non-selling tasks<br>• Number of new accounts being opened<br>• Mileage per sales call<br>• Cost of each order generated<br>• Total expenses over a specified period<br>• Salesperson selling skills, etc. |

**Table 10.2** continued

| Area of interest | Popular controls |
| --- | --- |
| Promotion analysis | • Awareness and recall of adverts used<br>• Response to consumer promotions used<br>• Popularity of trade promotions<br>• Nature of publicity generated<br>• Actual expenditure over a specific period of time<br>• Quality of creative work carried out by external consultants<br>• Reactions or sales relating to direct response campaigns<br>• Coverage and frequency achieved through advertising media used, etc. |
| Financial analysis | • Value of debtors<br>• Value of creditors<br>• Cash budgets<br>• Marketing expenses<br>• Profitability and profit trends (net profit)<br>• Cost of sales<br>• Gross margins<br>• Return on investment<br>• Return on capital employed, etc. |

evaluation purposes. The relative importance of each factor will vary from situation to situation but a simplified checklist of this nature serves as a reminder of the need to trace the cause of a problem. For example, lack of profitability could be attributed to poor stock handling in the company's stores, inadequate advertising, poor salesmanship, unsatisfactory distribution, etc. The factors listed provide a realistic picture of a situation, simplify the decision-making process, guide further planning and facilitate the achievement of overall objectives. As Theodore Leavitt indicated: '*All roads must lead to one specific, clearly set target*'. Efficient planning and effective control can make the target easier to reach.

# ■ SUMMARY

This has been a detailed chapter and to conclude, therefore, it seems appropriate to summarise the stages of developing a marketing plan as follows.

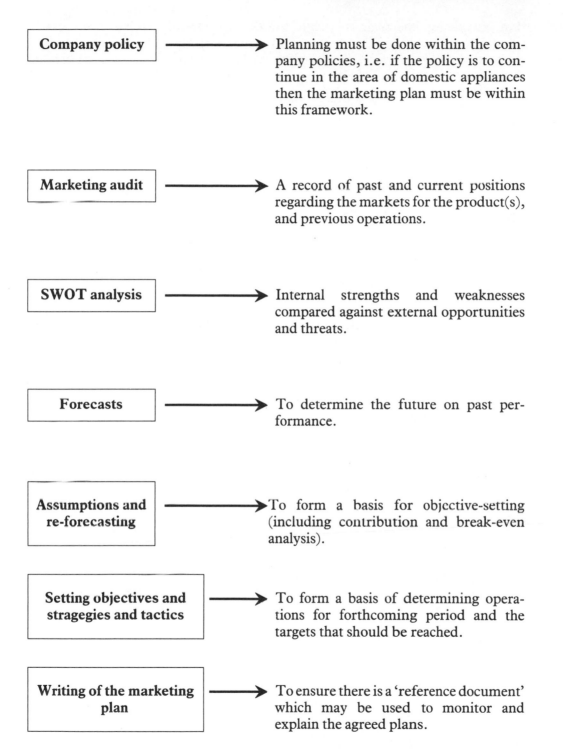

**Company policy** ⟶ Planning must be done within the company policies, i.e. if the policy is to continue in the area of domestic appliances then the marketing plan must be within this framework.

**Marketing audit** ⟶ A record of past and current positions regarding the markets for the product(s), and previous operations.

**SWOT analysis** ⟶ Internal strengths and weaknesses compared against external opportunities and threats.

**Forecasts** ⟶ To determine the future on past performance.

**Assumptions and re-forecasting** ⟶ To form a basis for objective-setting (including contribution and break-even analysis).

**Setting objectives and stragegies and tactics** ⟶ To form a basis of determining operations for forthcoming period and the targets that should be reached.

**Writing of the marketing plan** ⟶ To ensure there is a 'reference document' which may be used to monitor and explain the agreed plans.

On completion the plan is usually presented to the managing director who considers its merit in relation to the aims of the company. Adjustments may have to be made before the final version of the marketing plan becomes part of the total business plan, for which the managing director is responsible.

# ■ STUDY AND EXAM TIPS

**1** Remember that a marketing plan is not a simple document containing endless decisions on the elements of the marketing mix. It is a document which identifies, explains and justifies all actions to be taken over a period of time with regard to the marketing effort.

**2** Be prepared to discuss in detail the steps to be followed in developing a marketing plan.

**3** Questions on contribution and break-even analyses are extremely popular with examiners. You are expected to show an understanding of the contributions these techniques make to understanding profitability, cost control, objective-setting and product-mix decisions.

**4** Distinguish clearly between objectives, strategies and tactics.

**5** The growth share matrix developed by the Boston Consulting Group is an extremely valuable marketing tool so be prepared to discuss the implications of each quadrant identified. Market share and market growth implications are critical.

**6** Always use clear, informative and appealing diagrams to highlight your answers. Diagrams or illustrations should take up at least half an answer sheet.

**7** It is difficult to justify certain recommendations without the use of a simple but relevant example. Seek an example before the examinations and attempt to relate it to the key issues of this chapter.

**8** There are numerous 'controls' which different companies can or ought to use. Avoid the reproduction of endless lists of likely controls and concentrate on key areas of importance arising from the question.

**9** A marketing plan will relate to all elements of the marketing mix. Make sure you have carefully revised your notes on the marketing mix.

**10** Planning and control are two distinct functions of marketing management but they are totally dependent on each other.

# ■ SELF ASSESSMENT QUESTIONS

Answer the following questions awarding yourself one mark for each question that you answer correctly. If you answer less than six questions correctly reread the relevant parts of the chapter. The answers are on page 239.

**1** What does SWOT stand for?
a) S..................................................................................................................
b) W.................................................................................................................
c) O................
d) T................

**2** Identify three ingredients of an effective marketing plan, the fourth being 'specificity'.
a) ................
b) ................
c) ................

**3** One step of the marketing planning process is 'environmental analysis'. Name the other four.
a) ................
b ................
c ................
d ................

**4** One strategy identified by I. Ansoff is 'market penetration'.
Name the other three.
a) ................
b) ................
c) ................

**5** Complete the formula used to calculate contribution per unit.
Contribution per unit =

**6** Complete the formula used to calculate the break-even point in units.
B/E point (in units) =

**7** There are four types of products associated with the growth share matrix, one of which is 'dogs'. Name the other three.
a) ................
b) ................
c) ................

**8** Complete the sentence: Environmental analysis refers to the examination of the facts associated with macro, ................ and micro environmental layers.

# ■  PAST EXAMINATION QUESTIONS

### Chartered Institute of Marketing

1  Describe the main topics in an annual marketing plan for a business with which you are familiar. Show how each topic relates to the others and how the plan will be used as a basis for management action.

2  How do contribution analysis and break-even analysis relate to each other? What use is made of them in marketing?

3  What is the importance of the annual marketing plan? How should it be created and in particular what quantitative analysis should it contain?

4  By using an example, describe contribution analysis and justify its importance in profit planning.

5  Write a summary of a realistic (but not necessarily real) marketing plan for a product or service with which you are familiar.

# PART 4

# International marketing

# 11 International marketing

*International marketing is a little more complex than domestic marketing but the principles are still the same.*

You may at some time have travelled to another country for a holiday, to study or on business, and possibly felt a sense of 'belonging' when you came across a product, a service or an organisation which also exists in your country of origin. There is a sense of pride when this happens because you realise that a small part of your country is wanted by people in other countries to satisfy a specific need. You may have returned home with products from the country you visited because you view them as being better than the products available at home or because they are unique and exciting. Whatever the intentions of the individual and irrespective of the products or services actually purchased, the situation described represents a small example of the excitement and dimensions that may be associated with international marketing.

The simple fact is that a product or service popular in one country can be equally as popular in many others. This popularity is rarely the result of sheer luck; it is the result of a carefully planned marketing approach which identified the opportunity, developed the necessary information base through research, achieved market entry through the use of appropriate marketing channels and developed the required rate of success by using the conventional marketing activities described in this textbook for home market operations.

International marketing does not represent a completely different type of marketing technique; it is simply the correct application of the elements of the marketing mix in a new national environment. The actual operation and the overall complexity differ from the home market but the marketing philosophy and approach remain the same. Entering international markets either represents a **market development strategy** (the same product introduced into a new market) or a **diversification strategy** (the market is new and the product is adjusted to local requirements or a completely different product is introduced in order to satisfy local needs). This summarises the situation faced by companies or individuals considering international markets for the first time. Once involvement in these markets has been achieved growth can be pursued by adopting many of the strategies discussed in Chapter 10.

We cannot examine all the aspects of international marketing in the context of *Marketing in Practice* but the following issues are considered:

1 Differences between domestic and international marketing
2 Advantages and disadvantages of entering international markets
3 Investigating overseas markets
4 Direct and indirect methods of entering overseas markets
5 Organisational implications of international expansion.

# ■ COMPARISON OF DOMESTIC AND INTERNATIONAL MARKETING

International marketing implies a foreign environment within which a company may decide to operate but, as already explained, the philosophy of marketing does not change from domestic to international markets but the techniques used are adjusted to the environment being faced. There may, for example, be differences in the advertising media available, in the types of outlets consumers use in order to buy certain goods, in legislation covering the sale of goods, in language, religion or economic climate. The likely differences are too numerous to list but it is these differences which often make international marketing more complicated and unpredictable than marketing within the home market. The home market may be more problematic than selling to another country but it is rarely seen in this light as there is a better understanding of the market one has always lived in.

All the possible differences between home and foreign markets must be investigated before entry into the new market is justified. The research approach required is covered later in this section, but for now the main areas where differences may, or will, be found are summarised as follows:

1 **Language**
  ● Official language or languages of the country
  ● Existence of regional dialects
  ● Popularity of foreign languages
  ● Evidence of ethnic minorities using their native tongue.

2 **Religion**
  ● Religious taboos
  ● Variety and popularity of different religions
  ● Religious holidays
  ● Sacred objects used in the country
  ● Implications in the use of certain products (Muslims not eating pork, etc.)
  ● Power of the religious organisations.

3 **Political**
  ● Political system in operation
  ● Overall political stability
  ● General national ideologies

- Political relationships between 'home' and 'overseas' country which may enhance or deter trade.

## 4 Economic
- Size of potential markets
- Wealth per capita (purchasing power)
- Distribution of wealth among the social groups
- Inflation – or deflation – rate
- Stability of local currency
- Import taxes in operation
- Restrictions affecting the marketing of products from overseas
- Quality and intensity of local competition
- Availability of necessary raw materials, component parts, machinery, etc.
- Unemployment levels
- Availability and cost of suitable premises
- General economic stability.

## 5 Technological
- Transportation systems in operation
- Quality of communication system used: telex, telephone, fax and computer systems in existence
- Areas of expertise that the country is famous for (Japanese are, for instance, famous for electronics, Swiss for watches, etc.)
- Energy systems available. Electrical power may vary from country to country: this affects the operation of electrical goods
- General speed of technological development.

## 6 Social
- Authority and family structure
- Evidence of social institutions
- Values and attitudes towards changes, achievements, work and wealth
- Size of different social classes
- Social development of consumers within the country
- Attitudes towards products and people from abroad
- Eating and shopping habits and customs

## 7 Education
- Literacy levels
- Quality of general and higher education
- Evidence of academic or professional institutes or associations
- Overall quality of local labour force
- Availability of suitable skills for the company's operations.

All the areas identified above will collectively offer an adequate summary of a country's profile and can be used as indicators of likely opportunities or threats which may exist within an overseas country. Marketing does not change: it is the **environment** that must be faced which changes.

# ■ ENTERING INTERNATIONAL MARKETS

Entry into a new market, especially if the market is located thousands of kilometres away from the home market, will obviously present a company's decision-makers with a series of problems, worries, doubts, justified or unjustified optimism or fear. Every decision, product, service, market or company will obviously be affected differently but it is vital to consider in general terms the likely gains from 'going international' as well as the possible limitations of such a decision.

## ADVANTAGES

- An international market can offer the opportunity for a higher profit. Competition may be less intense, the product may be unique, a higher price may be possible and a greater profit may be generated.
- Products may lose their popularity in the home market and their useful life is extended by introducing them into overseas markets where demand may still exist. Many different markets can be entered over many years and companies can continue to successfully sell a product developed and launched a long time ago.
- By selling in many different countries, operating risks are spread over a wider market base and any failure in one market can be offset by successes in others.
- Success in overseas markets often improves a company's or product's reputation which will have a positive effect in both the domestic and international markets.
- Seasonal factors which affect the demand for a product in one country can be offset by operating in overseas markets. For example, the summer months in Australia coincide with the winter months in Europe. Seasonal products like sun protection products can be marketed throughout the year if the company successfully enters markets with different seasonal peaks.
- Changes in legislation, economic climate or political situations can be overcome by entering overseas markets where the conditions are more favourable to the company's operations.
- If fixed costs of production are covered by home sales it may then be possible to utilise excess productive capacity by selling at a lower price in another country, provided there is revenue generated beyond variable costs (see Contribution Analysis in Chapter 10).

## DISADVANTAGES

- International operations can prove extremely costly and can affect the overall profitability or liquidity of a company. The right method of entry for the particular company is, therefore, critical and this issue is examined in detail later in this chapter
- Exchange rates may fluctuate wildly and taxes imposed on imported products may affect demand and profitability adversely.

- Operating in overseas markets is risky because unexpected changes can lead to loss of profitability and investment in these markets.
- Competition may prove to be as intensive as in the home market or new market entries may limit the opportunities for growth and success.
- Involvement in overseas markets must often be supported by intensive management commitment. This often leads to neglecting the operations in the domestic market which can prove extremely problematic.
- Products or companies from overseas may be received with suspicion or even hostility and success may prove to be impossible to achieve, particularly if the company is exporting from a country that has a poor reputation for quality.
- Cultural and language barriers may prove difficult to overcome.

The dividing line between unacceptable risks and extensive rewards is clearly thin in international marketing and it is, therefore, critical to carry out a detailed examination of all the major environmental factors of a potential overseas market.

## ■ INVESTIGATING INTERNATIONAL MARKETS

It would be unacceptable to consider entry into an overseas market without carrying out an in-depth evaluation of its composition, trends, size and overall attractiveness. Conventional research techniques, concentrating on the collection of primary or secondary data, can be used as for the home market (see pages 22–7). The objective here is to identify the major problems associated with carrying out research in overseas markets. In order to appreciate the difficulties with information collection overseas, the following is a reminder of the major differences between domestic and international marketing:

1 Sources of data overseas may be less reliable than services available in the home market.
2 Advanced research methods, e.g. consumer panels and retail audits, may not be available in certain less-developed countries, depriving marketers of detailed information on market shares, profiles of users of major brands, regional preferences, etc.
3 Making contact with key decision makers may prove more problematic overseas. Their identity may not be known, they may be unwilling to respond, or even suspicious of information collection involving a company from overseas.
4 In certain countries it is often impossible to collect information from the potential users of the products which the company is thinking of launching. In strict Muslim countries, for example, it will be virtually impossible to interview adequate numbers of women on personal matters.
5 The quality of research organisations overseas may vary from country to country and the reliability of the information collected could prove questionable.
6 Research involving trial users of a new product or ratings of product features may also give biased results because the respondents used may be unable to

offer a reliable assessment or may be prejudiced for or against the product (new and exciting or new and untrustworthy or unproven).

7  The marketing terminology and its implications may vary from country to country. Socio-economic groupings accepted in the UK could prove meaningless overseas because a different system of classification may be used. The same problem could be evident with the classification of manufacturers, retailers, wholesalers, etc.

8  Cultural differences will have a direct effect on the importance of the 'family' as an economic unit and the relative role of individual members of the family. A woman's role, for instance, may be difficult to understand in different cultural environments.

9  Statements used by respondents to refer to the issues under MR investigation may lose their true meaning when they are translated into the language of the company paying for such research programmes.

10  Literacy levels may affect the methods of information collection to be used and may lead to long delays and often unacceptably high costs.

11  Test markets or information useful in selecting test markets may not be available so another useful research option may be lost by the company considering entry into the market.

12  Overall consumer development will affect the reliability of their responses. Products may prove too complex, concepts may be difficult to explain or evaluate and actual information may represent guesses, speculation or assumptions rather than much needed facts.

13  Climatic conditions will also affect people's preferences, priorities and actual needs. Information collected may fail to allow for the relative importance of such factors and may consequently be used wrongly.

14  Finally, the postal or telephone services may not be of the highest quality so the use of postal questionnaires or telephone interviewing may prove impossible. Attractive research techniques may be significantly limited.

The likely problems identified are not meant to be offensive to any developing or less developed nations, they simply represent a list of objective problems which can be encountered. In more advanced national markets the opposite could be the case where marketing organisations are faced with too much information, from a wide variety of sources, often providing conflicting facts on the same issues.

Generally speaking, any research programme undertaken in overseas markets should utilise the best research methods available, concentrate on the understanding of the overall profile of the country and attempt to discover as many relevant facts about the total market and the likely target market segments as possible.

Any research programme which fails to provide answers to the following questions is unlikely to prove beneficial to the information users and attempts to enter the market are likely to be problematic.

• How large is the market and are there any substantial segments?
• What is the value of the target market/s to the company?

- What is the competitor situation? Do a few companies have control of the market?
- Do the product, pack, brand, packaging need changing in any way to suit the needs of the market or to meet legal requirements? Often international companies will have to slightly change their product, e.g., taste, dimensions, colour, texture, strength, etc., and significantly change their brand pack and promotions to serve the needs of particular markets and to influence consumers in different countries.

- What is the trend in the market for similar products (if they exist)?
- Are trade credit and after sales servicing required?
- What are the promotional activities used by competitors?
- What price structure is needed?
- What promotions tend to be used to influence the market?
- Is there an adequate network for distribution?
- Why should potential customers buy the product? What are the benefits that purchasers in the particular country will receive?
- Do customers need credit facilities?
- Does the language in promotions require changing?

Some information may be available within the country of origin of the marketing organisation. Students are reminded that relevant desk research must always be undertaken before extensive funds are committed to field surveys in overseas markets.

The following list is a summary of the main sources of information which can be used by a UK based company seeking data on overseas markets:

1  The British Overseas Trade Board (BOTB)
2  Department of Industry Statistics and Market Intelligence Library
3  The Exporter's Bank
4  The local Chamber of Commerce
5  The exporter's Trade Association
6  The executives of the UK Forwarding Agents
7  UK market research organisations specialising in international trade such as the 'Economist Intelligence Unit'
8  The Export Credit Guarantee Department (ECGD)
9  The Confederation of British Industry (CBI)
10  The Institute of Export
11  UK embassies of foreign countries
12  Foreign Information Bureaux in the UK
13  The Statistics Office of the EC (EUROSTAT)
14  Appropriate newspapers and journals, e.g. *Export, Marketing, The Financial Times, The Economist.*

Similar sources of information will exist in most developed countries in the West. Many international organisations may also be added to this list depending on the information needed, e.g. the IMF, World Bank, UNICEF, etc.

# ■ DIRECT AND INDIRECT METHODS OF ENTERING OVERSEAS MARKETS

Assuming that a decision to enter overseas markets has been finalised and assuming the actual country to be entered has been selected, there is a need now to examine the different ways in which a company can enter the market. All methods offer marketers advantages, ideal for certain situations, but they also suffer from various limitations. The positive and negative aspects of the different methods are highlighted here so that comparisons of the methods can be facilitated.

The six most common methods of entering overseas markets are:

1  Direct exporting to overseas customers
2  Use of agents
3  Use of branch offices overseas
4  Use of manufacturing unit/company
5  Joint ventures
6  Franchising.

The first two tend to relate to exporting, the fourth to international business and the rest to marketing internationally, though they may be mixed, e.g. a manufacturing/marketing unit may be established from which a franchising system is set up.

## Direct exporting

Direct exporting can be defined as 'selling to customers in another country from your home base'. This method of entry does not involve any major financial risks. It helps a company to generate additional funds through extra sales to overseas customers and can also be seen as a way of testing the popularity of a product in international markets. There are, however, three serious marketing limitations which must be considered:

1  There is no control over the use, or even abuse, of the products sold to overseas customers. If a product is applied wrongly or is promoted inadequately to overseas consumers by the importing companies which have bought it, a poor reputation for the product may develop. If at a later stage the exporting company decides to commit itself to the overseas market and attempts to market the product on a large scale, adverse reactions by the consumers may prove extremely problematic.
2  Product imitation by overseas manufacturers may occur. When a product is sold to somebody overseas, there is a transfer of technology taking place. Somebody may buy it, examine it, test it, evaluate it, understand its technology and applications and imitate it. When we refer to imitation we do not imply a blatant copy of the product (same name, colour, shape, etc.), we imply imitation of the concept. Highly technical products may not be easily imitated but certain convenience or shopping goods may prove extremely easy to copy

(clothes, shoe designs, chocolates, etc.). Of course, imitation may take place under many conditions but the exporter has little knowledge of imitations when they do take place as he or she is not operating in the market and, therefore, may be too late with any counter-measures.

3 There is no reputation build up for the exporter. For example, imagine that a specialist machine has been exported solely to a manufacturer overseas for immediate profit, and improving the overall production capabilities of that company. This advantage may be a closely kept secret by the buyer and therefore there will be limited awareness among the rest of the market of the true qualities of the machine. The exporter may have gained a sale but there is no communication about the product, its functions, its origin, etc.

Likewise, if products are purchased only on the understanding that they are marketed under the brand decided by the importer, then the importer's reputation will develop but not that of the exporter who supplied the product.

The limitations of this method of entry can be overcome through a more committed marketing approach using one of the other methods.

## Use of overseas agents

The appointment of an agent, usually resident within the country the company wishes to sell to, enables a specialist company or agent to act as a representative of the company, and bring about vital contacts and sales in return for a pre-agreed sales commission. There are many types of agents but the following are the most regularly used.

### 1 COMMISSION AGENTS

A commission agent negotiates the sale of products with customers and places the orders with the manufacturer who in turn supplies the products ordered. A commission is received based on the value of the sales achieved by the agent.

### 2 STOCKING AGENTS

Stocking agents offer the services of a commission agent, but they also provide additional facilities of storing the exporter's products in their own premises. They can supply customers from stock, thus reducing delays in delivery which are often inevitable when supplying overseas markets from a home base. They receive commission on sales achieved but also charge a fee for the storage and distribution of the products.

### 3 REPAIR AND SERVICE AGENTS

Many products offered to overseas markets – such as cars, domestic appliances and small industrial machinery – require regular servicing and the availability of spare parts. Repair and service agents offer a further extension to the two previous types of agents by additionally holding stocks of spare parts and by providing repair and general maintenance services. Fees for these services are of course charged to customers.

## 4 DEL CREDERE AGENTS

When dealing with orders from overseas customers there is a risk of not receiving full payment for products supplied, receiving payments late, or even an overseas customer defaulting due to liquidation. The last is a particular problem where each item is very expensive, e.g. industrial equipment. Del credere agents are willing to accept the risk associated with payments by overseas customers in addition to providing the services offered by the other types of agents. This involves a separate contractual arrangement which an overseas agent may be willing to undertake due to familiarity with the overseas market and customers and the level of commission he or she will receive for accepting the risk.

Irrespective of the type of agent used for entering into an overseas market, certain advantages and disadvantages must be considered in relation to this approach before it is adopted.

### ADVANTAGES

- Acquisition of local expertise through the experience of the agent.
- The agent's operations and existing business contacts can ease the introduction of a new product from overseas.
- The approach involves minimal investment and it is consequently very attractive to small companies lacking the resources required for a more direct and committed market entry.
- The popularity of products can be measured in a very inexpensive way. Lack of success may cause the exporter to withdraw from the market, without suffering extensive losses. Success, on the other hand, may offer the necessary encouragement to invest heavily in an overseas market.

### DISADVANTAGES

- Agents tend to deal in a variety of related or even unrelated products. One cannot expect an agent to concentrate solely on a recently introduced product, so many opportunities may be lost due to the agent's inability to explore all likely options.
- Agents may insist on a sole agency contract and then not obtain any sales with the result that the exporting company cannot enter the market itself or appoint another agent, and yet it has lost sales opportunities.
- As already indicated, agents receive commission on all sales achieved. The products with the highest percentage or total commission will obviously attract the attention and efforts of the agents and any slow moving product lines offering limited or irregular commission may be neglected or even totally ignored after a certain period of time.
- Agents are unlikely to be able to exploit the potential of overseas markets fully, due to the nature and limitations of their operations.
- The activities of agents may not be totally ethical or marketing orientated. Marketing organisations may seek a long term relationship with a group of customers, while agents may settle for one-off commissions. Adverse reactions

from purchasers or users of the product will have a long term effect on the reputation of the products, making future growth problematic if not impossible.

Agents must be evaluated carefully before they are appointed and the following **screening criteria** are strongly recommended:

a) Agent's human and physical resources: particularly important where the agent must use a sales force and physically distribute the product
b) Years of experience: in a particular industry or with particular products
c) Agent's overall reputation
d) Financial stability
e) Proven performance, and/or evidence of contacts.

Never appoint a sole agency unless the agency is guaranteeing some success within a specific period or is willing to market in a manner agreed in writing. Never sign an agency agreement that does not clearly indicate the way in which the exporting company (the principal) and agency will settle disagreements between them.

Evaluate how much commission the agent may reasonably expect over a year and then determine if your company could obtain more customers through sending salespeople abroad or by advertising in the country, e.g. colleges often advertise abroad with students applying direct to the college for a prospectus and subsequent admission.

# Use of branch offices

This method of entry represents a more direct approach to international marketing. The company invests in the overseas market by setting up its own office, service company or unit to represent it overseas. The type of office will be dependent on the product or nature of operations sought and the likely options may include: repair centres, sales offices, distribution centres, retail outlets, marketing units, complaints centres, etc. It may be that a manufacturer in the country is also used to manufacture the product under the strict guidance and to the detailed specifications of the marketing branch, to reduce costs and dispense with transportation of the product from the parent company.

**ADVANTAGES**
- The cost associated with other methods of entry could be higher than the investment and costs associated with a branch office. As sales grow, the total commission of an agent could be extremely high making a more direct method of entry financially attractive.
- Branch offices offer a greater degree of marketing control because they represent a corporate extension of the company. Policies, objectives, strategies and tactics selected can be more consistent and more easily controlled.
- Through this direct representation overseas, the marketing philosophy can be implemented and pursued more effectively. Market information can be

collected, customer complaints can be handled more efficiently, business contacts can be developed, overseas customers can be made to feel more secure and the overall reputation of the company can be cultivated.

## DISADVANTAGES

- As already indicated it may make financial sense to actually set up a branch office, but unfortunately there is a need for some initial investment which may be beyond the means of a small exporting company.
- Setting up branch offices creates additional control burdens for the organisation. Controlling operating units in one country is much easier than keeping control of the operations of business units dispersed in many different countries.
- The major decision makers in branch offices overseas may have to be personnel of the parent company, relocated to overseas markets. Such relocation may cause problems because people are not always willing to move or stay overseas for a long time and may not speak the language adequately. Frequent changes of personnel may cause continuity problems because different people may be pursuing the accomplishment of objectives differently. In addition changes of personnel may not allow customer and employee relationships to blossom overseas and the efficiency of the operations may suffer. Finally, the operations of the company in the home market may also suffer because experienced personnel are transferred to overseas units.
- Branch offices overseas can rarely be staffed solely with people of the parent company. Local skills will have to be recruited and this could prove problematic in terms of costs and training.
- Employment laws, personnel motivation and employee expectations vary quite distinctly from country to country and as a result it may be difficult to keep the peace within overseas units.

# Establishing a manufacturing, marketing and service unit

Here a complete company is established – usually by a multinational – to reduce cost, acquire expertise and maximise marketing opportunities. Advantages and disadvantages are similar to those of branch offices but, in addition, the company has complete control and obtains all profits and it may be possible to export from the unit to other countries at lower costs than supplying from the home production unit. A disadvantage would be the addition of one more production unit to control in a culture, and possibly in a language, that is foreign.

# Joint ventures

Joint ventures are basically a form of international partnership between two or more companies from different countries. The partnership is set up in order to enable companies to operate within specific countries or in order to combine resources.

## ADVANTAGES

- A joint venture with a competent company operating in the market the exporter wishes to enter, will provide the exporter with ready knowledge of the market, facilitating easy entry to the market and promoting consumer satisfaction.
- Risks associated with this form of market entry and the actual costs faced may be shared.
- Many overseas governments do not allow foreign companies to invest directly in their countries and only permit market entry if a joint venture is set up. In other words, this method of entry could be the only way of operating in otherwise closed countries.
- The combination of resources of two or more companies may actually remove some operational weaknesses which the individual companies may have. A local firm, for instance, may have manufacturing, marketing, selling and research resources which are currently under-utilised while the foreign company wishing to enter may provide new ideas, products or services which could prove profitable. A resulting combination in the form of a joint venture may create a formidable force within the market.
- Political uncertainty or general hostility towards foreign companies or companies from one particular market can be overcome due to the presence of a local firm. Consumers may trust the product more and local business contacts can be cultivated further.

## DISADVANTAGES

- All forms of partnerships face problems rising from disagreements between the partners. It is difficult to find two companies with different expectations, origins, history, structure and procedures which can operate harmoniously on a permanent basis. The actual areas of conflict will vary and every effort will have to be made to remove the problems through clearly established objectives, regular meetings, review of procedures, positive management attitudes, clear and frequent communications and willingness by both parties to listen, to adapt and to compromise.
- As already indicated, risks and costs are shared but profits are also divided between the companies involved thus reducing the returns to the exporter.
- The overseas partner may accumulate the necessary expertise through the joint venture and become a direct competitor if and when the agreement is terminated.

# Franchising

The term franchising refers to the selling of a licence which allows a company to use somebody else's name, product or service in return for a pre-agreed premium payment (initial payment) and annual commission/royalty fee. A franchise agreement is made between the organisation that will provide its name, products, promotional support and expertise (the franchisor) and the person/company who is willing to pay a premium and commission (the franchisee) for the right to operate with the help and under the name of the franchisor. For example, Colonel Sanders introduced the idea for Kentucky Fried Chicken, determined how the product could best be prepared, marketed and sold. He retained control over how this was done, but left the operation of the majority of individual retail outlets to the self-employed proprietor of the premises. The franchisor becomes, in part, a partner with every franchisee operating and owning an outlet.

The franchisor remains a service organisation, without the massive overheads and complicated controlling systems of regional branches, retail staff and outlets while receiving ongoing payments from the franchisee.

The franchisee, on the other hand, can purchase a ready made business, with all the backup of a large and experienced organisation, but the business essentially remains his or her own. The major part of the profits generated remain with the franchisee.

To assess a successful franchising operation it is essential to evaluate the benefits to the franchisee, to ensure that what is offered as a marketable possibility appears attractive and worthwhile to the people who have to operate in the market place.

## ADVANTAGES TO THE FRANCHISEE

- Business ownership with limited risk and financial outlay.
- Training in product knowledge, and in the running of the business.
- Established image – the business starts from a position of strength with a well known name and reputation, backed up by large scale promotions and advertising – usually in the national media – normally beyond the sole proprietor's pocket.
- Professional help is provided in raising finance, recruiting and training staff, finding premises and advising ongoing operations.
- Purchasing benefits through the bulk buying power of the franchisor and consistency of quality.
- Reduced business risks, as the franchisor's problem solving team is on hand and is likely to have encountered similar situations before.
- Market research and product development is usually beyond the small business operation so the franchisor will keep the franchisee up-to-date with relevant, recent and future developments that will help the business.

## DISADVANTAGES TO FRANCHISEE

- Franchisor's control, essential to the successful operation, can prove constraining or rigid at times.
- Resentment of the ongoing commission payments may build up after a while, especially if the franchisee senses any lack of value for money.
- Poor support. Things may not turn up as expected or as promised. The franchisee may not get the backup needed or the original idea may not have been sound.
- Freedom to sell the business may well be restricted by the franchisor.
- Dependence; if the franchisee becomes too dependent on the franchisor's

support, some of the motivation and incentives associated with running one's own business may well be removed.

### ADVANTAGES TO FRANCHISOR

- The image of the franchisor's operation is maintained through strict control over the operations of the franchisee.
- Little to no financial outlay may be involved when adding one more franchisee to the current list.
- Useful where there is a widely dispersed consumer market as operations throughout the whole market place are made possible.
- Ensures motivation by the franchisee as the franchisee wants to earn as much as possible.

### DISADVANTAGES TO FRANCHISOR

- The franchisor must have a perfectly planned idea and preferably be already operating some units to reassure potential franchisees that their investment will be a success.
- The franchisor never owns the outlets and, therefore, does not enjoy all the profits.
- There can be great difficulty in convincing potential franchisees to part with a premium payment and also difficulty in finding franchisees who will most probably succeed and, therefore, keep up the good name of the franchise operation.
- The franchisor must be aggressively marketing-orientated and remain that way if he or she is to retain the support of the franchisees and expand the operation.

## ■ ORGANISATIONAL IMPLICATIONS OF INTERNATIONAL EXPANSION

Any reference to international marketing automatically brings to mind efforts made by a company to grow, achieve greater prosperity and widen its platform of operations. An adventurous overseas plan is a fine concept and can be very rewarding as long as the overall structure of the organisation can support such a growth.

The function of an organisational structure is to assist in the attainment of the company's objectives by grouping all the necessary functions and activities in a logical manner. It specifies the areas of authority, highlights the relationships between people working within the structure and represents a general framework within which the company is built and operates.

Entry into overseas markets automatically introduces a number of additional influences within the company and any structure already used must be able to accommodate the following:

1 Possible introduction of new personnel possessing the knowledge and skills required to tackle the challenges from abroad.

2 New working relationships with suppliers, distributors, media owners, institutes and associations, government departments, etc. which must be handled in a competent and professional manner.

3 Key personnel may need to travel extensively, some members of the staff may be sent overseas for specific periods of time and generally speaking the company must have at its disposal quality short-term replacements who can maintain continuity of operations in the absence of others. Failure to do this may lead to catastrophic results in the home market.

4 Bearing in mind that overseas markets represent new, complex and unfamiliar environments differences of opinion among key decision makers are often inevitable and the company's structure should be geared towards democratic debate, fruitful communication and flexibility which can maximise the quality of the company's response to the new market place/s.

5 International markets are often separated from the home market by thousands of miles and companies face the risk of highly fragmented operations. Control is the key to success here and modern company structures must allow for well-integrated operations.

6 Operations in overseas markets may be drastically different to the normal operations of the company and all marketing oriented companies must be prepared for such a variety of activities. The critical issue to consider here is whether all operations – home or overseas – are making a positive contribution towards the company's corporate objectives.

7 Any successes overseas may lead to jealousies and antagonisms between members of the staff dealing with the international operations and staff involved in the home market. Such problems must be eliminated quickly and the company's structure must allow for team spirit and internal synergy.

8 The likely prestige which may be enjoyed as a result of international success often blinds key decision makers within an organisation and some critical areas of the company's operations are often ignored or treated as minor tasks. Elimination of this problem can again be achieved through a flexible structure geared to accommodate all operations and able to support the needs of all employees.

The objective of this section of the chapter is not to identify and discuss all types of organisational structure which can be adopted by companies, but to identify a structure which can accommodate all the changes and challenges which international marketing may introduce to a company. This structure is known as the **grid structure** or **matrix structure** and its elements can be summarised as follows:

- It includes all the major management functions (production, marketing, finance, personnel, etc.) which concentrate on the overall integration of all activities undertaken at home or overseas. These functions represent the company's **central services** and they collectively control highly fragmented operations.
- It includes a number of specialist sub-units which are developed with specific projects, products, markets or functions in mind. An international company,

for instance, may develop a number of offices in overseas markets so that local needs are serviced effectively, quickly and in a marketing oriented manner. Each overseas office will have a manager who is given the freedom to decide and implement plans of action as long as his decisions are consistent with overall company expectations. The same principle can be applied in the case of product managers (people in charge of specific product lines), area managers (people responsible for specific geographic areas within which the company operates) or project managers (people given the responsibility to complete a specific assignment relating to research, product development, value analysis, etc.).

- The structure also allows individual departments or company units to develop according to their needs. A subsidiary of the company in an overseas market may have to develop its own marketing department, production facilities, personnel department or distribution operations. Such development can be accommodated because each function will be guided by the relevant central service.

A visual presentation of all the above is necessary in order to appreciate the quality of the structure, best presented as a 'net'. An imaginary matrix organisation may be presented as follows:

**Company Chairman**
(Central Services)

|  | Marketing | Production | Finance | Purchasing | Personnel |
|---|---|---|---|---|---|
| UK Manager |  |  |  |  |  |
| USA Manager |  |  |  |  |  |
| Australia Manager |  |  |  |  |  |
| Special Projects Manager |  |  |  |  |  |

Specialist Managers

Every intersection represents a point of communication between a central service and a specialist manager. Consultation, reporting, control and constructive disagreements represent likely communication areas but the flexibility of the structure can help in overcoming any problems faced.

A word of caution is necessary at this stage; a structure is only a framework within which people operate. Negative management philosophies, poor quality of staff, unwillingness to co-operate and inadequate internal communication are the major enemies of every organisational structure, including those with a matrix structure.

This structure offers the opportunity to control effectively overseas operations and it is in the hands of the people within it to make it work. When this is achieved, the company is ready to enter and grow successfully within many international markets.

# ■ STUDY AND EXAM TIPS

**1** International marketing does not represent a new dimension of the marketing concept. The philosophy is the same, but the environment changes and marketers must respond to it.

**2** The main methods of entering overseas markets represent popular examinable topics.

**3** Use examples from your own country to highlight any problems encountered by international marketers (language, religion, transportation systems, etc.)

**4** Distinguish clearly direct methods of entry from indirect methods of entry.

**5** Be prepared to discuss the different types of agents available and the criteria which must be used in selecting the 'right' agent.

**6** International marketing represents one of many strategic options available to marketing managers – particularly where home markets are saturated or are less profitable. Make sure you have revised the marketing strategies explained in Chapter 10.

**7** Seek to relate the theory to practical situations highlighted in magazines, newspapers, books, TV, etc., in order to appreciate the complexity, risks and rewards associated with international marketing operations.

**8** International marketing does not only apply to large corporations. It is a topic that interests all types of organisations.

## ■ SELF ASSESSMENT QUESTIONS

Answer the following questions awarding yourself one mark for each complete question that you answer correctly. If you answer less than six correctly reread the relevant parts of the chapter. The answers are given on page 239.

**1** Identify four possible differences between domestic markets and international markets apart from 'language'.

a) ................

b) ................

c) ................

d) ................

**2** Identify three major sources of information for UK-based desk research on overseas markets.

a) ................

b) ................

c) ................

**3** Name five common methods of entering overseas markets apart from 'franchising'.

a) ................

b) ................

c) ................

d) ................

e) ................

**4** Name three types of agents apart from commission agents.

a) ................

b) ................

c) ................

**5** Identify the alternative term used to refer to a matrix structure.

................................................................................

**6** What do the following abbreviations stand for?

a) BOTB ........................................................................

b) ECGD ........................................................................

c) CBI ...........................................................................

**7** International marketing represents either a market development strategy or a ................ strategy.

**8** Identify three screening criteria used to evaluate agents, apart from financial stability.

a) ................

b) ................

c) ................

# ■ PAST EXAMINATION QUESTIONS

### Chartered Institute of Marketing

1 Describe the main methods of export distribution and the circumstances under which you would choose each of them.

2 What are the first steps to be taken by a marketing manager on receipt of an enquiry from a firm in a country where he has not previously done business, offering their services as agents for his products?

3 For a company considering exporting for the first time, what advice would you give them on how they should proceed to select the most appropriate country or countries?

4 Describe the criteria you would use in order to evaluate and select overseas agents.

# ■ SPECIMEN QUESTION

A popular topic of conversation among marketing managers is the 'single market' of the EC. Explain what you understand by the 'single European market' and its implications to the marketing operations of companies based in the Community.

# ■ SUGGESTED ANSWER TO THE SPECIMEN QUESTION

The Single European Market (SEM) is a popular topic of conversation in marketing but it is unfortunately marred by confusion, misunderstanding, conflicting facts and masses of information regularly published which often lead to further confusion.

The SEM effectively constitutes 12 member states of the European Community trading without restrictions and thus allowing complete freedom in the movement of goods, capital and labour. The countries are the UK, Spain, Portugal, Italy, Greece, West Germany, France, Eire, Denmark, Holland, Belgium and Luxembourg.

The European Community is a Free Trade Area which has been developed over the last 30 years with the ultimate intention of creating a single market lacking physical, fiscal and technical frontiers and with a single currency. In other words products manufactured in any of 12 countries can be exported to any other member state without being subject to import taxes or quotas. The term quota refers to restrictions imposed on the quantity of products that will be allowed to be imported into a particular country. Thus, exporting continually becomes easier, quicker and cheaper as companies learn to trade within the bigger 'multi-country' market.

It is the removal of these barriers – between the member countries only – which has created many differences of opinion as to their implication for the marketing of products and services within the European Community. The following aspects should be taken into account:

a) Cultures between the 12 countries in question will remain different, though less defined, so many products sold internationally will still need to be adapted to the national and regional expectations of each country and the usual methods of marketing and distribution used internationally will still apply.

b) Even though a common language may be introduced (Esperanto) it will not be spoken by the masses for many years to come, so language barriers will continue to exist as before.

c) The freedom in the movement of money means that companies and individuals will seek money outside of their own country at the lowest rate possible.

d) The commercial benefits associated with the removal of trade barriers are likely to attract companies from outside the community so European companies will still need to maintain and improve their competitive posture if they are to survive.

e) Legislation covering product ingredients, health warnings, consumer protection, product protection, etc., will continue to unify so certain aspects of products and the marketing mix will become more standardised throughout Europe.

f) Companies have to watch the servicing of their home markets more closely as companies within the market attempt – without border restrictions – to enter markets in other countries within the Community.

g) European companies must not concentrate only on Europe; they must continue with their quest to enter and penetrate other national markets throughout the world to spread risk of downturn and to ensure that, like the Japanese and Americans, they remain internationally competitive.

h) Key decision makers must become familiar with the new environments to be faced if they are to meet the challenges in the home, as well as the Community's individual markets, effectively. Reading government and industrial bulletins, attending relevant seminars and reading trade periodicals will help.

i) Companies used to marketing internationally will continue to have a comparative advantage over companies which have always concentrated on their home markets due to their international marketing skills and knowledge.

j) As barriers still exist to countries outside the Community those inside will have a comparative advantage when dealing within the Community.

k) Competition will continue to take place on the labour front so companies must introduce effective training programmes to provide efficient staff.

l) Quality control, pollution-preventing measures and trading standards will continue to add costs to production which must affect the sales of companies selling within a market that has an elastic demand.

m) Competition between companies for skilled management staff with a track record in international markets will continue to grow.

Twelve European countries with a combined population of 320 million people become one large potential target market of interest to countries such as Japan, the USA, etc. and so vigilance is needed. Effective continuous research, professional assessment, realistic objective-setting, an effective marketing mix, adequate organisational structures and staffing and strict controls of the operations undertaken provide the guidelines for success in such a large and highly competitive environment.

# ■ MINI CASE STUDY

Test what you have learnt by reading the following case study and answering the questions. Submit your answers for assessment by your tutor.

## Wheelers Cars Ltd

Wheelers, a well established car distributor, has a total of five large showrooms located on prime sites in major cities throughout the UK. They are the main agents for an up-market German car. When the economy was buoyant sales went well but with the onset of recession the company is faced with major problems. In general, sales are falling and the amount of service and maintenance work that is done by the garages attached to the showrooms is also on the decline.

George Carter, previously a Marketing Manager of a larger car distributor group, has just taken over as Managing Director, Mr Race, the previous Managing Director, having just retired. Having had an opportunity to examine the various aspects of the company, George Carter has called a directors' meeting to discuss the current position of the company and prepare a plan of action to rectify matters. It would appear that the company has only £100 000 cash on deposit of which £20 000 is already accounted for if current debts are to be paid. Debts to the company are virtually non-existent as either the customer or HP company settles the cost of the car at the time of purchase.

The company has approximately 60 cars paid for in stock; with sales so slow the cars have had to be paid for before they were sold. The trade value of the cars is approximately £600 000. George Carter points out that these continuing losses in sales, servicing and maintenance may require the company to sell off a site to raise capital, causing redundancies. This must take place within four months. The market value of each site is:

Site 1   £780 000
Site 2   £700 000
Site 3   £430 000
Site 4   £400 000
Site 5   £230 000

Mr Carter also points out that the Birmingham site(s) had been losing money for two years and no decision has been made regarding its future. The site has been supported by sales made at the other sites. The Birmingham site used to be the leading profit-maker for the company but over the last 20 years local social and economic changes have meant a change in the local populace and also substantial unemployment. The new residents in the area are not of the social-economic group that tend to buy expensive German cars.

Mr Carter asks the Board of Directors for their initial comments before a two day meeting is arranged, where the problem can be dealt with in greater detail. He is given the following opinions:

The Production Director, Mr Banks, who is in charge of the garages' servicing and repairs, believes that the Birmingham site should be sold and staff laid off. In this way he believes the company can weather the recession and make itself efficient and ready for a recovery in the economy.

Mr Coates, the Marketing Director, believes that they should move down market, and become agents for a mass market car. The company should then be promoted nationally to attract more customers. Twenty per cent of the cost of such advertising will be paid for by the German manufacturers provided their cars are mentioned in any advertising.

Mr Jones, the Commercial Director, believes that they should promote the garages' servicing and repair services locally, for any make of car as this would be inexpensive and the garages overall are currently working at 65 per cent of their capacity. He also considers it wise to become agents for a less expensive car and drop current distribution of the German car as too much capital is tied up in each car.

Finally, Mrs Kalsi, the Accounts Director, gave her opinion. She also feels that they should sell the Birmingham site to ensure liquidity for the company and then buy a small company in the growth area of the economy to spread risk of investment. She also considers that their current premises could be used for other services but she wants to investigate finances further before making any suggestions.

Mr Carter thanked them for their comments and informed them that the company could raise up to £500 000 from the banks but at the cost of putting up their best site as a guarantee. A second two day meeting was arranged before the meeting was concluded at which time George Carter assured them he would evaluate their suggestions in further detail with them and subsequently outline a plan of action for the forthcoming year.

Answer any two questions from Part 1, *or* question 4 or 5 from Part 2. Time allowed 1 hour 15 minutes.

*Part 1*
1 Analyse the alternatives the company may have with regard to the future of the Birmingham site and suggest any research you consider relevant for making a final decision on the site.
2 Assuming the company chooses to retain its current market for high priced cars while moving down market, outline a promotions plan designed to promote its new image(s) and types of sales giving reasons for the methods that you suggest.
3 Diversification by extending current services, by selling cars meant for the mass

market and by purchasing another company were all suggested in the case. Evaluate these suggestions and put forward any ideas you may have on ways of extending the product/service range.

*Part 2*

**4** Assuming that you are George Carter, analyse and evaluate the suggestions made throughout the case for improving the trade position of the company.

**5** Outline a marketing plan for the company to cover the forthcoming year providing your reasons for the overall aims of the plan and any objectives and strategies that you suggest.

The case study was adapted from Wheelers case study presented in *How to Pass Exams* published by Stanley Thornes, and written by W. G. Leader for improving students' exam success.

# Answers to self assessment questions

## ■ CHAPTER 1

1 Marketing research may be defined as 'The planned and systematic gathering and collation of data and the analysis of information relating to all aspects of marketing and the final consumption of goods and services'.
2 a) Personnel department
   b) Marketing department (includes sales)
   c) Production department
   d) Purchasing department
3 a) Governmental
   b) International organisations
   c) Business publications
4 a) Statistics
   b) Abstracts
   c) Lists
5 Secondary
6 Ad-hoc
7 a) Defining the purpose and objectives
   b) Determining the methods of collecting information
   c) Collating, analysis and reporting on the findings
8 No
9 Reduction
10 a) Qualitative
    b) Desk

## ■ CHAPTER 3

1 Universe
2 Buyer behaviour
3 . . . consistent with a pre-determined research objective.
4 . . . statistical regularity.
5 . . . non-random samples.
6 a) Stratified
   b) Systematic
   c) Multi-stage and/or cluster sampling
7 Quota
8 Census
9 a) Postal questionnaires
   b) Telephone interviews
   c) Observation
10 Double
11 Qualitative
12 Sales for the period for each product
13 Retail audit
14 Consumer panel
15 a) Word association tests
    b) Sentence completion tests
    c) Blind tests
    d) In-depth interviews

## ■ CHAPTER 4

1 a) Sales promotions
   b) Public relations
   c) Personal selling

2 a) Television
   b) Radio
   c) Press
   d) Posters
3 False
4 Trade and technical
5 Trade (or 'Trade and Technical' will do)
6 Mail drop
7 A classification of residential neighbourhoods
8 Target Group Index
9 British Market Research Bureau
10 Post-testing
11 a) Association
   b) Completion

## ■ CHAPTER 5

1 Clients (*Note:* Even if the client is a media owner wishing to advertise in another media he would be classified as a client)
2 False
3 Media planner
4 Accounts Executive (or Accounts Director if he/she is responsible for all clients of the agency)
5 No to all questions
6 Pitch
7 False
8 Code of Advertising Practice
9 Advertising Standards Authority
10 Truthful

## ■ CHAPTER 6

1 a) Two for the price of one
   b) X per cent extra quantity for the price of one
2 You were expected to identify any four from the following six techniques.
   a) Competitions
   b) Free offers

   c) Coupons
   d) Reduced prices
   e) Refund offers
   f) Self-liquidating offers
3 Originality
4 Third party communications relating to newsworthy events regarding the company and/or its products and services
5 You were expected to remember any three from the following four
   a) Sponsorship
   b) Media relations
   c) Community relations
   d) Internal PR
6 a) Letters of apology
   b) Full refunds
   c) Open days
7 Events
8 Advertising and personal selling
9 Promotional mix
10 Point-of-sale
11 Short term incentives offered to consumers or members of the trade or the company's sales staff in an effort to boost sales.

## ■ CHAPTER 7

1 One or more prospective purchasers with the purpose of making a sale
2 Benefits
3 Product knowledge
4 a) Invoice
   b) Collection
5 a) Action function
   b) Control function
6 The skills and knowledge needed to do the job – current skills and knowledge of the potential trainee
7 f) Obtaining references
8 Qualitative
9 a) Word of mouth
   b) Advocate channels

# ■ CHAPTER 9

1 Projections
2 a) correlation
  b) Exponential smoothing
3 a) Salesforce estimates
  b) Buyers' estimates
4 ... of a national market in order to assess the level of success to the expected under real-life conditions
5 a) Accuracy required
  b) Replacement cycle of the product
  c) Number of marketing variables being tested
6 a) Use valid numerical data whenever possible
  b) Involve skilled people with an established knowledge of the market
  c) Be cautious of bias from opinions and faulty statistics
7 See page 168.

# ■ CHAPTER 10

1 a) Strengths
  b) Weaknesses
  c) Opportunities
  d) Threats
2 a) Measurability
  b) Flexibility
  c) Accountability
3 a) SWOT Analysis
  b) Marketing objectives
  c) Marketing strategies
  d) Marketing tactics
4 a) Market development
  b) Product development
  c) Diversification

5 Contribution per unit = Price per unit − Variable cost per unit
6 Break-even point (in units) = 

$$\frac{\text{Total fixed costs}}{\text{Contribution per unit}}$$

7 a) Problem children
  b) Stars
  c) Cash cows
8 Meso

# ■ CHAPTER 11

1 Possible differences include: religion, political, economic, technological, social or education
2 a) BOTB
  b) Chambers of Commerce
  c) Trade associations
3 a) Direct exporting
  b) Agents
  c) Branch offices
  d) Manufacturing unit/company
  e) Joint ventures
4 a) Stocking agents
  b) Repair service agents
  c) Del credere agents
5 Grid structure
6 a) British Overseas Trade Board
  b) Export Credit Guarantee Department
  c) Confederation of British Industry
7 Diversification
8 a) Human and physical resources of the agent
  b) Years of experience
  c) Agent's overall reputation

# Index